RAW FEELING

RAW FEELING

*A Philosophical Account of the
Essence of Consciousness*

ROBERT KIRK

CLARENDON PRESS · OXFORD

Oxford University Press, Walton Street, Oxford OX2 6DP
Oxford New York
Athens Auckland Bangkok Bogota Bombay
Buenos Aires Calcutta Cape Town Dar es Salaam
Delhi Florence Hong Kong Istanbul Karachi
Kuala Lumpur Madras Madrid Melbourne
Mexico City Nairobi Paris Singapore
Taipei Tokyo Toronto
and associated companies in
Berlin Ibadan

Oxford is a trade mark of Oxford University Press

Published in the United States
by Oxford University Press Inc., New York

© Robert Kirk 1994

First published 1994
First issued in paperback 1996

British Library Cataloguing in Publication Data
Data available

Library of Congress Cataloging in Publication Data
Kirk, Robert.
Raw feeling : a philosophical account of the essence of
consciousness / Robert Kirk.
Includes bibliographical references.
1. Consciousness. 2. Mind and body. 3. Philosophy of mind.
4. Metaphysics. I. Title.
B808.9.K57 1994 126—dc20 93-5278
ISBN 0–19–824081–3
ISBN 0–19–823679–4 (pbk)

Printed in Great Britain
on acid-free paper by
Bookcraft (Bath) Ltd.
Midsomer Norton, Avon

PREFACE

How could processes in the brain amount to conscious experiences? If you are perplexed, this book is for you. It is also for you if you claim there is nothing to be perplexed about. We have been right to be mystified by the mind—body problem, even after decades of philosophical activity with the benefit of progress in psychology and the neurosciences. Previous attempts to remove the mystery have depended on assumptions which no one would accept unless they had an axe to grind. Behaviourism is a conspicuous example, and it still has adherents. Behaviourists maintain that mental states are determined entirely by behaviour and behavioural dispositions: it doesn't matter at all what goes on inside the head so long as it produces the right patterns of behaviour. Although there are more sophisticated approaches than simple behaviourism, they still involve uncomfortable contortions. In this book I set out my own view of the most troublesome philosophical problems in this area, and offer solutions which don't require us to grit our teeth.

Work on the final version was temporarily halted by the appearance of Daniel Dennett's splendid book *Consciousness Explained*. Had I been wasting my efforts? Of course some disagreement was to be expected: no two philosophers will agree about everything. With some relief I found there are substantial divergences. Although he tackles the same problems, his approach is different. He is as much concerned to find an account of the empirical facts underlying human consciousness as he is with the philosophical problems. And on the central question of the 'essence' of consciousness, as I am calling it, I don't think he has actually cracked the problem. As I will explain in due course, his suggestions call for too much teeth-gritting.

The title needs some explanation. Tolman used the expression 'raw feels' in his book *Purposive Behaviour in Animals and Men* (1932) to refer to certain features of our mental life which he thought science could not capture. His phrase is by now familiar, suitably vague, and close to what I shall focus on: the essence of consciousness—itself a loose, 'folk' word. I have modified Tolman's expression to avoid any hint that being conscious is a matter of being related to a special class of entities. Raw feeling is not a thing but a process, which on my account is purely physical. Let me add that my use of 'raw' doesn't imply that it involves no interpretation—and my use of 'feeling' doesn't imply it is feeling in the ordinary sense either.

It is a pleasure to thank the many people who have helped: Greg McCulloch, who generously offered penetrating detailed comments on the whole of an earlier version and stimulated much necessary rethinking; my former research student Nick Buckley; other colleagues and students at Nottingham and elsewhere who have forced me to sharpen my ideas; two anonymous readers for the Oxford University Press; and my wife Janet, who has improved my English and put up with frequent episodes when my own consciousness seemed to have been switched off.

CONTENTS

Contents

Contents

I

Raw Feeling and the Intelligibility Gap

A few people suffer from the extreme of colour-blindness, achromatic vision. Most were born that way; but occasionally someone who started life with normal colour vision loses it. Conceivably the reverse might happen,[1] so let us imagine it has happened to Anna, and she tells us her thoughts.

I.I   ANNA

'Until a few days ago I saw only the relative lightnesses of things, not their colours. Of course that didn't stop me using a lot of colour words correctly quite often. I knew that blood is red, clear skies blue, oranges orange, and so on. But I couldn't have told you the colour of anything just by looking at it. A few days ago everything changed. Suddenly I found I had full colour vision like other people. I know that's what it is because I can match colour samples just by looking at them. So I'm quickly learning to name the colours of things that otherwise look alike. I use a chart for hard cases, and I expect I'll soon be able to use colour words as well as anyone.

'But some odd ideas occurred to me as I was colouring a sketch of the scene outside my window. Everyone agreed that I'd got the colours right, and that things must look to me to have the colours they really do have. But then I coloured in a second sketch of the same scene, changing the colours round systematically, replacing each colour by its complementary—red by green, blue by yellow, and so on. My first odd idea is that although the colours in this second picture didn't match the ones of the scene outside, the world might have been coloured that way instead of the way it is. I mean the actual objective colours of things might have

---

[1] Something *like* the reverse actually happens. Judith Taylor lost her sight as a child and was blind for thirty years. After a recent operation she regained her sight. At first it was monochrome. 'It was at least a month before I began to see colours again. I began to notice the colour of my children's hair and the blue velvet curtains of the local church. Over the next few months, like a child, I had to re-learn colours.' Reported in *The Observer Magazine*, 28 May 1988, 36 f.

been different in that systematic way—and, coloured that way round, the world wouldn't have looked any more strange to me than it does now.

'And then the second odd idea struck me. The colours out there might have stayed as they are—but the way I saw them might have been different. I might just as well have acquired colour vision in a different way, one which made the scene outside my window give me the same pattern of colour experiences as the second picture gives me now. If I had acquired colour vision in that different way, my first picture would have looked to me as the second one does now. Yet my behaviour would have been exactly as it actually has been. There would have been an inner difference—in the character of my colour experiences—but no outer one. The inner difference wouldn't have been detectable except, perhaps, by a detailed examination of my brain.'

Anna's first idea helps to make the second more plausible, and it is the second that I will focus on. She is talking about the subjective character of experience, and so about what I am calling raw feeling. She believes it involves something 'inner' which is not reducible to behaviour. And she has been struck by an old idea: the apparent possibility of the 'inverted spectrum'.[2] This may look like a trivial puzzle—in fact it irritates some philosophers. Certainly the idea in question needs to be set out with some care. But it turns out to be a crucial test of any account of the nature of consciousness.

1.2 PROBLEMS

Whether or not Anna is right about what is possible, she has led us into a thicket of problems. Suppose she is right. Then ordinary perceptual consciousness involves something remarkable, something that is 'inner' in a special way, not just literally inside the head, like the firing of neurones. This special kind of innerness

---

[2] The *locus classicus* is John Locke: 'Neither would it carry any Imputation of *Falshood* to our simple *Ideas*, *if* by the different structure of our Organs, it were so ordered, That *the same Object should produce in several Men's Minds different* Ideas at the same time; *v.g.* if the *Idea*, that a *Violet* produced in one Man's Mind by his Eyes, were the same that a *Marigold* produced in another Man's, and *vice versa*. For since this could never be known . . .; neither the Ideas hereby, nor the Names, would be at all confounded, or any *Falshood* be in either.' (*Essay*, II. xxxii. 15.) A related thought, without the explicit introduction of systematic transposition, is ascribed to the Cyrenaics by Sextus Empiricus, *Against the Logicians*, I. 196–8.

shows up with subjects of experience—things it is like something to be.[3] But what does it involve? Traditional theories invoke special non-physical items—'ideas', 'sense data', and so on. But that is just a mistake, as we shall soon see. We shall also see that it doesn't help to go to the other extreme and maintain that nothing is involved beyond the behaviour and dispositions of organisms.

You might expect that answers to our questions would eventually emerge from further work in the neurosciences. But that is at any rate not obvious. Parts of the scientific story covering perceptual experience are familiar. In the case of colour vision, for example, patterns of light from the surfaces of objects are focused on to the retinas, which consist essentially of three types of nerve-endings, sensitive to three groups of wavelengths: long (red light), intermediate (green), and short (blue). Electrochemical impulses from these nerve-endings are subtly processed and the resulting impulses transmitted along the optic nerves to the visual cortex. There further processing takes place, of kinds that are still unknown, and somehow the result is our experience of colour. But when you think about this sort of perceptual consciousness it is hard to resist the idea that further explanations are needed on top of the scientific ones—on top, even, of whatever the most detailed scientific account may eventually turn out to be. There is an *intelligibility gap*. It is nicely illustrated by a famous passage from Leibniz's *Monadologie*:

We have to admit that perception, and what depends on it, cannot be explained mechanically, that is, by means of shapes and movements. If we imagine a machine whose construction ensures that it has thoughts, feelings, and perceptions, we can conceive it to be so enlarged, while keeping the same proportions, that we could enter it like a mill. On that supposition, when visiting it we shall find inside only components pushing one another, and never anything that could explain a perception.[4]

I believe that consciousness is somehow constituted by physiological processes. The trouble is that even a complete physiological

---

[3] The phrase has been made famous by Thomas Nagel in his 'What Is It Like to Be a Bat?'. But see the seminal though perplexing earlier discussion of what it would be like to be a Martian/a bat in Brian Farrell's 'Experience'.

[4] G. W. Leibniz, *Monadologie*, sect. 17. In his article 'Form, Function, and Feel', William Lycan neatly inverts both the idea and its application. He imagines a submicroscopically tiny person inside a normal-sized brain and uses the example in support of physicalistic functionalism.

description would not remove our perplexities. One reason is that the description seems unlikely to provide any indication of whether systems other than those with our particular type of nervous system might also have that kind of consciousness. What about Martians or robots? The description would not necessarily have enough generality. But the main reason is that the physiological story by itself does nothing to explain how the events it describes could be *like* anything for the subject. How could that sort of thing—neurones firing in complex patterns—yield THIS? This intelligibility gap provides the main philosophical problem to be tackled in this book. It is perhaps the last really perplexing component of the mind–body problem.

Anna expected that the subjective differences which she envisaged would be associated with physiological ones. It seems easy to think up suitable kinds of physical differences—something like crossed wires, for example. But such stories stop short of explaining what many people find the most puzzling facts. What is it about a given physical set-up which yields this particular kind of experience rather than the kind which is actually yielded by the other set-up? What could possibly link these physiological facts to this type of experience? There is a further perplexing idea. Science-fictional stories about automata and zombies face us with the unsettling question: how is it that these physical events bring consciousness with them *at all*?

Still on the assumption that Anna is right about what is possible, further questions arise. How far is the nature of consciousness an empirical matter, and how far does it depend on our ways of conceptualizing our mental lives? Will developments in psychology and the neurosciences inevitably pass our questions by? Or do we, perhaps, need a whole new science to deal with the phenomena of consciousness? Again, how is it possible to know what kinds of experiences other people have? Or, if that isn't possible, how can the notion be even intelligible? Could it be that our ordinary notions of conscious experience are in a hopeless mess, as some philosophers maintain?

Anna's intuitions—what she unreflectively finds it natural to believe—may well be mistaken, like our ancestors' intuitions about the shape and motion of the earth, or the geometry of space. More than one philosophical approach to the nature of consciousness has it that she is indeed fundamentally wrong. We shall have to take these approaches seriously. In any case, since we are all against sin, we mustn't rely on our intuitions.

I have three aims. One is to tease out the most serious problems from among those I have roughly indicated. Part of this task will be to justify my contention that the notion of raw feeling is sound. I shall also have to make clear what the intelligibility gap is. Another aim—the main one—is to develop solutions to the real problems, thereby showing how the intelligibility gap can be closed. Here let me emphasize that I will focus quite narrowly on the problems stated, which means that many important and fascinating related issues will not be discussed. The third aim is to make clear that the proposed solutions are solutions—to show that they require no leaps of faith. Resistance is likely from opposite directions. On one side are those who stick by the intuitions and find it hard to conceive how they could possibly be provided for by the means that will be employed. On the other side stand behaviourists, verificationists, Wittgensteinians and eliminativists—a mixed yet daunting line-up—who reject the contention that there is a problem about consciousness. Throughout we shall have to anticipate likely objections from both sides.

1.3   THE PLOT

It would be nice if I could explain straightaway just what I think the intelligibility gap is. But that explanation depends on other ones: it will evolve in the course of the book. A preliminary task is to clarify the notion of raw feeling itself, and I will start on it in this chapter by clearing some excessively crude theories out of the way. But you may wonder whether any such notion could be sound. Is it, perhaps, just a survivor of primitive Cartesian ways of thinking? In the next chapter I will examine two very different philosophical approaches which threaten to undermine my whole project. One is inspired by Wittgenstein, the other is utterly alien to his philosophical temperament: eliminative materialism. I will argue that, contrary to appearances, neither of these approaches has any force against the notion I am actually defending. Evidently this notion has something in common with the old conception of sense data. But it is significantly different. Crucially, raw feeling doesn't call for anything beyond the physical; and it doesn't involve the conscious subject's being related to a special class of entities. It is a state or process, not a thing.

One way in which the notion of raw feeling is akin to that of sense data is that it permits Anna's intuitions to be essentially correct. Something like the different ways of seeing colours that she envisages turn out to be at least a theoretical possibility. This possibility, expressed in what I will call the Transformation thesis, forms one component of the intelligibility gap. For it is obscure how such a claim could be either ruled out, or fitted into a satisfactory account of perceptual consciousness. The main component of the intelligibility gap, though, will emerge only when we have considered relations between the facts of consciousness and the facts that can be stated in austerely physical terms. Our intuitions, massaged by stories like Anna's, tend to suggest that the physically statable facts inevitably fall short of fixing the facts about perceptual consciousness. How *could* they determine that my experiences of the blue sky, for example, are exactly like THIS? How could they even determine that there is consciousness at all? (Years ago I was roused from dogmatic Rylean slumbers by one of my first tutorial students. To some brash assertion she politely objected, 'But there are zombies, aren't there?' I could neither refute nor vindicate her assumption—hence, indirectly, this book.)

In Chapter 3 I will argue that these intuitions of contingency are mistaken. The link from the physically statable facts to the facts about raw feeling is necessary—or at any rate we might as well assume that it is. I shall argue that the totality of truths statable in an austere physical vocabulary strictly implies the totality of mental truths, including those about raw feeling: it is impossible that all of the former should be true while any of the latter was false. That is the Strict Implication thesis. Many philosophers today will accept it, although there are still some who think physicalism is compatible with a less than absolutely necessary link from physical facts to consciousness. But the Strict Implication thesis, though important, cannot pretend to be a solution to our problems. On the contrary, it is no more than a contribution to clarifying what those problems are. It just helps us to get clear about one crucial component of the intelligibility gap. Even if the Strict Implication thesis is true, what we need is an explanation of how it could be true.

Not that I am presupposing physicalism. Our problems must

be capable of being solved without our being forced to commit ourselves to physicalism or dualism—though if I am right there would not be much point in taking up dualism. To make this clear I will reinforce the principle that, in Putnam's words, 'we could be made of Swiss cheese and it wouldn't matter'.[5] It is not for philosophy to attempt to explain the actual mechanisms of consciousness. But the Swiss Cheese principle lets us proceed on the assumption that raw feeling is constituted by something physical, whatever that something may eventually turn out to be. Even if, quite unexpectedly, our own consciousness proved to involve something over and above the physical, the Swiss Cheese principle would still justify the claim that there *could* have been consciousness in a purely physical world. In this way it enables us to see that the issue of dualism versus physicalism is irrelevant to our problems. To support the principle I will use an argument which will make it easier to see how an objective description of complicated machinery might also be a specification of a centre of consciousness—something with its own subjective point of view. The argument will help to unfreeze the mind-set exemplified by Leibniz's remarks about mental machinery.

Still, how *could* the facts of consciousness possibly be determined by the physical facts alone? Answering this question will go far towards bridging the intelligibility gap. My answer comes in Chapters 4 and 5. There I shall be chiefly concerned to give an account of what it takes for something to be a subject of perceptual consciousness. Of course it is so far unclear what such an account must actually do, but I will try to have clarified that question when the time comes.

My account will be, in a very broad sense, functionalist. But here we find the Transformation thesis leering up at us again. Many people think the inverted spectrum idea cannot be fitted into a functionalist account, in which case Anna's thoughts may seem to undermine Chapters 4 and 5. However, in Chapter 6 I will complete my case for the claim that the Transformation thesis cannot be ruled out a priori. The apparent difficulties can be smoothly overcome by further developing the account already given. By then I think the intelligibility gap will have been bridged. But there will still be resistance. In the final chapter, therefore, I

[5] H. Putnam, 'The Nature of Mental States', 191.

will recapitulate the various components of the intelligibility gap and attempt to make clear that they have all been dealt with. It will then be useful to examine Thomas Nagel's challenge to physicalism. As a minimal physicalist myself, but not a reductionist, I think he has a sound and important point about what we are able to know. There is a sense in which he is right to maintain that 'there are facts which do not consist in the truth of propositions expressible in a human language'.[6] But I will argue that he has not provided any considerations which threaten the account to be presented here.

I.4   RELATIONAL ACCOUNTS AND THE INFINITE REGRESS OBJECTION

Brooding over ideas like Anna's has led to some strange theories. Some are excessively familiar, and I won't linger long over well-trodden ground. But I do want to deal fairly with any reasonable opposition. The following sections will be devoted to preliminary weeding and pest-control. 'Sense datum' theories and behaviourism had better be cleared out of the way first. Each of these violently opposed and fundamentally mistaken approaches offers clues about what an adequate treatment will have to include. Their discussion will lead to a partial definition of raw feeling at the end of the chapter.

By reflecting on visual illusions, hallucinations, and ideas like the inverted spectrum, early thinkers were nudged towards a simple relational account of experience. There are subjects, whatever they might be, and there is a special class of items to which subjects are related. These 'ideas', 'sense data', 'qualia', or whatever are intermediaries between us and the world out there. Caused to occur by ordinary things like houses, the sky, stars, rabbits, they themselves are not also 'out there' because they can occur, as in hallucinations, when their typical causes are absent. They are 'inner' and very mysterious. Not even the most delicate brain surgery could reveal your sense datum of a rabbit. Yet we are supposed to face these picture-like inner items rather as we face the images on our television screens. At first such relational or

---

[6] Nagel, 'What Is It Like to Be a Bat?', 396.

'act-object' accounts appear to provide for intersubjective differences of the kind envisaged by Anna. Systematic differences
between you and me in respect of the internal objects typically
produced in us by red things, for example, would be no more
problematic than differences between the tiles in our respective
bathrooms. But all such theories are demolished by a powerful
objection deployed by Ryle in *The Concept of Mind*.[7] Though
familiar, it is worth restating because even reasonable 'qualia
freaks' seem unaware of its power.

The crucial question is how far the putative inner perception is
supposed to resemble ordinary perception of external objects. The
more closely it does so, the stronger becomes the pressure to
apply to it the same relational story as is proposed for ordinary
perception. If perceiving mental objects is like ordinary perception,
then if the relational story is needed to explain ordinary perception it must also be needed to explain the perception of these
mental objects themselves. So a second level of mental objects is
brought into play and we have an infinite regress. But such a
regress would leave no room for any explanation of perception at
all. For this story says nothing about what inner perception is; it
merely exploits our pre-theoretical grasp of the notion: perception
is explained by perception and therefore not explained. A comparison helps to clinch the point. In a camera, an image is focused
on to the film. But of course the camera does not see. Suppose,
then, we fix a further camera inside the first, so that it can
photograph the image on the first film. No matter how many
times this absurd procedure were repeated, the result could never
be that there was vision. The same goes for the replication of
levels of mental image-making. So if inner perception in the relational story is like ordinary external perception, the relational
story cannot explain perception. On the other hand, the more
inner perception is held to differ from ordinary external perception, the more obscure becomes this notion of inner perception,
on which the whole story is based.

You might now suppose that all the relational story needs
is a satisfactory explanation of inner perception. Paradoxically,
though, that would wreck the story. For if the idea of inner
perception could be elucidated without invoking a regress of

---

[7] G. Ryle, *The Concept of Mind*, 113 ff.

internal mental objects, their introduction at any level would be made explanatorily idle. If the inner perception of sense data can be satisfactorily explained without invoking ranks of quasi sense data further back, it must be possible to construct a similar explanation, dispensing with sense data, for the ways in which the mind deals with the patterns of stimulation that come from our retinas (and, for cases of hallucination, with similar patterns caused in other ways). For according to the mental object story, the objects of inner perception share their perceptible properties with external objects. (Believe it or not, the doctrine is that a sense datum may be round or yellow like a balloon.[8]) It follows that any adequate account of the inner perception of sense data must be capable of being adapted so as to apply to the physical images on our retinas.

The theorist might reply that even if that is right, it doesn't absolutely rule out an account in which there is a single level of mental objects or sense data. Perhaps so; but this is no help to the relational theorist. For then, given that the account of inner perception really is adequate, we have the following possibility. Two people could have exactly the same subjective experiences in perception, illusion, hallucination, and so on, yet while the one had sense data (in the strong relational sense) the other lacked them. This shows that although the special inner items might conceivably form part of the mechanisms of perception, they would make no contribution to the character of experience. So relational theories are in principle incapable of doing their intended job.

1.5 JACKSON'S DEFENCE OF A RELATIONAL ANALYSIS

The general form of relational theories leaves room for the possibility that the internal mental objects should be physical. (In a later chapter we shall examine a recent relational theory where they are indeed physical.[9]) However, as we have noted, traditional

---

[8] According to Frank Jackson in his book *Perception*, visual sense data have shapes and colours in the same sense as that in which external objects do. See 1.5 below.

[9] See 6.3 below.

relational theories have been dualistic. That is because they ascribe spatial and other properties, such as colours, to the internal
objects—and there seem to be no physical items with the right
properties in the right place. If I have a round greenish sense
datum—a real object to which I am related—then since everyone
agrees that no such round greenish object exists in my brain, the
sense datum, if internal at all, must be non-physical. Although
I think the infinite regress argument demolishes all relational
theories, we shall benefit from a look at Frank Jackson's careful
defence of this type of theory in his book *Perception*. He arrives at
his dualistic sense datum doctrine on the basis of two main considerations. One is the claim that descriptions of shape and colour
are univocal when applied to both external objects and sense data;
the other is his view that there can be no adequate alternative
to a relational analysis because statements about hallucinations
and sensations cannot be non-relationally paraphrased. I will
argue that the univocality claim gives no support to a relational
analysis because Jackson's reasoning is based on a mistaken
presupposition.

The 'univocality thesis' is that ' "red", "square", "five inches
across", and the like mean the same when applied to visual hallucinations as they do when applied to physical objects; and . . . "in
my foot", "in my stomach", and the like mean the same when
applied to bodily sensations as they do when applied to physical
objects'.[10]

By itself this thesis seems unproblematic, and clearly has no
tendency to support a dualistic doctrine. That is just as well, since
'red' or 'in my foot', as used in connection with hallucinations or
bodily sensations, could hardly be understood at all unless they
had the same meaning as they have when applied straightforwardly
to physical objects. The trouble with Jackson's position is that
even behaviourists could accept those points. 'I am hallucinating a
pink elephant', for example, might be paraphrased in dispositional
terms which included the expression 'pink elephant' used in
exactly the same sense as it would have when applied to a pink
elephant—something on the lines of: 'I have some of the behavioural dispositions I should have if I were faced with a pink
elephant.' So the univocality thesis raises no problems for those

[10] Jackson, *Perception*, 74.

who reject the sense datum doctrine. However, Jackson argues
that it is impossible to provide adequate *paraphrases* of sensation
statements which both respect the univocality thesis and involve
no commitment to a relational analysis.

One interesting consideration he offers in favour of the univocality thesis is that I might be unable to tell whether my experience was of a phosphene or of a real flash of light. (Phosphenes
can happen when a small electric current is passed through a
certain region of the cortex.) Then, he says, 'I will not know
whether to describe my experience as seeing a yellow flash of light
or as having an hallucination of one; but I will know that "bright
yellow" is the term to use to describe my experience *whether or
not* it is a phosphene or a flash of light'.[11] He points out that if the
univocality thesis doesn't hold in such cases, I don't know what
my words 'bright yellow' mean because I don't know whether or
not I am hallucinating, which he rightly describes as absurd.
And that does seem to support the univocality thesis. But does
it also support the much stronger thesis (which Jackson also
maintains) that in both possible cases—a real flash of light and a
phosphene—*there is something*, a sense datum, which is yellow?
You might think it did. For you might think that unless there
were a yellow something in each case, the fact that the word
'yellow' was used univocally would be mysterious. Jackson doesn't
explicitly state this argument. Instead he goes on to attack non-
relational paraphrases of the statements we might use to describe
our possibly hallucinatory experiences. But in any case the example of uncertainty in such situations does nothing to support
the view that in both cases there is something which is yellow.

The main question at issue in Jackson's discussions is whether
the metaphysical facts about perception and sensation involve a
relation between a subject on the one hand and an object—a non-
physical sense datum—on the other. Yet the statements whose
analysis he discusses are not, after all, attempts to characterize the
metaphysical facts of the matter. They are statements made by
or about people in ordinary mental language. Admittedly these
statements, such as 'I am having a greenish after-image', are attempts to characterize perceptual and other experiences—not
about unrelated topics like the cost of living. More to the point, it

[11] Ibid. 75.

is not irrelevant to see if adequate non-relational paraphrases can be devised. Still, there is at any rate no obvious reason why difficulties over finding convincing non-relational paraphrases of such statements should bring with them difficulties over non-relational metaphysical analyses of the facts of perception. Jackson, however, presupposes that difficulties of the first kind do entail difficulties of the second kind.

This presupposition is mistaken. Think of statements like 'I was looking for the rabbit', said when, as it happens, there is no rabbit to be referred to. We can't construe such statements relationally, and we may have difficulty paraphrasing them non-relationally. But that is no reason to suppose that the metaphysical facts are essentially relational. Similarly, if people's characterizations of their hallucinations or bodily sensations involved a commitment to a relational analysis, so that it was hard to paraphrase their content except in terms of such an analysis, it wouldn't follow that a relational analysis of experience was correct. People's theories pervade their psychological reports; but our accounts of what is really going on don't have to respect those theories.

Now Jackson might reply that he doesn't actually assume that the people whose statements are up for paraphrase hold any particular psychological theory. But the point is that the move from 'no possible non-relational paraphrase' to 'no non-relational account' is by no means automatic. Justification is needed; and he has not supplied it. He might also add that the idea of paraphrases is not his: it has been a feature in the literature of physicalism at least as far back as Carnap.[12] That is true. But the fact that some of his opponents have shared his dubious presupposition does nothing to justify it.

As Armstrong has insisted, an adequate account of consciousness or mental states in general need not attempt to find analytical equivalents or even logically necessary and sufficient conditions for true statements about them. I will discuss and support the claim later.[13] For the present, let me just note that if it is correct, Jackson's strategy fails for that reason alone. Even if he is right in maintaining that no adequate non-relational paraphrases of

---

[12] See e.g. R. Carnap, 'Psychology in Physical Language', J. J. C. Smart, 'Sensations and Brain Processes', and 7.5 below.

[13] D. M. Armstrong, *A Materialist Theory of the Mind*, 84 f. See 3.4 below.

statements about hallucinations and sensations are possible, it doesn't follow that no adequate non-relational account of the facts of hallucination and sensation is possible either. I will return to this issue in the final chapter.

1.6 STATES, PROCESSES, AND ONTOLOGY

In the teeth of the infinite regress argument Jackson urges that there can be no adequate alternative to a relational scheme of analysis for perception and sensation. Apart from rejecting various proposed paraphrases of descriptions of experience, he also attacks the idea that talk of sensations can be adequately handled by talk of 'states', 'conditions', or 'processes', or by adverbial accounts. Now, I have said why I think the question of paraphrases doesn't arise. But since I believe we do have to think of perception in terms of states or processes, it will be worth noting what he says.

His main worry seems to be that a state theorist cannot improve ontologically on a relational theorist. He thinks the state or process theorist is threatened by ontological commitments no less objectionable than those of the theorist of mental objects. For example, he says: 'If we may have many sensings for one person at a time, sensings must clearly be strongly distinct from persons and to have a sensation will be, as on the act-object theory, to be related to something other than oneself.'[14] But here I suggest he has confused two distinct questions. One is whether there is any sense at all in which a state or process theorist is committed to the existence of states or processes of persons, over and above the existence of persons. The other is whether such a commitment, assuming it obtains, threatens the goals the state theorist has in rejecting relational analyses of sensation and experience. The answer to the first question is Yes; but to the second it is No.

Words like 'state', 'process', and 'condition' are ontologically cheap. Consider, for example, a car. Such a thing poses no problems even for the most austere physicalism. It would be a remarkable argument which showed that it involved the existence of anything over and above systems of elementary physical particles,

---

[14] Jackson, *Perception*, 60.

organized in certain well-understood ways, the various larger-scale components performing various different functions thanks to their construction and the laws of physics and chemistry. Yet we can characterize any number of different states and conditions that a car may be in, and any number of different processes that may occur in it—all without jeopardizing our physicalistic view of the vehicle. It might be in a clean state or condition, or a rusty one; or one of having worn piston rings, or . . . 'State' and 'condition' are so non-committal that for virtually any description that could be true of the car we can characterize a corresponding possible state or condition. Since the original descriptions are admittedly consistent with physicalism, the alternative ones cannot introduce any ontological extras—or at any rate none that need worry the physicalist.

Evidently each state, condition, and process is, in Jackson's phrase, 'strongly distinct' from the car itself. That is, although their existence depends logically on the car's, the car's existence doesn't depend on theirs. In a very similar way the state or process theorist in the philosophy of mind can admit that each possible state or process of a person, when it occurs, actually exists, and is strongly distinct from the person. My having the auditory experiences I do have as I hear the cat outside is strongly distinct from me, since my existence does not (thank goodness) depend on my having those particular experiences.

The state or process theorist's commitment to the existence of mental states and processes of persons does not therefore undermine the purposes of the theory itself, and does not introduce ontological commitments that have no advantage over those of a relational account. Given the devastating power of the infinite regress objection to the latter, that is just as well. So if we reject relational accounts, as I think we must, we can happily take it that for something to have experiences is for it to be in certain kinds of states, or to undergo certain types of processes.

1.7 BUNDLE THEORIES

One way to avoid the difficulties of relational theories of the mind might be to renounce one side of the relation altogether. According to bundle theories, instead of a subject related to special internal objects, mental life is supposed to be nothing but a collection of such objects, changing through time. Just what those objects are depends on the details of the particular theory, but they will include sense impressions and sensations. They will have to be non-physical, since no one who accepts a physicalist position needs to take on the crushing burdens of the bundle theory. I know of no serious exponents of bundle theories of the mind today.[15] But, as is often the case with unattractive theories, the objections to them bring out some useful points. The ones I shall concentrate on help to emphasize, in particular, certain points about the essential role of causal relationships among mental states.

One well-known difficulty for bundle theories is the question of what unites the members of one bundle—what makes this experience mine rather than someone else's or no one's? No satisfactory answer has been devised. Another familiar objection, perhaps even more compelling, is that the idea that a pain, for example, could exist all by itself, without any subject whose pain it was, is unintelligible. The only way we can understand the notion of a pain is as an experience that some subject has. Nor does putting a lot of such things together make the idea more palatable.

Now consider whether the members of a given bundle interact causally. Suppose they do not. In that case, when I claim to be recalling some experience I had yesterday—hearing someone speaking, for example—the experience of actually hearing the other person speaking yesterday is not, contrary to what one would tend to suppose, a causal factor in the experience I have now when I recall that earlier experience. Perhaps this idea isn't exactly unintelligible. But clearly no one would adopt it unless they were forced by very powerful considerations indeed, and

---

[15] No one, that is, who holds a view of the nature of consciousness such as I have just sketched, one on the lines indicated by Hume's statement that we are 'nothing but a bundle or collection of different perceptions, which succeed each other with an inconceivable rapidity, and are in a perpetual flux and movement' (*A Treatise of Human Nature*, I. iv. vi. 252). An attractive but different kind of bundle theory, applied to the question of personal identity rather than consciousness, and emphasizing Hume's comparison of a person with a nation, club, or political party, is compellingly urged by Derek Parfit in *Reasons and Persons*. Dennett's position on 'selves' in his *Consciousness Explained* has affinities with this view, and, again, is not what I am attacking here.

these seem to be lacking. So no doubt the bundle theorist will concede that the members of a given bundle do interact causally. (If not, the theory runs into some of the same difficulties as epiphenomenalism: see the next section.) But now consider the case of a bundle that at present includes a pain. Normally that pain will act on other components of the bundle, causing thoughts about the pain, hopes that it will soon go away, decisions to take an aspirin, and so on. However, something which normally causes something else can, logically, fail to do so. So suppose that happens with a pain I now have. The pain component of the bundle is there but simply fails to have any effects on other components. It follows that I would have no thoughts about my pain, no desire for it to go away, wouldn't take aspirins; and if you asked me whether I was in pain I would say I wasn't. So the bundle theory allows for the possibility that we are all in extreme pain all the time without realizing it. But that again is, if not simply false, scarcely intelligible. (Nor can this objection be avoided by the suggestion that a 'pain component' not appropriately linked with other components doesn't count as a pain at all. The objection would then be that we couldn't sensibly be said to have all the time, without noticing it, the sort of sense datum typically associated with pain.)

The only merit of bundle theories of consciousness seems to be that they avoid the pitfalls of relational theories. The objections we have noted make clear, though, that keeping the 'object' side of the relation while rejecting a distinct subject is no solution. We must not construe the having of experiences as a matter of a subject's standing in a relation to 'inner' particulars. But neither can they be mere subjectless orphans. Apart from other considerations, the causal interrelations of mental states preclude this.

1.8 EPIPHENOMENALISM

If you are impressed by the seemingly universal explanatory power of physics, and by the wealth of evidence for the view that all behaviour is somehow caused by physical processes in the central nervous system, yet at the same time you can't see how consciousness could be accounted for by just those physical processes, then you may bite the bullet and take up epiphenomenalism.

Epiphenomenalism notoriously and self-consciously defies common assumptions about the causal relations of mental states. Since a recent defence overlooks one or two of the most telling objections to this doctrine I will give them here. They too will help us to attend to what an adequate account of consciousness must include.

It is Jackson again who defends the view that 'certain *properties* of certain mental states, ... [properties which he calls qualia], are such that their possession or absence makes no difference to the physical world'.[16] To the objection that it is 'just obvious that the hurtfulness of pain is partly responsible for the subject seeking to avoid pain, saying "It hurts" and so on' he replies that what at first looks like an obvious case of causation may turn out to be, instead, a case of two distinct effects of a common cause. That is true; but it hardly meets the point of the objection.

Consider my utterance of 'It hurts', produced when asked how my burnt hand feels. Two key points must be kept in mind. First, if the hurtfulness of pain never has any physical effects at all, it won't explain such physical events as the occasional utterance by English speakers of such words as 'hurtfulness'. Second, epiphenomenalists are nevertheless committed to the view that such utterances do *refer* to hurtfulness, otherwise they would be unable to state their doctrine. These implications make epiphenomenalism incapable of a satisfactory explanation of the facts that the word 'hurtfulness' both gets uttered and refers to hurtfulness.

An attractive and widely accepted view is that, typically, an expression which refers to a thing or kind does so partly on account of the latter's causal role in the expression's having acquired a use.[17] Epiphenomenalism rules out any such theory of reference; yet exponents of the doctrine have offered no convincing alternative. There is an acute problem here, given that they cannot appeal to magic. This becomes clear when you consider how they

---

[16] F. Jackson, 'Epiphenomenal Qualia', 133. It may be as well to note here a point that has been emphasized by Dennett: we are talking about 'epiphenomena' in the special *philosophical* sense, according to which they have no effects on the physical world, not in the psychological sense, according to which they are defined merely as features lacking functions.

[17] See S. Kripke, *Naming and Necessity*; H. Putnam, 'The Meaning of "Meaning"'.

could consistently explain how 'hurtfulness' refers to hurtfulness
rather than to what they maintain is something completely different: the processes they regard as only its concomitant physical
causes. Since a causal theory of reference is not available to them,
presumably they must have recourse to a descriptive one. But
if the supporting descriptions don't explicitly mention that they
apply to something non-physical, the difficulty just noted applies:
'hurtfulness' might just as well refer to the physical concomitants.
You might try to escape this difficulty by requiring the descriptions
to specify explicitly that hurtfulness is non-physical. But that
seems unjustified. It is hard to see how the non-physicality of
hurtfulness could have been built into our ways of talking.

There is a more devastating objection, which further illustrates
the vital role of causal relations among mental states. The usual
version of the doctrine has it that epiphenomena don't cause other
epiphenomena. (Here epiphenomenalists are obliged to take the
contrary view to bundle theorists.) Instead, each is caused by
concomitant physical processes. Nor does it seem that epiphenomenalists could give up this view. For if one epiphenomenon
causes others, the doctrine is exposed to the objection against the
bundle theory noted earlier. If an epiphenomenal pain quale is
supposed to cause epiphenomena involved in thoughts about the
pain, then the doctrine allows something to be genuinely possible
when it is scarcely intelligible: that each of us should be in extreme
pain all the time without realizing it. So it seems they had better
stay with the usual version of the doctrine.

But now consider the question of what constitutes our knowledge or awareness of our own epiphenomenal qualia. Epiphenomenalists are committed to the logical possibility that all or some
of a person's qualia should suddenly cease, remain absent for a
few minutes, hours, or years, and as suddenly return—all without
the slightest effects on behaviour. Of course they will insist that
the laws of psychophysical nature would always prevent such a
thing actually happening; but the objection requires only the bare
possibility. That being so, our knowledge or awareness of our
qualia could not on their view be constituted by any of the purely
physical processes occurring in us. For exactly similar processes
would occur in beings that were physically just like us yet completely lacked qualia—it would occur in Zombies who had no

qualia to be aware of. (Epiphenomenalists are bound to concede
that such creatures could exist. Otherwise they would be committed to the inconsistent view that qualia involved nothing over
and above the physical: see Chapter 3.) Nor could the awareness
in question consist purely in the presence of the relevant qualia
together with those same physical processes. For that would imply
that such awareness involved no sensitivity to qualia. To be aware
of the presence or absence of something seems to require as a
minimum some kind of sensitivity to its presence or absence. Yet
the doctrine cannot allow this sensitivity to be constituted by
any physical states or processes. So for epiphenomenalists, our
awareness of our pains can consist only in the occurrence of
certain other *non*-physical processes, distinct from the pains themselves. Similarly our awareness of the *absence* of pains can consist
only in the occurrence of certain non-physical processes. However,
in order for these processes to be sensitive to the presence or
absence of pain they would have to be causally affected by the
presence or absence of the epiphenomenal qualia in question. And
that contradicts the conclusion of the last paragraph.

So it seems that epiphenomenalism self-destructs. If epiphenomenal qualia cause other qualia, all of us could be in extreme
pain all the time without realizing it. If they don't, we can't be
aware of our own pains. To abandon the doctrine would appear
less painful than to maintain it in the face of such difficulties.
Apart from those objections, there is a more general consideration
which ought to make people resist what they see as pressures to
accept epiphenomenalism. It is simply that those aspects of mental
life which they classify as epiphenomena are in fact among the
most significant components of our existence. The actual nature
of our experiences matters to us. So the suggestion that it has
absolutely no effects on what we do or say is almost unintelligible.
In any case, if my account of consciousness is correct there will be
no need to resort to epiphenomenalism.

The varieties of dualism I have discussed evidently provide no
adequate basis for grappling with our problems, although they do
at least attempt to do justice to important aspects of consciousness
that some other theories have played down. Later, in Chapter 3, I
will consider Cartesian dualism, and have some less unkind things
to say about it than about these other varieties. But now let us
look at the opposite end of the theoretical spectrum.

1.9 BEHAVIOURISM

I take 'analytical' or 'philosophical' behaviourism to be the view that there is no more to the existence of mental states than the existence of something with the right behavioural dispositions or capacities.[18] Analytical behaviourism has the following considerations in its favour. It provides for a straightforward explanation of our ability to talk about other people's mental states: we can do it because we can learn which kinds of behaviour go with which mental states. It thereby disposes of the epistemological problem of our knowledge of other minds. And it enables puzzles like Anna's, and all the philosophical difficulties they appear to generate, to be dismissed as misconceptions. So if this doctrine is correct, the only residual problem is to account for those misconceptions and bring pretty well everyone back into the path of truth. For not many people explicitly maintain a straight behaviourist position today. In any case I don't know how the objections to it could be met. Two are specially noteworthy. The first is that it is obvious that headaches, phosphenes, or tinnitus are not just a matter of behaviour or behavioural dispositions: they are episodic. The second is that there are powerful arguments for what Ned Block calls 'psychologism': the view that even if something had all the right behavioural dispositions and capacities to be counted as intelligent, or as otherwise a genuine psychological subject, it would still not be so if it lacked the right kinds of internal processing.

Several possible non-conscious devices appear to be behaviourally equivalent to sentient beings. One candidate would be an artificial giant operated by a crew inside its head—fanatics, they would have to be, dedicated to ensuring that the giant behaved appropriately regardless of their own interests. I will return to it in Chapter 4.

Another candidate is the computer-driven robot Block describes

---

[18] This is the least problematic version of (analytical) behaviourism. It avoids the objectionable claim that each type of mental state is constituted by its own proprietary behavioural disposition. It also avoids the gratuitously odd claim that there are no mental states at all. Note that this view need not maintain that the relevant kinds of behaviour must be specifiable in non-psychological terms: only that descriptions of behaviour, however deeply they involve psychological language, do not depend for their truth on the nature of the processes that lie under the subject's skin.

in his article 'Psychologism and Behaviourism'. Since I shall refer
to this ingenious system more than once in the course of the book,
I will mention its key features now. Its sentient-seeming behaviour
results from having the computer's memory stocked with *all
possible* 'sensible life-histories' (of not longer than some pre-
determined duration: say seventy years). These life-histories are
represented in terms of two sets of complex patterns. On the one
hand are sequences of possible total patterns of instantaneous
input from its 'sense-receptors'. On the other there are sequences
of possible total patterns of instantaneous output to the motors
that drive its limbs. At each instant its behaviour is produced by a
very simple program. This program (*a*) is at each instant linked to
one or other of the many stored possible sensible life-histories
whose initial segment coincides with its actual life-history so far,
(*b*) searches for the alphanumerically-next such stored history in
which that same initial segment is immediately followed by the
current instant's total pattern of input, (*c*) puts out whatever may
be the next output pattern in that stored history—and so on,
until its seventy years of life (or whatever the limit may be) are
exhausted.

The stored life-histories are all 'sensible'. That is, they are all
such that, whatever the system's input–output history so far may
be, the next programmed output ensures that its overall pattern of
behaviour would be counted as sensible in its total context. These
incredibly vast possible life-histories might conceivably have been
laboriously worked out over centuries by armies of research
students, or they might have come into existence as the chance
effects of an electric storm in the computer centre. Either way, the
two key considerations are these. First, the stored life-histories
cover the *totality* of possible sequences of sensory inputs—they
cover all possible worlds in which the robot might have had to
operate. So no matter what actually happens, its behaviour is
guaranteed to be sensible. Second, there are no processes inside
the system which could constitute the system's *own* assessment of
its situation, or its deliberation about what to do next.

The point of this story is not to prove anything by itself—by a
crude appeal to intuition. It is, rather, to illustrate something
about our ordinary ascriptions of intelligence to systems. Although
normally made in ignorance of the details of internal processing,
these ascriptions are by no means purely behaviouristic. They

are not completely insulated from consideration of the internal processes by which behaviour is produced. In particular we surely require, for intelligence, that the system's behaviour result from its own assessment of its current situation. So if we look inside it and find that in this case its behaviour was produced in a way incompatible with that requirement, we shall tend to abandon the claim that it is intelligent—in spite of its behaviour. (That doesn't prevent our calling it shmintelligent, of course. But it might well prevent our treating it with the consideration we should give to a system that really did improvise its own responses.) The Block machine fails that test.

Of course you might still insist that talking about deliberation and calculation need be no more than a fancy way of talking about behaviour and dispositions. But in view of the work that would have been required from the armies of research assistants, and since we know of systems that really do deliberate and calculate on the spot (ourselves), that line is at best hard to sustain.

A third candidate for a non-conscious but intelligently-behaving system is another robot: the Machine Table robot, to be described in a later chapter.

All such entities have the right dispositions and capacities, but cannot plausibly be described as conscious—or so I maintain.[19] I take them to be counter-examples to analytical behaviourism.

1.10 A ROUGH FIX ON RAW FEELING

It does seem that perceptual experience and sensation involve something 'inner' which survives the behaviourist bludgeon. Admittedly, sense datum theories badly misconstrue the nature of that inner something. Having an experience isn't a matter of being faced with an ethereal television screen. The relational model must go. Nor is the mind a bundle of sense data. But at least sense

---

[19] For discussion of the artificial giant, see 4.5 below. Block's machine is described in his 'Psychologism and Behaviourism'. The Machine Table robot is discussed in 4.3 below and in my 'Sentience, Causation, and Some Robots'. For useful statements of the standard case against analytical behaviourism, see Armstrong, *A Materialist Theory of the Mind*, ch. 3; W. G. Lycan, *Consciousness*, ch. 1.

datum theories attempt to do justice to the special inner some-thing. They treat experiences and sensations as having intrinsic features independent of their causal or other relations with ex-ternal things. They thereby provide room for the kinds of be-haviourally undetectable interpersonal differences in people's ways of perceiving that were imagined by Anna. In these respects, I will try to show, sense datum theories were right.

Not that behaviourism is altogether wrong, even though it is an over-reaction to the quirks of dualistic theories. Behaviour is crucially important in the ascription of *content* to mental states. We could hardly have learnt how to use psychological descriptions except through their multifarious links with patterns of behaviour. And this point applies to experiences and sensations as much as to beliefs, desires, and other intentional states. For it would seem to make no sense to talk of experiences and sensations without content. Their having content, in turn, seems to require them to stand in certain kinds of relation, via behaviour, to external things.

So there is substantial truth in behaviourism. All the same, for there to be experiences or sensations at all it seems there must be something inner (in that special sense) which has a character independent of any particular relation to external things, or so I will argue. If that is right, the inner something could be present even if experiences and sensations in the full sense were not. It could even be instantiated in a brain in a vat. Now there are good reasons for doubting that an entity which had never been capable of any sort of behaviour, such as a brain in a vat, could have mental states with content, could conceptualize or indeed have any sort of mind. But that only means that the inner something which I am talking about doesn't automatically bring content with it. It is necessary, but not sufficient, for experience and sensation. In that sense it is the essence of consciousness. Because it is not necessarily coextensive with experiences and sensations, I pick it out with the specially devised phrase 'raw feeling'.[20]

In the world as we know it a subject of raw feeling is also a subject of perceptual experiences and sensations, interacting with things in the world. These interactions play a vital part in giving experiences and sensations their content. Often we introduce the

---

[20] Of course the expression is to be thought of as a gerund like 'thinking', not as a mass term like 'pudding'.

content of experiences by saying what they are 'of'; and often what they are of is what typically causes them. For me to have the experience of smelling freshly ground coffee, for example, requires me and my experience to stand in some appropriate causal relation to freshly ground coffee. An investigation of the nature of such relations helps to explain what it takes for experiences and sensations to have the contents they do. However, it will not be necessary to pursue that investigation here. This is not another book about content. It is about something without which, if I am right, there would be no content.

Raw feeling does not, I think, involve anything over and above physical events in brains, or in whatever Martians or suitably constructed robots may have instead of brains. But to *say* that something is a subject of raw feeling is not to say that it is a locus of various kinds of physical events. On my account a subject of raw feeling need not be a full-blown psychological subject, need not have a mind. Yet it does have an inner life. It is something it is like something to be. So merely to describe the physical processes inside it in physical terms would fail to capture something about it that is interesting, important, and perplexing.

The six statements below extract the main points about raw feeling from what I have said so far. They are not intended as a definition, still less do they explain what it takes for something to be a subject of raw feeling. But they may help to make my subject-matter clearer.

I. Whenever we use any of our senses something is caused to occur—raw feeling, or, as I shall alternatively say, the having of raw feels—which has a general character associated with that sense and a specific character partly but not entirely determined by the things acting on that sense at the time.

Visual raw feeling has one general character, auditory raw feeling has a different one, and so for each sense. The *specific* character of my experience of a ripe tomato, for example, is partly dependent on the tomato itself, but partly on me. (I) is comparable with the claim of sense datum theorists that sense data are part of any normal sensory experience.

II. To be a subject of raw feeling involves having at least minimal consciousness, hence being something it is like something to be.

Bear in mind, though, that for the reasons noted earlier a subject of raw feeling might not be a full-blown psychological subject. It might lack contentful thoughts and experiences and the ability to conceptualize.

> III. The various kinds of raw feeling could occur independently of any external items which might actually cause instances of them to occur, and also of any behaviour or behavioural dispositions which those instances may cause.

For reasons already noted, this doesn't commit me to reject externalism about the *content* of experiences and sensations: the view that such content depends logically on causal or other relations with external things.

> IV. There is also raw feeling outside perception. It is a constituent of dreaming, of hallucinations, and of mental imagery of all kinds.

This again parallels a view typically held by sense datum theorists.

> V. A subject of raw feeling can detect its occurrence in a way that others cannot, except perhaps in special cases—for example as a result of connections between brains.

This point serves no epistemological purposes here. But it needs to be noted. I can detect my own sensory experiences without having to note my behaviour or brain processes. But this need not give me a special epistemological authority as to the character of my raw feels, much less make me incorrigible. Note especially that it is no part of my position that we are normally *aware* of our raw feels. The point is rather that awareness involves raw feeling.

> VI. Raw feeling is not to be construed on the relational model, as a matter of there being particulars to which the subject is related; nor as a matter of such particulars being somehow bundled together.

Raw feeling is a process which makes it easy for us to speak in terms of our 'raw feels'. But that phrase is not to be taken to imply that some mysterious kind of entity is involved. It is a way of talking about features of the processes which constitute raw feeling.

I am not using the expression 'raw feeling' in the hope that it corresponds exactly to some notion already current in folk psychology or the philosophical literature. I think it helps us to pick out something which still needs attention. Dennett has claimed that 'traditional analyses' of qualia suggest they have four remarkable properties. They are, he says, supposed to be 'ineffable', 'intrinsic', 'private', and 'directly or immediately apprehensible in consciousness'.[21] He has some fun showing that nothing could have all these properties. But according to my account of raw feeling, it isn't supposed to have any of them. It is a different notion. (Of course I don't expect anyone to concede immediately that it's a sound one.)

As I explained in the Preface, the expression 'raw feeling' is adapted from Tolman.[22] But too much must not be read into its components. 'Raw' seems appropriate because it suggests that the phenomenon in question doesn't depend for its existence either on having content or on being conceptualized. But it mustn't be taken to imply that raw feeling is free from interpretation or processing, or in any way simple or unitary. On the contrary it involves a great deal of interpretation—of a kind—and it is far from simple. Again, although there is some aptness about the word 'feeling' in this connection, I do not intend to imply that the phenomenon I am talking about qualifies as a kind of feeling in the ordinary sense.[23]

Tolman's own phrase 'raw feels' will still sometimes be useful. But it has to be understood with (VI) in mind. Raw feeling is a process; and when for convenience I write of raw feels, that does not imply that they are items to which the subject is related. They are features of the process. The phrase 'raw feels' has to be accepted as essentially vague—a bit like 'clouds' and 'waves'. As I write, for example, I have some raw feels caused by the shapes and colours of the characters on my word-processor screen and others caused by freshly ground coffee. That is to say I can

---

[21] D. C. Dennett, 'Quining Qualia', 46 f. Cf. his *Consciousness Explained*, 373, 390, 450.

[22] See E. C. Tolman, *Purposive Behaviour in Animals and Men*.

[23] 'Pain is a feeling', according to David Lewis in 'Mad Pain and Martian Pain', 130. But although pain involves what I call raw feeling, raw feeling in general includes vastly more than is ordinarily covered by 'feeling'. On the way interpretation is involved, see Chs. 4, 5, and 6.

distinguish features of the heterogeneous flux of raw feeling and characterize them in terms of their actual or typical causes. Such talk is convenient as far as it goes. But obviously there is no basis for sharp answers to questions like 'How long does a raw feel last?', 'Does a change in apparent colour result in a change in raw feel?', 'Is the shape raw feel distinct from the colour raw feel?', 'How many raw feels did you have before breakfast?'—any more than there are, generally, sharp answers to such questions as 'How long does a cloud last?' or 'How many waves can you see?'. Still, we can give rough answers to those questions about raw feels, just as we can to the others.

To conclude this chapter let us return to Anna's thought about the inverted spectrum. I will formulate a thesis on the lines of her suggestions. It will help further to clarify the notion of raw feeling and to remind us of the problems we need to deal with. Roughly, my view is that Anna was right, or at any rate more right than those who regard the whole idea as nonsensical. Statements I–VI imply that the various kinds of raw feeling really occur at a certain stage in the causal chain from publicly observable input to behavioural output, and so are *logically* independent (under some description) of their causal or other relations to things outside the subject. Suppose, then, that in fact red things typically cause a certain kind of raw feeling, X, in Anna, and green things typically cause a different kind, Y. If we simplify a bit and assume the symmetry of the spectrum, there seems no reason a priori why the nervous pathways from her retinas should not have been differently organized, so that red things caused Y instead of X, green things caused X instead of Y, and so on systematically through the spectrum, respecting complementarity. If that had been the case, then when she saw a ripe tomato in normal light, her visual raw feel would have been of the kind she now actually has when she sees an unripe tomato, and vice versa, without any relevant differences in her behavioural capacities.

This suggestion evidently depends on an assumption additional to the one about symmetry. It is that for each individual with normal colour vision, each discriminable hue is correlated with a different kind of raw feel. On that assumption, the spectral ordering of the actual colours of things induces a corresponding ordering of associated raw feels. The key idea, then, is that each hue could have been correlated throughout a person's lifetime with the kind of raw feel which is actually correlated with another hue—perhaps the former's complementary hue—without making any difference to the person's discriminatory capacities. The whole array of kinds of raw feel could have been permanently switched round, or otherwise transformed, relative to its connections with external hues. Given enough symmetry, all relevant relationships of sameness and difference would have been preserved, so the subject's use of language would seem normal.

In fact the colour solid has asymmetries which appear to preclude the exact preservation of all discriminatory capacities through such transformations.[24] However, my notion of raw feeling doesn't require this familiar example to be entirely sound. Indeed, it doesn't depend on there being any dimension of any actual human sense modality which has the necessary symmetry. A fortiori it doesn't entail that there actually are any instances of individuals whose ways of perceiving differ in the manner envisaged. Even so, if the doctrine of raw feeling itself is correct, something analogous to the inverted spectrum case remains a genuine possibility. This more cautious claim is embodied in the *Transformation* thesis:

The following is logically possible: that there should be a dimension of perception, a sense modality, a subject of perceptual experience in that modality and a transformation of the pattern of kinds of raw feels correlated with the features registered by that sense modality, such that if the transformed pattern had obtained throughout the subject's lifetime, there would have been no differences in any of the subject's discriminatory capacities.

So much by way of a rough fix on raw feeling. My central problem is to explain how there could be such a thing. The theories we have noticed so far leave the intelligibility gap as wide as ever. But is there really a problem here at all?

---

[24] Asymmetries of the colour solid are exploited by Bernard Harrison in *Form and Content*. However, his solution seems to me to be undermined by its reliance on what I shall argue are merely contingent asymmetries (see 6.7 below). C. L. Hardin, in *Color for Philosophers*, 134–54, provides a detailed discussion of this issue. Incidentally, the need for symmetry seems to rule out even the bare possibility of some types of experience, notably pain, instantiating the Transformation thesis.

2

Is the Notion Sound?

The whole idea of raw feeling may strike you as fishy, especially when linked with the Transformation thesis. Does it really make sense? Or is it just a symptom of confusion—a relic of a fundamentally wrong-headed Cartesian outlook?[1] In this chapter I will examine two sets of considerations that might appear to reinforce these doubts. One is Wittgenstein's private language argument, which you might think would demolish the notion. Yet, I will argue, even the Transformation thesis survives Wittgensteinian assault. The other considerations are inspired chiefly by science. It seems reasonable to suppose that science has no use for the notion of raw feeling. If so, you might wonder how it can be worth taking seriously. But I will argue that the notion helps us to get clear about genuine problems, which would not vanish even if we gave up talking in those terms.

This chapter will not, of course, allay all possible doubts about the notion of raw feeling. My aim is to show that it is not vulnerable to certain familiar types of objection. I suspect that the lack of a satisfactory philosophical account of anything like that notion tends to make the objections seem more compelling than they are. The account in later chapters will, I hope, overcome any lingering resistance.

2.1 WITTGENSTEIN AND THE INVERTED SPECTRUM

Although Wittgenstein might well have rejected the notion of raw feeling, the considerations he offers do not justify such rejection. This is largely because the notion does not involve the ideas and assumptions he was trying to demolish. At various times he

---

[1] I used to think of it that way myself. See R. Kirk, 'Goodbye to Transposed Qualia'.

attacked the idea of sense data, and more generally the relational analysis of perception. He also attacked the idea that the character of our experiences is 'private' in the strong sense that none of us can really know what other people's experiences are like. But some of the considerations he himself offers can be seen as providing an account of how what I am calling our raw feels are *not* private in that strong sense. So if Wittgenstein is right, my position offers no support for the sceptic. And if he is wrong, the notion of raw feeling is not after all vulnerable from that quarter. I will elaborate these claims in this and the following sections. The inverted spectrum idea will continue as a catalyst. Let us start with some of Wittgenstein's remarks from 'Notes for Lectures on "Private Experience" and "Sense Data"':

We said that one reason for introducing the idea of the sense datum was that people, as we say, sometimes see different things, colours, e.g., looking at the same object. Cases in which we say 'he sees dark red whereas I see light red'. We are inclined to talk about an object other than the physical object which the person sees who is said to see the physical object. It is further clear that we only gather from the other person's behaviour (e.g., what he tells us) what that object looks like, and so it lies near to say that he has this object before his mind's eye and that we don't see it . . . Now I want to draw your attention to one particular difficulty about the use of the 'sense datum'. We said that there were cases in which we should say that the person sees green what I see red. Now the question suggests itself: if this can be so at all, why should it not be always the case? It seems, if once we have admitted that it can happen under peculiar circumstances, that it may always happen. But then it is clear that the very idea of seeing red loses its use if we can never know if the other does not see something utterly different. So what are we to do: Are we to say that this can only happen in a limited number of cases? This is a very serious situation.—We introduced the expression that *A* sees something else than *B* and we mustn't forget that this had use only under the circumstances under which we introduced it . . .[2]

___

[2] 'Wittgenstein's Notes for Lectures on "Private Experience" and "Sense Data"', 316. (Rhees tells us these notes seem to have been written between the end of 1934 and March 1936. He remarks: 'I have left the Germanisms even when I felt sure he would have corrected them, as one reminder that these are rough notes' (274).) The cases Wittgenstein describes in this and related passages are illuminatingly discussed by David Pears in *The False Prison*, ii.402–22. However, for the reasons to be noted in this and the following section, none of the cases he discusses coincides with what is envisaged by the Transformation thesis.

Clearly, one of his chief targets here is the relational analysis of perception, involving internal objects 'before the mind's eye'. We have already seen that such analyses are mistaken. So if my version of the inverted spectrum idea—the Transformation thesis— requires a relational analysis, it fails for that reason. But I don't think it does require that sort of analysis. Nor do I think it commits us to any form of dualism. The essentials of the *legitimate* inverted spectrum idea can be accommodated within a physicalistic ontology. But let us look further at what Wittgenstein says.

The version of the inverted spectrum idea which he criticizes here is significantly different from the Transformation thesis. An earlier passage helps us to get clear about this difference. He imagines someone saying: 'I can't understand it, I see everything red blue today and vice versa'—and finds this intelligible, given the right circumstances. Such a sudden intrasubjective switch does seem conceivable. 'We should say we know that he means by the words "blue" and "red" what we do as he has always used them as we do.' I expect most people would agree with this conclusion. In any case I know of no compelling objection to it, so let us move on. The case is different, Wittgenstein continues, if the person claims *always* to have seen everything red blue, and so on, even when he agrees with the rest of us in his use of colour words.[3] And indeed, against this second alleged possibility the argument in the quoted passage is surely effective. How can it make sense to say that someone sees green where they and everyone else says they see red? But again the Transformation thesis implies no such possibility.

Those of us who think the inverted spectrum idea is essentially correct are not committed to the view that what is inverted is full-blown *experiences of colour*. The Transformation thesis concerns relations between kinds of *raw feeling* and their typical external causes, not relations between experiences or sensations and their causes. It is not my contention that if a person says, to no one's surprise, that they have an experience of red when they see a ripe tomato, they might perhaps actually be having an experience of green instead. Indeed, I believe that in order to be able to have an experience of green (if that idiom is acceptable) or to see anything *as green*, you must normally see red things, green things, and

---

[3] 'Wittgenstein's Notes', 284.

colours generally as other people do. And that includes having the same raw feels in the same perceptual situations. So I don't want to suggest that one of the behaviourally undetectable alternative ways of seeing red things is *seeing them (as) green.* On the contrary, I think we know that when people with normal colour vision see ripe tomatoes in normal circumstances they see them as red and have an experience of red. What I am saying is that in spite of the fact that everyone with normal colour vision actually has one kind of raw feel on seeing a ripe tomato in normal conditions, it is possible they should have had a different one. The kinds of raw feeling associated with the various colours might always have been transposed, without any effects on people's behavioural capacities.

Later I will argue that if there were many actual instances of the Transformation thesis, some of our ways of talking about one another's experiences would be undermined. Much of the power of that language rests on a presupposition to the effect that in general the relevant facts about our internal workings—facts which are detectable, though not behaviourally—are alike. The Transformation thesis, I will argue, does nothing to undermine that presupposition. That being so, it is entirely consistent with our knowing that we have similar experiences, including similar raw feels, in similar perceptual situations. If that is right, it is another reason why Wittgenstein's argument in the quoted passage—that 'the very idea of seeing red loses its use if we can never know if the other does not see something utterly different'—leaves the Transformation thesis untouched.

A large component of the motivation for the sense datum doctrine was epistemological. And much of the original motivation for discussing the idea of a private sensation language was in order to crystallize certain epistemological concerns. Could knowledge of the external world be founded on knowledge of our own sensations? Could we know other people's sensations? The position to be defended here, in contrast, has no such motivation. It has been devised in the attempt to understand the nature of experience; so we might broadly describe its motivation as metaphysical. It makes no commitment to the view that it is impossible to know what one another's raw feels are like.

Still, in the *Investigations* Wittgenstein surely envisaged, and rejected, something very like the Transformation thesis:

272. The essential thing about private experience is really not that each person possesses his own exemplar, but that nobody knows whether other people also have *this* or something else. The assumption would thus be possible—though unverifiable—that one section of mankind had one sensation of red and another section another.

The context shows that he rejected the assumption mentioned in the second sentence. Let us examine his reasons.

2.2   DOES RAW FEELING FALL FOUL OF THE PRIVATE LANGUAGE ARGUMENT?

Suppose there were an actual instance of the Transformation thesis, however improbable that might be. Suppose, for example, that you and I saw red things differently. How could anyone possibly find out? Not from our behaviour, because *ex hypothesi* there could be no behavioural clues. There might be corresponding subtle physical differences; indeed I am sure there would be. But it is at any rate hard to see how any such differences could be *necessarily* linked with the character of raw feels. The latter appear to float free from the physical: that is a large part of our problem. In fact, without the sort of investigations we shall soon be plunged into, it is hard to see why the physical goings-on, whatever they may turn out to be, should necessarily involve raw feeling at all. So the whole idea of raw feeling, with its burden of the Transformation thesis, may well appear to bring an impenetrable privacy with it.

If that conclusion were correct, presumably I would be able to speak inscrutably of the way I saw red things, and you of the way you saw red things. Each would understand their own individual private use of expressions like 'the way I see red things', but no one else could tell what either of us meant. I might describe my experience as 'red-K', you might describe yours as 'red-Y', and we should have private languages within the meaning of the act. So if this reasoning were sound you might think that the Transformation thesis, and with it the whole notion of raw feeling, would fall foul of Wittgenstein's private language argument.

But in fact it doesn't. As a preliminary to noting the flaws in that reasoning, let me set out what I take to be the heart of the private language argument. There are two main sets of considerations. One is directed against the possibility of the actual use of a private language, as follows.

1. Speaking a language is, in Pears's words, 'an artificial accomplishment with standards of correctness which have to be learned and maintained'.[4] So it involves the ability to use the expressions of the language correctly.

2. Using the expressions of a language correctly involves the ability to tell, at least on occasions, whether or not we are doing so—whether we are successfully conforming to the appropriate standards.

3. For this to be so, there must be a difference between being right and just thinking one is right. There must be a difference between what has to conform to a standard, and what constitutes the standard itself.

4. But if only I can understand my private language, so that only I can possibly check my use of its expressions, there will be no difference between being right and merely thinking I am right: 'and that only means that here we can't talk about "right"'.[5] If the only possible check on whether I am successfully conforming to the appropriate standards of correctness is my own judgement of my own behaviour, there is no difference between the check and what has to be checked—which means there is no check at all.

5. So there can be no such thing as private success or correctness, and therefore no possibility of a private language.

The other main set of considerations is to the effect that there is no way for a private language to get started, no way for a person to give meaning to its expressions. Clearly its expressions could not be 'tied up with my natural expressions of sensation', since in that case the language wouldn't be private in the right sense.[6] But neither could they be defined or otherwise usefully associated with what they have to refer to. Any such procedures would have to

---

[4] Pears, *The False Prison*, ii.333. Language need not necessarily be learned, so 'learned' is not quite general. But in the context of the private language argument it certainly applies: the private sensation language is not supposed to be innate.

[5] Wittgenstein, *Philosophical Investigations* I, sect. 258.

[6] See ibid., sect. 256.

ensure that the private linguist remembered the connections right in the future. And step 4 has ruled that out.

I find the private language argument compelling. However, I have summarized it here only as a preliminary to arguing that it grounds no solid objection to the notion of raw feeling. It would do so if that notion, plus the Transformation thesis, implied radical privacy: that we couldn't know what one another's raw feels were like. But it has no such implication. For, as I will explain, we have every reason to suppose that the possibility envisaged by the Transformation thesis is not instantiated. Knowing something is possible is quite consistent with knowing it is not the case. (There might have been a rabbit in my desk drawer, but in fact I know there isn't one.)

But what about the reasoning at the beginning of this section? One flaw in it is that it assumes without argument that the character of our raw feels somehow floats free from the physical facts: that physical differences couldn't possibly reveal that two people's ways of seeing red things were the same, or that they were different. Later I will try to show that the assumption is false.[7] For the present I will just state this aspect of my position and go on to discuss other flaws in the reasoning, and other ways that Wittgensteinian considerations may still appear to undermine the notion of raw feeling.

Dogmatically, then, the totality of truths statable in narrowly physical terms *strictly implies* all truths about raw feeling, or at any rate can legitimately be assumed to do so. (See Chapter 3.) If that is correct, there are at least some conceivable situations where acquaintance with certain physical facts, together with sound conceptual reasoning, could reveal whether your ways of raw feeling were like mine or different, and if different, how. If I knew you were a particle-for-particle replica of me, then, given we were purely physical systems, I should if necessary be able to reassure myself that your way of seeing red things was the same as mine. Further, if I knew you were a particle-for-particle replica of me

---

[7] See Ch. 6. I am using the phrase 'see red things' as a way of avoiding the commitments of 'seeing red'. Monochromats see red things—they see tomatoes, etc.—but presumably they don't see red. Later I shall suggest that if the possibility envisaged by the Transformation thesis were widely actualized there might be no sense in describing anyone as seeing red; but that would be entirely consistent with describing people as seeing red things, and that in different ways.

except for certain kinds of difference in the ways our respective retinas were hooked up with the rest of our central nervous systems (together with whatever further differences those differences had caused), I could learn that the raw feels you had when you saw something red differed from mine; and not only that, but in what the difference consisted.[8] Since the reasoning under discussion presupposes that these contentions are false, it fails to show that the notion of raw feeling involves the possibility of a private language.

However, I don't wish to press those considerations just now because they may seem to miss the point. From the Wittgensteinian perspective the point is to explain how the notion of raw feeling can be intelligible *now.* How can it be intelligible so long as we are ignorant of whatever physiological processes might underlie differences of raw feeling? And how can expressions such as 'same ways of raw feeling' be understood if we can't tell whether or not pairs of individuals share the same ways of raw feeling? I maintain that we can already, as things are, justifiably claim that the possibility envisaged by the Transformation thesis is not actualized. I think we can be said to know that human beings who share the same sensory capacities share the same ways of raw feeling—and that we can be said to know this without knowing the details of the underlying physiology. So I don't think an understanding of the expression 'raw feeling' requires a knowledge of the physiological facts. However, the challenge is to explain how the knowledge in question is possible. Before meeting it I want to emphasize two points.

The first is that in spite of being explicable in terms of ordinary mental language, the expression 'raw feeling' depends for its application on a certain amount of theorizing. As we reflect on perceptual experience we come to realize that there are aspects which are not merely dispositional but involve actual episodes, which the subject can detect in a way that others do not. I don't have to study my own behaviour to tell whether or not I am

---

[8] These two cases appear to be counter-examples to Cynthia Macdonald's assertion that 'such physical differences as might occur within the confines of bodies could not ground the belief that they differ psychologically' (*Mind–Body Identity Theories*, 149; cf. also 34, 222). Of course these cases are very special. It remains generally true that physical differences do not necessarily entail psychological ones.

having a certain kind of experience; but others do: the episode of raw feeling involved in that experience does not itself lie open to public view. The second point is that episodes of raw feeling stand in causal relations to sensory stimulation, to other mental states, and to behaviour. Grinding coffee, for example, may cause an episode of raw feeling which in turn may cause me to exclaim that the freshly ground coffee smells good. And of course this episode's standing in such causal relations entails that it is something real, which really has certain features.

Now Wittgenstein is sometimes supposed to have been an anti-realist with respect to statements about sensations. He is supposed to have held that knowing the meaning of such statements consists in knowing the conditions in which they are assertible, when these involve only what is open to public view: things like behaviour, facial expressions, features of the passing scene. On that account the truth or falsity of such statements would also have to be understood in terms of what was open to public view. Let us consider it in relation to my realist conception of raw feeling as a causal factor in the production of behaviour.

2.3   ANTI-REALISM ABOUT SENSATION LANGUAGE

On the basis of Wittgenstein's argument against the possibility of a private ostensive definition, Dummett has maintained that the untenability of a realistic construal of statements such as 'John is in pain' has been 'definitively demonstrated'.[9] However, he assumes the realist is committed to the view that 'only the man who experiences the pain has conclusive reasons for saying that he is in pain'.[10] Since that in turn surely requires you to hold that the central use of the word 'pain'—the use which gives it its essential meaning—is its use in connection with your own case, that view is indeed exposed to the private language argument. But my variety of realism is not open to this objection. Certainly I maintain that experiences involve real events, 'inner' events of raw feeling. But it is consistent with this position to hold that others often have

---

[9] M. Dummett, *Truth and Other Enigmas*, p. xxxiii.
[10] Ibid., p. xxxv. See also pp. xxxiv, xxxvi.

conclusive reasons for saying that I am in pain. It is therefore also consistent to hold that a grasp of the meaning of 'pain' depends on a grasp of the publicly accessible circumstances in which the word is used, as well as a grasp of the connections between those circumstances and the 'inner' event which, in the right relations, constitutes my feeling pain. So my position seems not to be exposed to Dummett's attack.

However, people sometimes ascribe to Wittgenstein a more extreme version of anti-realism, one that comes close to behaviourism. According to this version, to understand statements about sensation and experience is merely to know in what publicly observable situations their assertion would be justified. Since what is stated cannot go beyond what is understood, the truth values of such statements cannot depend on anything hidden: it is a misunderstanding of the nature of such statements to suppose they even involve reference to hidden states or processes, let alone their characterization. On this reading, Wittgenstein's position was flatly incompatible with the doctrine of raw feeling.

This incompatibility is highlighted by the fact that the Transformation thesis allows room for all the *external*, *overt* criteria for (at any rate) some kinds of raw feeling to be satisfied in their absence. Indeed, the notion allows room for the external criteria for raw feeling to be satisfied in the absence of raw feeling of any kind. That is the lesson of systems such as the Block robot described in Chapter 1. So now it is clear how I must respond to the extreme anti-realist reading of Wittgenstein's views. If that reading were correct I should have to maintain that he was just wrong, and for the same reason that behaviourism is wrong. Behaviourism is wrong if only because it implies that the Block robot and its kin are subjects of experience when they are no such thing. It implies that deliberately constructed simulacra of sentient beings would be sentient merely because they were guaranteed to produce the right sorts of behaviour. Similarly, if Wittgenstein's position were anti-realist in the present sense, it too would wrongly imply that such things would be sentient. It would insist that everything relevant to an understanding of the language of experience and sensation must be available for ordinary external public inspection, without going beneath the system's surface. But that would overlook the fact that our ordinary understanding of talk of experiences and sensations has a theoretical component. It treats experiences and sensations as internal changes which their subjects can detect in ways that others cannot. To the extent that any Wittgensteinian objections to my position presuppose that kind of anti-realism about the language of experience and sensation, then, I will disregard them on the ground that the presupposition is false.[11]

I will assume that Wittgenstein was not that kind of anti-realist. This is compatible with the private language argument and at least some of his other views. The private language argument doesn't impose that kind of anti-realism, still less behaviourism. It doesn't rule out the possibility of talking about raw feels, only that such talk should be impenetrably private. But now, how can we construe Wittgenstein's position if it was not in that sense anti-realist?

2.4   HOW WE CAN KNOW WHAT OTHERS' RAW FEELS ARE LIKE

In the interpretation I favour, which seems consistent with Wittgenstein's other main views as well as with common assumptions, I follow David Pears. Wittgenstein's thought is that the institution of talking about experiences and sensations depends on their being causally enmeshed in patterns of publicly accessible events and behaviour. For example, there are the patterns we exploit in teaching little children to use the vocabulary of pain: injury followed by crying, followed by adult concern and attention. But these patterns enable us to talk of experiences and sensations only in ways that render them generally knowable. They do not permit private classifications. We cannot for example each have a private word for red in addition to 'red', nor can the same word mean one thing for everyone, and in addition, for each person, something known only to that person.[12] Such suggestions make no sense because they would require the possibility of a second institution of talking about experiences and sensations that some-

[11] The extreme interpretation I have just rejected is quite often advanced in conversation, if not in print. It is noteworthy that Hacker, the most comprehensive and compelling interpreter of Wittgenstein's views in this area, rejects the suggestion that Wittgenstein was an anti-realist at all. See *Wittgenstein: Meaning and Mind*, for example 545 f., 561.

[12] For Pears's interpretation, see *The False Prison*, ii.331. For the Wittgensteinian view just outlined, see *Philosophical Investigations* I, sects. 273–80.

how shadowed the public one, yet, unlike the public one, was completely independent of publicly accessible criteria and therefore left us incapable of telling whether or not we were using its vocabulary successfully.

Pears neatly summarizes some crucial points when he says, in connection with a dialogue occurring in Wittgenstein's 'Notes for Lectures',

> the interlocutor protested that all sensations have 'intrinsic' properties which cannot possibly be captured by any 'extrinsic' criteria derived from the circumstances that bracket them. But that did not work, because all the available criteria had been pre-empted, and so, if these 'intrinsic' properties really did remain uncaptured, they would only be wheels that could be spun independently of the rest of the mechanism.[13]

This reasoning is no threat to the doctrine of raw feeling. On the contrary, it helps it out of an apparent difficulty. The doctrine certainly has it that experiences and sensations involve intrinsic properties. But it doesn't entail that these properties are unknowable—uncapturable by publicly available criteria. The interpretation just sketched helps to make clear how this is so. However, we must not require such criteria to do more than they possibly could.

Wittgenstein's famous slogan, 'An "inner process" stands in need of outward criteria',[14] lends itself to the extreme kind of anti-realist interpretation rejected earlier. But it doesn't force that interpretation on us. It is consistent with the interpretation just endorsed, including the view that there is something about experiences and sensations which goes beyond what is manifest in publicly observable behaviour and circumstances, something which, as a result of its causal relations with behaviour and other externals, is normally 'captured' by public criteria, yet logically capable of eluding them. What Pears calls 'all the available criteria'—behavioural and other external criteria—cannot *absolutely* guarantee that the intrinsic raw feel properties are captured, since the relevant internal workings are not themselves among those criteria, as we have noticed. Nevertheless, on the present interpretation Wittgenstein's position is consistent with

---

[13] *The False Prison*, ii.340. The dialogue alluded to is on pp. 316–18 of 'Wittgenstein's Notes'.

[14] Wittgenstein, *Philosophical Investigations* I, sect. 580.

the claim that the available criteria do capture the character of the sensations and experiences that are actually present, hence of the raw feels. But how can this be so, especially since most of us are completely ignorant of the details of one another's physiology?

The answer is a justified presupposition that reality is co-operating with us. We have every reason to believe we are not surrounded by such science-fictional entities as Block's robots. Apart from other considerations, we know that the sheer technical difficulties are too great. Similarly, as I will explain, we have every reason to believe there are no instantiations of the Transformation thesis. There still remains *logical* room for situations where the usual external criteria are satisfied yet there are no experiences at all. And, given that we cannot normally burrow about inside people's heads, outward criteria are all we have to go on. So if we are to avoid gross error, the part of reality which lies inside people's heads has to co-operate. And it does co-operate. We have good reasons for supposing that those internal processes which are not among the criteria are relevantly similar for all human beings who share the same perceptual capacities. Some of those reasons have become available only recently, with the discovery of information about the structure and workings of the brain. But that scientific information has never been accessible to more than a handful of the masses of people who have claimed to know, on occasions, what one another's experiences were like. So let's leave those reasons aside: the main ones are simpler. We have known for ages that, having come into existence as a result of similar processes, we share similar internal organs. Few of us have ever known what those processes are, or just what internal organs we share, or even what functions those organs perform. But the evidence of everyday life, not to mention what sometimes becomes visible as a result of accidents, war, and surgery, has given us a reasonable basis for the presupposition that any differences between human beings in respect of the nature and modes of functioning of their internal organs are relatively slight. Of course there still are differences, many of which tend to show up in behaviour. But in general we have been justified in presupposing that one another's internal organs are similar and function similarly. And we have been justified in making this assumption in spite of our ignorance of the physiological facts.

These considerations seem to me to justify the assumption that we are not surrounded by mere simulacra of sentient beings, such as robots, with significantly different internal arrangements from ours. They are roughly analogous to the considerations which, before the advent of modern geology, justified the assumption that mountains consist of the usual sorts of solid rocks rather than a thin crust draped over a hollow framework of steel girders.

It should be clear that these considerations are not at all the same as the so-called 'argument from analogy'. That argument goes: I know I have certain experiences in certain circumstances. For example I know I feel pain when I trap my fingers in the door and wince or exclaim; others behave similarly in similar situations; therefore, by analogy, others have similar experiences to mine in those situations. The objectionable feature of the argument from analogy is its presupposition that I could start off knowing that I had experiences while not knowing whether others did. It mistakenly supposes that I could know what pain is, for example, entirely from my own case. The objection is not that the generalization from a single case is risky. It is that no such generalization is possible because I couldn't understand it if I didn't already know it was true; which means the argument is useless. In contrast, the considerations I have mentioned presuppose nothing of the kind. They concern only our assumption that other people's insides are like our own in matters relating to their psychology. We don't make an impossible generalization from our own case. We have normal inductive evidence based on many cases, together with general knowledge about the kind of organisms we are. And the conclusion is straightforwardly testable.

Do these considerations go far enough to preclude instances of the Transformation thesis? I suggest they don't. It still seems that the workings of your brain could have been so related to the workings of mine that we jointly constituted an instance of it. However, given our knowledge of our common origins, together with some conception of the baroque internal arrangements that would seem to have been necessary for there to have been actual cases of Transformation, we seem justified in assuming there are *in fact* no such instances. If so, we are presumably entitled to say we know there are none.

But is the evidence I have alluded to, together with general assumptions about the similarity of internal organs and their workings, a solid enough basis for *knowledge* of the character

of other people's experiences? And if it isn't, how can I avoid
conceding that the character of our experiences is radically private
after all? Perhaps the sort of evidence I have mentioned could be
reinforced. However, I don't want to deny that there is room for
error. If complete certainty is required, I don't think we could get
it without knowledge of the physiological facts—facts about the
internal reality whose co-operation we have usually presupposed.
Still, we shall eventually see how the physiological facts could in
favourable cases yield that kind of certainty, so the space available
for scepticism is strictly limited.

If there is a difficulty here for my own position, there is a
related difficulty for Wittgenstein's—still on the assumption that
he is not that extreme type of anti-realist. Since all the right
patterns of overt behaviour and behavioural capacities could be
shared by mere insentient simulacra of sentient beings, he too
needs an explanation of how we can know—or at any rate justifiably presuppose—that other people are not such simulacra. The
suggestions I have made seem to me to be acceptable in that role.
But they might well not be so for Wittgenstein. And in fact he has
an alternative. In *On Certainty* he outlines a view according to
which some propositions constitute what can be thought of as a
framework for intelligible discourse. Unless they are accepted,
our ordinary use of language would be incapable of serving our
purposes. Put thus crudely, the view may seem to resemble the
traditional doctrine of analytic propositions. But it is altogether
different. For one thing, the propositions forming the framework
include a great deal more than the traditional analytic ones: they
include some of the non-analytic propositions that Moore claimed
to know for certain, for example that the earth had existed long
before his birth, or that he had never been on the moon. For
another thing, part of the view Wittgenstein outlines is that even
the framework propositions may in certain contexts be up for
question, and may cease to be part of the framework and become
subject to revision.[15] Now, the statement that other human beings
have thoughts and feelings is of just the kind that belongs to
the framework. Our whole way of talking about ourselves and
others presupposes that it and related propositions are true. For
Wittgenstein these propositions cannot properly be described as

[15] See e.g. *On Certainty*, sects. 83, 95, 96, 97.

items of knowledge because, it seems, what is known must be capable of being intelligibly doubted.[16] But they are as certain as anything can be.

Whether or not you agree with that position, it appears to supply what is needed if we reject the behaviouristically extreme anti-realist construal of Wittgenstein's views. And so far as I can see it can be applied, if necessary, to the presupposition that similar people in the same perceptual situation have the same kinds of perceptual experience. That seems to be a likely framework proposition for talk about the character of one another's experiences. If so, we have here an alternative justification for the claim that, although it is possible—just—that you and I should have instantiated the Transformation thesis, we know that in fact we do not instantiate it.

But we must not pursue epistemological issues beyond necessity. The main point is that Wittgenstein's own remarks about criteria, understood as suggested at the beginning of this section, help to explain how we can know what other people's raw feels are like, and why the Transformation thesis doesn't automatically open the door to scepticism. Since those remarks must not be interpreted in the extreme anti-realist way, satisfaction of the criteria still leaves room for error. That is why I mentioned that our success in applying the criteria depends on the co-operation of reality. The past few paragraphs have been directed at the worry that our presupposition—that in fact reality is co-operating—might not be justified. Two ways of backing it up have been noted. Either way, the doctrine of raw feeling isn't prevented by Wittgensteinian reasoning from embracing the commonsense view that we can penetrate other people's inner lives. I conclude that we can often know what other people's raw feels are like. (There are limits. It is said that Tiresias, having experienced life both as a man and as a woman—at different times—reported that women got more pleasure from sex than men. Nothing I have said implies that such knowledge could be common.)

The considerations in this section also explain how it is that we are able to characterize one another's raw feels in spite of the fact that they are logically independent of things outside us. Raw feeling is the core of ordinary perceptual experience. So we

---

[16] Cf. *On Certainty*, sects. 219 ff., 231 ff.

characterize our raw feels whenever we describe our experiences, not just on those rare occasions when we use some special jargon. Diverse expressions like 'the taste of that soup', 'the smell of freshly ground coffee', 'like hearing rushing water', 'the kind of visual experience you have when you see a ripe tomato or an English pillar-box', 'a shooting pain' will all, in their different ways, serve to characterize raw feels. It is true that the occurrence of raw feels is usually only part of what is involved in having an experience of a particular kind, since kinds of experiences typically depend on their contents, which in turn depend partly on relations between their associated raw feels and other things. (There may be odd cases where there is no more to an experience than the occurrence of certain raw feels. The brain in a vat is an extreme example: see below.) Indeed, it is only because raw feels typically stand in fairly regular relations to other things that we can characterize our experiences and raw feels at all. However, the present point is that by characterizing an experience we are nevertheless characterizing the raw feels involved in it. And although our being able to do this depends on its standing in certain relations to other things, its character is independent of those relations, as is made clear by our ability to use expressions such as 'the kind of experience you have when . . .'.

2.5   BEETLES IN BOXES AND TRANSFORMATION

You may wonder whether Wittgenstein's beetle-in-the-box story undermines the Transformation thesis. The context of that story is the idea that I know what pain is only from my own case. We are to suppose that everybody has a box containing what we call a 'beetle'. But 'no one can look into anyone else's box, and everyone says he knows what a beetle is only by looking at *his* beetle'. The things in the box might be different, or might even be constantly changing. Even if 'beetle' had a use in these people's language, 'it would not be used as the name of a thing. The thing in the box has no place in the language-game at all.'[17] The exact points he is trying to make with this analogy are debatable. But it may seem relevant. Perhaps the analogue of no one's being able to look into

---

[17] Wittgenstein, *Philosophical Investigations* I, sect. 293.

anyone else's box is the impossibility of having anyone else's raw feels. And the idea of Transformation seems to be analogous to the possibility that the things in different people's boxes should be different. However, the analogy is crucially incomplete.

We have seen that our not being able to *have* one another's raw feels doesn't prevent our being able to tell what they are like—by hearing what people say and observing their situation, for example. In complete contrast, the beetle story starts from the discredited assumption of radical privacy; and it is from that assumption that the absurdities indicated by Wittgenstein arise. So nothing commits me to the view he is attacking: that it is only from my own case that I can know what pain is. On the contrary, I accept that we cannot know what pain is, or for that matter what it is like to see ripe tomatoes, unless we are in touch with a language and conceptual scheme in which the relevant words are used. An infant or a cat may feel pain; but they don't know *what pain is* because they lack a basis for making the relevant distinctions between what counts as pain and what doesn't—between pains and tickles, for example. Wittgenstein can say that the thing in the box has 'no place in the language-game' only because it is supposed to be radically private. So his remarks don't apply to raw feels, which are not radically private and do have a place in the language-game.

We can now deal with the suggestion that the Transformation thesis implies that there could be private ways of classifying experiences—for example, 'red-K' for my experience of red, 'red-Y' for yours. The thesis is only to the effect that differences of the kinds envisaged are possible, not that they actually exist. So if, as I think, there are no actual instances, expressions like 'red-K' and 'red-Y' would be meaningful but not private. In fact they would be synonymous, and would mean the same as 'of red' (said of an experience). For in that case we should know we shared the same experience, hence the same raw feel, when we saw red things in similar situations.

But what if there actually were numerous instances of the Transformation thesis in our linguistic community, while we knew nothing about them? In that case the linguistic position would be rather peculiar. We should continue to use the same expressions as we do now, with equal practical success, since according to the original assumption our behavioural capacities would be unaf-

fected. But because the relevant parts of reality wouldn't be co-
operating, our words would fail to penetrate one another's inner
lives as they do now. Even our understanding of words like 'red'
would be affected, on the assumption that the understanding we
actually have of such words involves knowing what red things are
like.

This last point needs clarification. It is widely assumed that a
full understanding of 'red' requires us to know what it is like to
see red things. (I am not assuming that this view is correct. A
related point will be discussed in Chapter 7.) On that assumption
there has to be such a thing as what it is like for normally sighted
people to see red things in normal circumstances: it has to be the
same for most of us. But if there were no such thing, as would be
the case if different people had different kinds of raw feel in the
same perceptual situations, there would be nothing it was like to
see red things, and hence, on the assumption, no understanding of
'red'. Of course the assumption might be mistaken. But in that
bizarre situation, even though raw feeling would still be associated
with colour vision, it would be beyond the reach of characterization in public language. The conditions for playing that particular
language-game would not be satisfied.[18] Such characterization
would then call for a genuinely private language. Since I think
Wittgensteinian considerations rule that out, I will not discuss the
alternative further. (Of course there are no Wittgensteinian considerations that could force me to accept it.) The assumption that
a full understanding of an ordinary colour word such as 'red'

---

[18] This helps to explain why Pears's valuable discussion of Wittgenstein's views
(*The False Prison*, ii.402–22) does not undermine the Transformation thesis. Even
when he comes closest to discussing the thesis itself (ibid. 417–20) he presupposes
with Wittgenstein that the latter's adversaries aspire 'to decant all the meaning of
the phrase "impression of blue" into its "intrinsic character" and then to argue
that, as things are, it is entirely possible that this "intrinsic character" varies in
complete independence of its physical setting' (418). As I have tried to show, the
Transformation thesis by no means requires the phrase 'impression of blue' to
derive its whole meaning from the intrinsic character of the associated raw feel
type. For the same reason, as well as for others that will emerge later, I do not feel
threatened by McDowell's reasoning in 'Values and Secondary Qualities' and
'Singular Thought and the Extent of Inner Space'. He seems to reject the sort of
position I am defending. However, I am not committed to the view that all aspects
of objective reality, including secondary qualities, are independent of human
sensibility. Nor do I see why 'experience's openness to objective reality' ('Values
and Secondary Qualities', 117) should be inconsistent with the central role I
ascribe to raw feeling. See n. 24 below.

requires a knowledge of what it is like to see the colours in question links the meanings of those words with the 'inner' aspect of experience; but not in a sense threatened by Wittgenstein's reasoning.

You might think that in the situation imagined the 'thing in the box'—the raw feel—really would have 'no place in the language-game at all'. But putting the situation in those terms would be misleading. We have seen that if there were massive instantiation of the Transformation thesis, that would prevent our being able to *characterize* one another's raw feels in the sense modalities that were affected. It would not impair our ability to *refer* to them. When asked to 'describe the after-image you get from staring at these sunflowers', for example, I couldn't characterize it success-fully. But there would be no failure of reference. And what I was thus able to refer to could hardly be regarded as having no place in the language-game. (Referring to raw feels must not of course be construed on the model of referring to physical objects. A raw feel is 'not a something, but not a nothing either'.[19])

I am not denying that Wittgenstein himself would have rejected the Transformation thesis. He certainly rejected something like it, as we saw early in this chapter. But I have been trying to show that if he rejected it, rather than something crucially different, he gave us no good reasons for doing so. Recall the passage quoted earlier, about the assumption that one section of mankind might have one sensation of red and another section another. There now seems every reason to suppose that this rejected assumption is in fact crucially different from the Transformation thesis. The thesis doesn't imply that our experiences are inaccessible to others. Wittgenstein himself has provided the means to understand how we can know the character of one another's experience, hence of their raw feeling. And some actual instances of Transformation, if they existed, would be discoverable, not unverifiable. So ex-ponents of the Transformation thesis can consistently accept that the notion of impenetrably private experience, and with it that of an unverifiable difference in the way different people see red, is unintelligible. The difference between the doctrine of raw feeling and some of the views Wittgenstein actually attacks may not be great, but clearly it matters.

---

[19] Wittgenstein, *Philosophical Investigations* I, sect. 304.

2.6   A BRAIN IN A VAT

Raw feeling is a sort of lowest common denominator of consciousness. Any conscious subject has it, while whatever has it, even if not a full-blown conscious subject, has something 'inner' in the special sense indicated by Anna. There is something it is like to be it.

The well-worn but still potent idea of brains in vats is usually brought to bear on issues in epistemology and the philosophy of propositional attitudes. But it also helps to focus our thoughts in connection with raw feeling.[20] Suppose *b* is a brain in a vat, supplied with adequate nutrients and coherent patterns of inputs to its afferent nerves. It is an exact replica of my own brain. At any instant, the inputs to *b*'s afferent nerves exactly replicate the inputs to my brain, and its total state exactly matches the state of my own brain. *b*, however, is on Mars. Its inputs are caused by the workings of a powerful machine, and have always been so caused. They are unrelated to the world outside the machine, still less to the causes of my own experiences. The similarity in our neural inputs is just a monstrous coincidence.

I contend that *b* is the brain of something it is like something to be, and so of a subject of raw feeling. Many readers will probably accept this straight off. Others will have objections. But I am not setting out to justify the contention at this stage. It helps to bring out a central feature of the doctrine of raw feeling: that raw feeling is logically and conceptually independent of its causal and other relations to things in the outside world. Towards the end of Chapter 1 I remarked that the doctrine of raw feeling doesn't require rejection of externalism about the *content* of experiences and sensations, according to which such content depends on causal or other relations with external things. What it does require is rejection of a more extreme view, more akin to behaviourism, which I will discuss shortly. I suspect that part of the motivation for this more extreme view may be the difficulty of explaining *how* the excitation of neurones could constitute an inner life. If so, I hope the position to be developed in Chapters 4, 5, and 6 will remove the difficulty. But in any case I want to meet the most

[20] The earliest use of the idea of a brain *in vitro* for this purpose that I know of is in J. J. C. Smart's article, 'Materialism'. Smart notes (659) that D. M. Armstrong had also been using the same example to make the same point.

likely non-dualistic objections to my contention that *b* is the brain of something it is like something to be—objections from those who accept minimal physicalism but reject behaviourism. (Minimal physicalism, I take it, is the fairly innocuous view that there is nothing in the world except the physical. I will discuss it more fully in the next chapter with the help of the Strict Implication thesis.)

We need to distinguish *b* from that putative subject of raw feeling whose brain *b* is. Not that any of us could get by without a brain; but a given subject of experience could have had a different body or even a different brain from the one they actually do have. This does not imply that the person is physically distinct from body or brain: only that the person could have been *constituted* by a different body or brain. I follow Aristotle and Wiggins in regarding the notion of constitution as indispensable when sorting out questions of identity.[21] Hobbes posed the question whether a ship constructed from the original individual timbers of the ship of Theseus, discarded in the course of successive refits over many years, would itself also have to be counted as the ship of Theseus. I favour the suggestion that it would not. Originally the ship was constituted by that individual collection of timbers arranged in certain ways. But at later times it was constituted by different collections. The ship built from the discarded original components of the ship of Theseus would have been just that, and not the ship of Theseus, because it wouldn't satisfy the conditions for continuous existence as a ship that we require for identity. Analogously, the brain that now helps to constitute me could conceivably have lost its identity as the same brain—perhaps because its components had been gradually replaced by quantities of electronic circuitry—without any effects on my own identity. So the brain *b* had better not be assumed to be identical with the putative subject of raw feeling whose brain it is. For convenience I will call that putative subject Boris.

There are likely to be three main sources of resistance to the idea that there is something it is like to be Boris. One will appeal to Wittgenstein's remark that 'only of a living human being and what resembles (behaves like) a living human being can one say:

---

[21] Aristotle conceived of a concrete object in the category of substance as being constituted by a certain form imposed on a certain parcel of matter. Wiggins develops the idea in *Sameness and Substance*.

it has sensations; it sees; is blind; hears; is deaf; is conscious or unconscious'.[22] Clearly this remark must not be supposed to exclude people who are paralysed. Ordinary psychological talk certainly reaches out far enough to include them as full-blown subjects of behaviour. Part of the reason, I take it, is that it makes some assumptions about the causes of behaviour. Treating experiences as potential causes of behaviour, it allows that in some circumstances what would normally cause certain sorts of behaviour may fail to do so, yet still be present. Still, a mere brain like *b* is a lot further away from human behaviour than a paralysed person is. Even on a very liberal interpretation the putative Boris does not 'resemble (behave like) a living human being'. The question, however, is not whether Boris is a full-blown subject of experience, but whether there is something it is like to be it. So although it does not resemble human beings in those respects which matter for the ordinary notions of sense perception and consciousness, or even the ordinary notion of the mental, that is beside the point.

After all, Wittgenstein wasn't talking about raw feeling, or only very indirectly. He seems to have been making two main points. First, words such as 'sensation', 'consciousness', and 'thought' *derive their uses* from their application to living human beings and whatever relevantly resembles human beings. If you try to apply them to significantly different kinds of things you risk talking nonsense: they float without support. But second, and more importantly, what enables these words to do their work is their links with behaviour. Only certain patterns of behaviour warrant our saying of something that it 'sees'; and the usefulness of the word depends on there being other patterns of behaviour which do not warrant its application. I take it that Wittgenstein's position here is correct. But it doesn't show that other words, not themselves part of the ordinary psychological vocabulary, yet ascribing some kind of 'inner' life and explicable on the basis of that ordinary vocabulary, couldn't possibly be applied to anything but living human beings or other actual behavers. So it doesn't rule out Boris's having that lowest common denominator of consciousness which I call raw feeling.

---

[22] Wittgenstein, *Philosophical Investigations* I, sect. 281. Cf. sects. 283, 284, 357, 360.

The second line of objection appeals to the idea that in order for a descriptive expression to be meaningful there must be ways of telling whether or not it applies, hence whether we are faced with something of the same type or different. But in cases like that of Boris—the objection might go—either we can't tell that there is raw feeling present at all, or (since it is suggested that physiological information will enable us to tell us that much) we can't claim that it will tell us just which kinds of raw feeling are present. However, at the end of Chapter 5 I will argue that, on the contrary, purely physiological information could enable us to tell that *b* was the brain of a subject of raw feeling. Moreover the processes inside *b* are exactly similar to the processes inside my own brain. We may assume for the moment (minimal physicalism) that ontologically the only processes going on are physical: there are no parallel or interacting non-physical processes. So on that assumption we can infer that the raw feel facts about Boris exactly parallel the raw feel facts about me. In that case, if my later arguments are sound, although we start off with purely physical information about Boris, we end up with information about Boris's states of consciousness. (I don't claim that these points establish that Boris is a subject of raw feeling: only that they undermine the suggested line of objection.)

The third source of possible resistance is the thought that the *content* of any possible characterizations of raw feels can come only from their connections with the outside world. Since Boris lacks all plausibly relevant connections, there is no basis for characterizing raw feels in Boris's case. We need to distinguish a crude and a refined version of this line of thought. The crude version would be supported by the plausible claim that you can't have the experience of suddenly recalling the appearance of the Eiffel Tower, for example, unless you stand in the right causal relations to the Eiffel Tower itself; similarly you can't experience redness unless you stand in the right causal relations to red things. Since Boris has no such causal links, Boris can't have such experiences. That seems right. But by now it should be clear that these points are irrelevant. My contention is that there is an ineliminable component of such experiences, the raw feel component, which Boris *can* have.

However, there is a more refined and interesting version of this line of objection. It is that there is no sharp cut-off point in the spectrum of cases stretching from thoughts about the Eiffel Tower at one end to pains and other sensations at the other. The content of thoughts about the Eiffel Tower surely depends on causal connections with that particular structure. It may seem that the content of thoughts about pains has no such dependence; but in fact (the argument goes) even these thoughts require some hooks on to external reality if they are to be contentful.[23] Since *b* lacks all such hooks, we can't characterize any of Boris's raw feels. But this objection fails for the same reason as the second. In normal circumstances we can know what one another's raw feels are because on the one hand we can know their causal and spatio-temporal links with external circumstances, and on the other we can count on the co-operation of reality (regarding their internal natures). That is why our thoughts about raw feels are rather unproblematically contentful. And we can apply such statements to Boris on the basis of the physiological information we have about Boris compared with similar information about me. The objection fails because it assumes that the only possible source of content for our thoughts about Boris's raw feels would have to be direct links between Boris's raw feels and the outside world. But in dealing with the previous objection we saw that that is not so.

Behaviourism was one over-optimistic project for dealing with the difficulties posed by consciousness. Behaviouristic anti-realism in respect of statements about experience and sensation was another. Just now we have in effect been resisting a third: the project of giving a philosophical account of all aspects of consciousness purely on the basis of the externally determined content of mental states. If this *ultra-externalist* project had been successful, then since Boris lacks all relations which could plausibly be supposed to have been relevant, Boris would have lacked all consciousness. But it will eventually become clear, I think, that ultra-externalism does not work. If it is combined with behaviourism, it is open to the objections noted in the last chapter. Even if it rejects behaviourism, it lacks the resources for an adequate treatment of the Transformation thesis. Like be-

---

[23] Something like this line of thought emerges from Pears's discussions of Wittgenstein's private language argument. See *The False Prison*, ii, especially 331 f., 411–17. Pears is not considering the notion of raw feeling any more than Wittgenstein was; but it is important to make clear that these Wittgensteinian points pass that notion by.

haviourism, ultra-externalism is also seriously embarrassed by headaches, phosphenes, tinnitus, dream imagery. Unlike experiences of colour or shape, for example, these are caused within the brain. Yet they cannot be dismissed as being *merely* the firing of neurones. They are 'inner' in a sense not exhausted by the fact that they are constituted by processes which are literally internal.[24]

2.7 CAN RAW FEELING BE 'QUINED'?

In explaining raw feeling I have made free use of common-sense expressions. But it is not itself a commonsense or folk-psychological notion. Nor is it scientific. It is an invention or term of art—philosophical or psychological art. But if this invention leads to difficulties, why should anyone be concerned? The history of thought is littered with the skeletons of philosophers' notions which have turned out to lead to difficulties and eventually been abandoned. Isn't there something perverse in using commonsense expressions to define a non-commonsense, non-scientific notion, and then devoting a book to dealing with the difficulties this notion raises? How could this exercise have any relevance to serious psychological or other scientific concerns—how could it even make a useful contribution to philosophy?

These worries spring from a misconception. It is not the *notion* of raw feeling that generates philosophical difficulties (although notions superficially like it certainly do). Most of the problems of consciousness arise whether or not anyone troubles to define such a notion. They arise from the difficulties we have in understanding

[24] As we shall see shortly, Dennett is one philosopher who appears to be committed to ultra-externalism. John McDowell's position has some affinity with ultra-externalism, although it seems to me that he does not discuss raw feeling as I am trying to explain it. He rejects the idea that 'intrinsic features of experience function as vehicles for particular aspects of representational content'; in fact 'we need to reject these supposed vehicles of content altogether' ('Values and Secondary Qualities', 114). However, although I think that an isolated brain could yield a subject of raw feeling, I do not hold that it could have the experience of colour. So it is not clear how far McDowell's position conflicts with mine; nor do I think his arguments tell against my position. In developing a position similar to McDowell's, Gregory McCulloch goes further: 'one can and probably should champion the phenomenological and what it is like, yet reject altogether talk of the phenomenal, qualia, raw feels, etc.' ('The Very Idea of the Phenomenological', 55). In reply to the suggestion that qualia and the like may be useful as 'explanatory elements in the account of these things' (loc. cit.), he appeals to Dennett—an ultra-externalist.

how there could be the sorts of objective phenomena that make the
notion worth bothering about. The true situation is that the idea of
raw feeling helps us along the way towards removing the difficulties, not least by avoiding the gratuitous metaphysical and epistemological commitments of its predecessors. Of course we could
always evade philosophical difficulties by not answering questions;
but no one still reading would be likely to favour that way out.
However, some philosophers—eliminative materialists—attempt
to bulldoze the difficulties out of the way by rejecting commonsense or folk-psychological notions in the hope that anything
those notions do which is worth doing will eventually be far better
done by a mature neuroscience. I will examine their claims later.
First I want to discuss the more sophisticated approach taken by
Dennett in his paper 'Quining Qualia' and his recent book *Consciousness Explained.*[25]

Dennett claims 'there is no secure foundation in ordinary "folk
psychology" for a concept of qualia. We normally think in a
confused and potentially incoherent way when we think about the
ways things seem to us.'[26] Because the notion of qualia that he is
attacking is hard to pin down, his method is to discuss a series of
fifteen 'intuition pumps', the first few appearing to reinforce the
idea of qualia, the rest appearing to undermine it. Much of what
he says in the course of his discussion can be accepted, even
welcomed, without having to give up the doctrine of raw feeling.
Notably we can accept his claim that there is nothing which has
the four properties that he claims qualia are supposed to have
on 'traditional analyses'. Qualia, he says, are supposed to be:
ineffable, at least partly on account of their being *intrinsic*, 'which
seems to imply inter alia that they are somehow atomic and
unanalysable'; *private* because 'all interpersonal comparisons of
these ways of appearing are (apparently) systematically impossible'; *directly or immediately apprehensible in consciousness*:
'essentially directly accessible to the consciousness of their ex-
periencer...'.[27] We need not pursue the details of his comments
on these properties and their relations. The thing to notice is that

[25] Dennett quotes from his *Philosophical Lexicon*: 'quine, v. To deny resolutely
the existence or importance of something real or significant' ('Quining Qualia',
42). In a note on p. 44 he describes his position on qualia as an instance of
eliminative materialism. In other respects he is not a typical proponent.

[26] Dennett, 'Quining Qualia', 62.

[27] Ibid. 46 f. See also his *Consciousness Explained*, 373, 390, 450.

the doctrine of raw feeling is quite consistent with his claim that nothing actually has those properties. The most important consideration is that we can know what one another's raw feels are like. Raw feels are neither ineffable nor private in the sense he intends. But it is also worth noting that although raw feels are intrinsic in a certain sense, that sense is not one according to which they are atomic or unanalysable.[28] And although my notion of raw feeling wouldn't altogether rule out the applicability of descriptions such as 'directly apprehensible', raw feels are not objects to which the subject's consciousness stands in some special relation. To the extent that it is this relational conception which he actually attacks, then, there is a sense in which raw feeling does not have even that property. Much of his discussion therefore leaves the notion unscathed.

Still, Dennett is clearly committed to oppose anything like the notion of raw feeling. He maintains that 'conscious experience has *no* properties that are special in any of the ways qualia have been supposed to be special',[29] whereas I insist that raw feeling is 'inner' in a special way. The disagreement is sharply exposed in connection with the idea of spectrum inversion. In *Consciousness Explained* he describes that idea as 'one of philosophy's most virulent memes'.[30] And in the earlier paper he claims that 'spectrum inversion as classically debated is impossible',[31] although he concedes that something like it is perfectly possible. Now, what he concedes to be possible is essentially the same as Wittgenstein concedes to be possible: sudden intrasubjective inversion resulting perhaps from neurosurgical intervention. But like Wittgenstein he rejects the kind of interpersonal difference contemplated by the Transformation thesis. I will focus on this position and try to make clear how Dennett is mistaken.

[28] I will not discuss Dennett's assumptions about the connections between being 'intrinsic', 'atomic', and 'unanalysable', although I think he disregards some relevant distinctions. The sense in which raw feels are intrinsic is that in which the character of an individual's raw feeling is logically independent of its relations to external things. Since a thing's shape, for example, is intrinsic to it in this sense, it is clear that this kind of intrinsicality by no means implies atomicity or unanalysability. See below.

[29] Dennett, 'Quining Qualia', 43.

[30] Dennett, *Consciousness Explained*, 389. 'Meme' is Richard Dawkins's word for a 'unit of cultural transmission', e.g. an idea, tune, fashion, argument, that survives and gets replicated much as genes do.

[31] Dennett, 'Quining Qualia', 63.

A crucial argument in his discussion starts from the familiar case of visual field inversion resulting from wearing inverting spectacles. When these are worn for the first time they make everything look upside down. As time passes, especially if the subject is permitted to move about, touch things, and generally interact with the environment, things come to look the right way up again. On the face of it, then, you might suppose that this case ought to be counted, together with the case of spectrum inversion, as support for the Transformation thesis. Now Dennett rejects the naïve idea that there are such properties as 'right-side-upness' or 'upside-downness'. So in this case, at any rate, although there is certainly the possibility of a sudden intrasubjective switch in the 'way round' things look to us, there is no possibility of an absolute interpersonal difference not reflected in behavioural capacities and not related to any such switch. Here let me make clear that I agree the Transformation thesis could not be instantiated in that way. However, Dennett is operating a slippery slope argument. His contention is that there is no relevant distinction between this spatial case and the case of colours. In the spatial case no absolute interpersonal difference is possible. So the only way there could be such a difference in the case of colour perception would be if there were some relevant distinction between the two. (He says there would have to be a distinction between a 'qualitative or phenomenal subclass' of properties on the one hand, and properties such as spatial ones on the other.[32] I won't discuss the issue in those terms.) In effect he defies the friends of qualia to provide a sound basis for such a distinction. He rejects the suggestion that the apparent imaginability of spectrum inversion provides a sound basis, and I would agree. But he doesn't really discuss other suggestions. Anyway, I will now try to show that there is a sound basis for a suitable distinction.

First let us note that Dennett omits from his battery of intuition pumps one which might have prompted him to reconsider. This is the case of individuals who at birth were particle-for-particle replicas of one another with the difference that they had relatively 'crossed wires' (together with whatever further differences had resulted from that). So far as I can see, he has not provided the materials for an adequate response to such stories. Yet this

[32] Ibid. 64.

particular sort of example can be elaborated so as to focus attention on a crucial point where he appears to be reduced to bald assertion. The following fantasy will make clear what I mean. Although it is not by itself enough to establish my case—for that, Chapters 4, 5, and 6 are necessary—it is not a mere appeal to intuition.

My name is K1 and I have an identical twin called K2. We have each been brought up in the strictly controlled environment of a windowless house where no natural objects other than ourselves and our attendants have been allowed to enter. The colours in my house are normal, but those in K2's house are systematically inverted relative to mine. However, in his house everyone uses a correspondingly inverted colour vocabulary. In this respect alone they don't speak English. What we would call a picture of a green rose with red leaves, for example, they describe as a 'picture of a red rose with green leaves'. By any account, then (still assuming minimal physicalism, and that at birth we were identical in all physical details), K2's experiential history differs strikingly from my own.

But now consider a somewhat different story. This time K2 has been brought up in a *normally* coloured environment like mine. However, at birth the nerves from his retinas were systematically transposed, so that the types of afferent impulse which in the first story are caused in him by red light are here caused by green light, and vice versa, and so on through the spectrum (assuming some simplification of the mechanisms). Clearly his internal history, downstream of the site of the retinal operations, is in all relevant respects exactly as in the first story. And since it is inverted relative to that of my own brain in the respects that matter for the perception of colour, this second story appears to illustrate the Transformation thesis. Suppose that in this story K2 is looking at a red rose, to which he applies the word 'red'. Since the state of the whole of his brain downstream from the site of the operations is in all relevant respects as it is when in the first story he is looking at a *green* rose (to which he similarly applies the word 'red'), the raw feel he has is the one I have when *I* see a green rose. And so on.

To make the point more dramatic, we may suppose not only that we are identical twins brought up in exactly similar surroundings, but also that our external life-histories are exactly similar.

The point is that in spite of this similarity, which would leave us with exactly similar behavioural capacities and dispositions, it seems that our experiences of the colours of things must be systematically different.

So much for the fantasy. Now for the argument which underlies these stories. I assume the first story is unobjectionable. It relies wholly on publicly checkable facts. There can be no serious objection to the idea of someone whose history of colour experiences, in the most full-blooded sense, was the reverse of that of a certain normal person because their micro-world was colour-reversed relative to the latter's. So if Dennett wished to challenge my conclusion he would presumably have to challenge the second story, where I assume that transposed nerves would provide K2 in the circumstances with an 'inner' life just like the one in the first story—one that was colour-reversed relative to my own. But how could he challenge that?

He might insist that the second story merely exploits our 'confused and potentially incoherent' intuitions. But if he denies that the operation would have made that difference to the way K2 saw colours, he must maintain that in that case we should both have had *the same* colour experiences when we were in the same situations—when we were both in my (normally coloured) house, for example. He must maintain that when we were both looking at a ripe tomato, K2's colour experiences would have been in all interesting respects just like mine—in spite of the fact that, downstream of the switched nerves just behind his retinas, the processes inside his brain would have been of exactly the same types as they are in the first story. Yet in the first story the processes inside K2's brain are certainly those of someone whose colour experiences are inverted relative to my own. Clearly, then, the present response to the story will work only on the assumption that *such internal differences are irrelevant* to the character of the colour experiences concerned.

Now of course this assumption would flow automatically from behaviourism and from ultra-externalism. And in fact Dennett's position is close to both of these.[33] But I have explained why I

---

[33] e.g. he says in *Consciousness Explained* that 'any entity that could pass the Turing test would operate under the (mis?)apprehension that it was conscious' (311); 'When you say "*This* is my quale", what you are singling out, or referring to . . . is your idiosyncratic complex of dispositions' (389); '*If* there are no qualia

reject these positions: it would be question-begging to appeal to them against my present argument. And there is a rather powerful objection to the assumption. The internal differences between K2's brain and K1's brain can be made to show up in behavioural differences relevant to colour perception.

We may suppose that in both stories the external life-histories of K2 are type-identical except in respect of the colours of his environment. So, for example, at the same point in his life when he first comes across a balloon in the first story, he comes across a balloon in the second story—although if in the first story it happens to be red, in the second it is green. But the operation on his retinas in the second story ensures that, inwards of the site of the operation, the physical history of his brain is exactly the same as it is in the first story. Of course that exact similarity of internal physical history is entirely consistent with the exact similarity of his behaviour in both stories. But now suppose that, one dark night, K2's brain were removed—the optic nerves having been carefully severed at a point inwards of the site of the operation— and substituted for the brain of K1 (my own brain). The resulting individual would behave like a victim of sudden intrasubjective spectrum inversion. For in both stories the history of K2's brain is in relevant respects different from that of K1, and on minimal physicalist assumptions these differences would result, via differ- ences in corresponding memories, in characteristic differences in behaviour. ('Great Scott, overnight things have changed colour— or else I'm seeing colours differently. Seeing ripe tomatoes now is like what seeing unripe ones was like yesterday.') The internal differences would be like those which would have resulted if K1 had simply been deposited in the colour-reversed house of the first story. Since the differences between K2's brain and K1's brain would actually show up in behaviour in the counterfactual situ- ation just described, that is a reason for concluding that they are not after all irrelevant to the question of the nature of our colour experiences, in spite of the fact that they underlie exactly similar behavioural dispositions and capacities. So we have at least a prima facie refutation of Dennett's position. Of course it matters that the retinas (which may be counted as part of the surface of the brain) are not included in the brain-swap. Transplanting them

over and above the sum total of dispositions to react, the idea of holding the qualia constant while adjusting the dispositions is self-contradictory' (398).

with K2's brain in the first story would have made true the hypothesis that in effect the colours of external things had been transposed. Transplanting them with his brain in the second story would have had no behavioural effects. But the point is that the whole of the brain inwards of the site of the operations is indifferent to the external causes of stimulations reaching it along the optic nerves. (Special colour-transposing lenses would have had the same effects on the brain as the operation.) So, short of an appeal to magic, it is hard to see how *what it was like for K2* could fail to be the same in *both* stories.

Dennett will no doubt want to press two other objections. One is that evolution has left us with innate patterns of response to some colours. (For example, he tells us we tend not to hang around in rooms with red walls.[34]) Assuming that is right, K2 would not share quite the same behavioural dispositions as mine. This empirical point must be accepted, but is it damaging? The innate links between particular colours and particular patterns of response seem in any case to be severely limited in scope. More to the point, it must be possible for them to be absent in particular individuals without the latter thereby being rendered incapable of colour discrimination. So Dennett's first likely objection seems to miss the target.

His second likely objection is that we have all had enough of such fanciful stories. The whole topic of qualia is 'a tormented snarl of increasingly convoluted and bizarre thought experiments, jargon, in-jokes, allusions to putative refutations, "received" results that should be returned to sender, and a bounty of other sidetrackers and time-wasters. Some messes are best walked away from . . .'[35] The reader must decide whether the particular story I have told is, in the context of the wider discussion, just part of the mess or a step on the way to clearing it up. It seems to me that you have to grit your teeth quite hard if you want to stay with Dennett's strongly behaviouristic view, while the position I am defending presents no great strain.

Back then to Dennett's slippery slope argument. Can I provide a sound basis for a relevant distinction between the case of actual spatial inversion, which could not possibly have a correlate in raw feeling that instantiated the Transformation thesis, and cases like

[34] Dennett, *Consciousness Explained*, 383–6.
[35] Ibid. 369.

that of external-world colour transposition, which possibly could have such a correlate? We are now in a position to identify a solid distinction here. Recall the first story about K2, who lived with normal vision in a colour-inverted house. He was able to get along perfectly well: just as well as I was able to get on in my normally coloured house. Why was that? Why did he suffer no disadvantage compared with the disadvantage he would certainly have suffered if his house had been upside down, for example, while he remained the right way up?

The crucial factor is that the colour differences between our two houses had no effects on our behavioural dispositions or capacities. From that point of view the two distributions of colours were equivalent. All the identifications and discriminations that I was able to make with respect to the items in my surroundings on the basis of their colours were ones that K2 was able to make with respect to the corresponding items in his surroundings on the basis of their colours. Indeed, every truth-stating sentence that either of us was able to produce about the colours of his surroundings was also a truth-stating sentence in the other's language—translatable into it by simple substitution of 'green' for 'red', 'orange' for 'blue', and so on.

Contrast the case where the house is upside down. If K2's house had been upside down relative to mine, while his feet stayed pressed downwards, he would have been in trouble. From our point of view the striking consideration is that he would have had no way of talking about 'up' and 'down' which could be translated into my way of talking by some simple substitution. This is because there is no simple isomorphism between his situation and mine as there is in the case of myself and K2 in the first story. You might suggest that the new story ought to include a reversal of the direction of gravity for the space bounded by his house. But that wouldn't help. Certainly it would get over the difficulty of having his feet on the ceiling—but only at the cost of having his head pressed against the floor. Nor, of course, would it help to say that he must have his *feet* pressed against the floor instead. For in that case there is no longer any difference between how things are for him and how they are for me, and we have left the case of spatial inversion altogether.

So a systematic difference in colours between two otherwise exactly similar environments would have no significant effects on people's behavioural capacities, while a total spatial inversion would have very significant effects. 'Total spatial inversion' here means the sort of thing envisaged earlier in the last paragraph, where the subject is not included in the inversion. It is only in that case that the situation would produce a difference perceptible to the subject. If environment, inhabitants, and gravity too were inverted relative to some other environment, as envisaged at the end of the paragraph, there would be no perceptible difference between the two environments. This point emerges particularly clearly when we notice that being transported from one to the other would leave your behavioural dispositions and capacities completely unaffected.

I suggest that Dennett's challenge has now been met. We have found a clear distinction between the case of spatial inversion and cases like that of the inverted spectrum. *Seeing things the right way round* consists entirely in being able to make the right co-ordinations between, on the one hand, our capacities to move about, handle objects, and describe the scene, and on the other hand, objects and their positions in space. For example, moving your hand objectively upwards as you watch it must seem to you to be just that, so that the parts of the background which successively appear just below the hand as it rises must actually be above one another. What spatially inverting lenses do is to upset the established coordinations between capacities to move and describe, and positions in space. Such is the plasticity of the mind that in time these co-ordinations tend to be re-established, so that the subject comes to see things the right way round again. Clearly this happens only as a result of a detected failure of co-ordination—it is crucial that in the case of K2 there could be no corresponding pressure to change his behaviour. But nothing is involved over and above these capacities to co-ordinate behaviour and descriptions.[36] *Seeing the colours of things*, in striking con-

[36] People are sometimes puzzled by the fact that although the image projected on to the retina is 'upside down'—the image of the tree-tops is inverted relative to the tree-tops themselves, and so on—we still see things the right way round. The removal of this puzzlement follows the lines indicated above. The spatial relation between the retinal image and its external causes is irrelevant, by itself, to how things look. Seeing things the right way round requires no more than the right relations between your ability to move and describe things, and the distribution of things in space. These relations can be right regardless of the position of the retinal image, a point made vivid by considering what would be the effect on vision of turning the whole brain upside down: nothing.

trast, does not consist entirely in having the right behavioural capacities. If it did, there could be no objection to behaviourism or ultra-externalism. Behaviourism and ultra-externalism have to be rejected precisely because there is a component in perception beyond the acquisition of the right behavioural capacities—a point illustrated earlier by the behavioural differences that we saw would result from substituting K2's brain for K1's. So Dennett's argument has been blocked. He may have 'quined' *qualia*, since the particular notion of qualia that he attacks is, as he characterizes it, certainly unsound. But he has not at the same time undermined the notion of raw feeling.

There should be nothing remarkable about this conclusion. Everyone agrees that perception involves the acquisition of information about the world; and the point we have been dwelling on is that our acquisition of this information has two main components. One is the acquisition and modification of various capacities to interact with things in the world. The other is certain internal changes which affect us in ways they do not affect others—the changes which constitute raw feeling. It is only behaviourists and ultra-externalists who will find this hard to accept.

We have noticed that Dennett rejects the idea that qualia could be 'intrinsic'. In this connection he argues that qualia could not be 'non-relational'. But it is important to be clear about the sense in which he makes this claim. He is particularly impressed by Bennett's example of the chemical phenol-thio-urea, which three-quarters of mankind find bitter, while the rest do not. Breed out those who don't find it bitter, he argues, and the stuff is bitter. Breed out those who do find it bitter, and it isn't.[37] So in that sense such properties as bitterness, and for that matter redness, may be said to be relational: whether or not a given thing has such a property depends on how it would strike the members of a given reference class. I would agree that these properties are relational in that sense. But notice that it is a sense in which something can have a certain colour, taste, or whatever, quite independently of whether it actually stands in any particular causal or spatio-temporal relations to other things, including people. There could

---

[37] Dennett, 'Quining Qualia', 61. This is his tenth intuition pump. Bennett's discussion is in his 'Substance, Reality and Primary Qualities'.

be things like red pillar-boxes on Mars even if no one ever knew about them. Since the character of our raw feels is not supposed to be intrinsic in anything stronger than this sense, the concept is not vulnerable to the considerations Dennett brings against the specific notion of the intrinsicality of qualia that he attacks.

2.8   ELIMINATIVISM IN GENERAL

According to some philosophers, folk psychology is 'a serious candidate for outright elimination'.[38] Since I have been trying to explain the notion of raw feeling in terms of the ordinary language of psychological description and explanation, it may seem exposed to attacks on folk psychology. But the eliminativist case is not only weak in general: it seems beside the point when applied to the doctrine of raw feeling.

The general weakness of the eliminativist case stems partly from its reliance on an excessively narrow conception of what is required for the existence of a class of entities to be consistent with a given scientific corpus. Churchland, in particular, assumes that unless the categories of folk psychology can be reduced to those of a future developed neuroscience, they lack application altogether—they don't apply to anything real.[39]

There is of course no generally accepted conception of reduction (which is one reason why I shall avoid using the word). At one extreme would be the thought that all statements in the reduced theory must have translations—actual synonyms—in the reducing theory. Only slightly weaker would be a conception according to which the reducing theory must supply logically equivalent statements to those of the reduced theory. A more widely accepted idea is that there must be 'bridge laws' or 'correspondence rules' connecting the terms of the two theories. At the other extreme are notions like supervenience and strict implication, to be discussed

---

[38] P. M. Churchland, 'Eliminative Materialism and the Propositional Attitudes', 76.

[39] See Churchland, 'Eliminative Materialism'. Quine holds similar views. For example, he regards it as the task of science to tell us what there is (see e.g. *Word and Object*, 22). So far as folk psychology is concerned, he has a special reason: his doctrine of the indeterminacy of translation. If sound, this would entail that beliefs and desires are not real states of persons. However, for reasons given in R. Kirk, *Translation Determined*, I believe it to be mistaken.

in the next chapter. Churchland's conception of reduction is not particularly strong. He does not, for example, insist that the reduction involve 'correspondence rules' between reduced and reducing terms. He suggests we can get a useful notion of theory reduction by imposing the condition that the reducing theory (suitably restricted if necessary) logically entails a system of statements that are *relevantly isomorphic* with the reduced theory.[40] However, even if a developed neuroscience is eventually able to cover in this way all the phenomena that are covered by folk psychology, while the latter's categories are not in Churchland's sense smoothly reducible to those of the former, that would not entail that folk psychology was dispensable in favour of neuroscience, still less that the categories of folk psychology don't pick out realities. At any rate it would not entail this without an assumption which makes the claim merely trivial.

To see why not, compare physics with the vocabulary and folk theory of landscape and its formation. Whatever we may say about the landscape, there is no doubt that we are talking about states of affairs which are all capable in principle of being described and explained, in its special way, in terms of physics. But there seems no way to *reduce* our landscape vocabulary to the vocabulary of physics (not in any sense of 'reduce' stronger than the limiting one given by supervenience or strict implication), and indeed no point in even attempting to do so. Why? Is it because the landscape vocabulary doesn't deal with realities at all, while physics does? Not unless we assume that whatever can't be categorized by means of the vocabulary of physics doesn't exist for that reason alone. The case of our landscape vocabulary is itself a counter-example to that assumption. To deny that there are hills or mountains or rivers because these concepts are not found in the conceptual scheme of physics, and are not reducible to that scheme, would not only make it hard to describe and explain many ordinary phenomena. It would overlook the point that each individual hill, mountain, or whatever is actually *constituted* by things describable in terms of the narrow vocabulary of physics. So the mere fact that physics lacks, for example, the concept *mountain* could hardly be a reason for refusing to accept

[40] P. Churchland, 'Reduction, Qualia, and the Direct Introspection of Brain States'.

the existence of things falling under that concept. In general, the non-reducibility of a given theory or quasi-theory to physics, or indeed to some other specified science, does not entail that its terms do not apply to existing things.

Why is there no way to reduce the landscape vocabulary to the narrow vocabulary of physics? Clearly because the two ways of talking and thinking have been arrived at from different starting points, for different purposes, with different interests in view. So different in these respects, indeed, that there is no reason why anyone should have expected there to be any congruity between the two schemes. Now, it is a familiar point that something very similar holds for the case of folk psychology and neuroscience. The principles according to which folk-psychological kinds are individuated are quite alien to neuroscience. Eliminativists see this as a justification for their position. But for the reasons just noted, this incongruity between the two schemes gives us no reason to conclude that the fact that the latter deals with realities entails that the former does not.

A more potent-seeming objection to the claim that folk psychology describes realities is that it is unscientific, so that its explanations are at best superficial. A scientific psychology may properly be supposed to describe and explain realities, and so can the neurosciences; but not folk psychology. Now certainly folk psychology *is* unscientific. But so is much of our ordinary talk about the landscape. If the objection is sound, therefore, it ought to show that our unscientific landscape concepts don't apply to realities—that there are no such things as mountains, hills, rivers, valleys, rolling country, and so on. But why should we accept that conclusion? No doubt our unscientific ways of talking don't analyse or explain things along the lines that science discovers: they don't cut nature at the joints. They don't describe natural kinds, perhaps. But it is easy to find counter-examples to show that the desired conclusion will not follow. Science tells us that stars are one kind of thing, planets another. But until children have learnt the difference they tend to call both stars and planets 'stars'. Used in that way—a piece of folk description if ever there was one—the word 'star' doesn't pick out a natural kind. Yet it still picks out things whose reality is guaranteed by science. 'Jade' is another word that picks out scientifically guaranteed realities in spite of not being an officially approved natural-kind word. For, as Putnam tells us, it applies to two distinct minerals, nephrite and jadeite.[41] So the mere fact that folk psychology is unscientific doesn't preclude its describing and explaining realities.

I have said that raw feeling is a component not only of ordinary sense perception, but also of bodily sensation, of dreaming, of hallucination, and of mental imagery of all kinds. But I should not expect a developed neuroscience or even a scientific psychology to treat this heterogeneous collection of states as a unity. They are united only, perhaps, in that they are salient to us as reflective subjects. Since for these sciences the very notion of a subject seems alien, their interests are widely different from my philosophical interests in pursuing my present investigations. So I should not expect them to be at all concerned with the notion of raw feeling. The notion seems impossible to explain except in folk-psychological terms, via the notion of a subject; and it is only from the general point of view of folk psychology that the philosophical problems it raises can be discerned. From the standpoint of neuroscience, and perhaps also from that of a scientific psychology, those problems can safely be ignored. But as we have seen, that does not mean they can be ignored from the philosophical point of view.[42] Still less does it mean that there is something wrong with the notion of raw feeling.

It is perhaps conceivable that folk psychology should eventually be superseded by a scientific psychology. But even that wouldn't mean that folk psychology didn't describe realities. There is a great difference between the case where a theory is superseded because it is less convenient or more superficial than its successor, and the case where it is superseded because it is false. We gave up using words like 'witch' and 'phlogiston' because we found good reasons for thinking there were no such things. But if in the future we found it convenient to give up using the word 'jade', it wouldn't follow that we thought there was no such thing as jade. Similarly, even if we eventually found scientific psychology and the neurosciences more convenient or intellectually hygienic than folk psychology, that would not imply that we regarded folk psy-

---

[41] See Putnam, 'The Meaning of "Meaning"', 241.

[42] I would agree with Kathleen Wilkes in 'Is Consciousness Important?' when she urges that the neurosciences as such need not concern themselves with qualia, raw feels, and so on. But as I have argued, that is not to say that these thoughts can be ignored altogether. See also E. Bisiach, 'The (Haunted) Brain and Consciousness'.

chology as false. Nor do the other considerations we have discussed have any tendency to that conclusion.

There is a further consideration, which seems to make the issue of eliminativism, in the end, beside the point. This is that even if the notion of raw feeling eventually turned out to be unsatisfactory, an explanation would still be required of how it nevertheless *appeared* to capture an important component of our mental lives. What is it about us and our experiences that makes such notions so appealing? Why is it that when we are faced by a scientific story of what goes on in sensation and perception, we are still inclined to wonder: 'How on earth could THIS be just a matter of all that?' Even the eliminativists owe us an explanation of the plausibility of such notions—and so far as I can see they must make at least provisional use of folk-psychological concepts to do so.[43]

2.9 CONCLUSION

We have examined two disparate lines of objection to the notion of raw feeling. Both have turned out to be seriously defective. In the course of the examination the notion has been to some extent clarified. It doesn't involve the assumptions which Wittgensteinian objections presupposed. Notably it doesn't involve any radical epistemological privacy or ineffability. We can characterize one another's raw feels reasonably well, even if our characterizations are always capable of further elaboration. Nor does the notion involve any clearly objectionable ontological commitments. It doesn't involve a relational conception of perception, still less does it involve any commitment to dualism.

As for eliminativist objections, raw feeling has turned out to have something of the rough and ready robustness of folk notions such as those of *mountain* and *river*. It is most unlikely to be smoothly reducible to the concepts of a developed neuroscience; but we have seen that that is no objection. In any case it helps to focus attention on some seemingly intractable problems.

---

[43] The article by Patricia and Paul Churchland to be discussed in Ch. 6 is evidence in favour of this claim.

3

Strict Implication and the Swiss Cheese Principle

Philosophy is not in the business of discovering the mechanisms of the brain. But it can aspire to understand how the workings of any mere mechanisms could produce something so mysterious as raw feeling. If raw feeling involves only physical processes, those processes must determine not only that it occurs, but what it is like. So—as I will argue if it is not already clear—the connection from physical processes to raw feeling must be an absolutely necessary one. Yet if the Transformation thesis is true, it is hard to understand how that can be so. In this chapter I will defend two propositions which, taken together, will help to make this understanding possible.

3.1 THE ZOMBIE IDEA

We can start from a thought of G. F. Stout's.

In general, if the materialist [he is referring to the epiphenomenalist] is right, it ought to be quite credible that the constitution and course of nature would be otherwise just the same as it is if there were not and never had been any experiencing individuals. Human bodies would still have gone through the motions of making and using bridges, telephones and telegraphs, of writing and reading books, of speaking in Parliament, of arguing about materialism, and so on. There can be no doubt that this is *prima facie* incredible to Common Sense.[1]

We might suspect that some people who speak in Parliament exemplify the possibility Stout has in mind—but just what is that possibility? To start with, imagine that an idealized version of

---

[1] G. F. Stout, *Mind and Matter*, 138 f. William James has a rather similar argument in *The Principles of Psychology*, i.132−6; but he does not point out, what gives extra bite to Stout's argument, that epiphenomenalists ought to accept the credibility of a world physically like ours, yet without sentience.

today's physics is capable of truly describing the whole of the actual physical universe, past, present, and future, and includes all true physical laws. Assume physicalists and epiphenomenalists are right in maintaining that all physical events fall under physical laws—the universe is physically closed—and let P be the set of all true statements in the austere vocabulary of that idealized physics. P is the totality of true physical statements and describes the physical situation at every place and time past, present, and future. Now let R be the set of all statements truly or falsely ascribing raw feels to items in the physical universe specified by P. The essence of Stout's idea may be stated as follows:

A. It is possible that P should have been true while there was no consistent subset of R all of whose members were true.[2]

That is, the world might have been just as it actually is in all physically describable respects (or at any rate just as physicalists and epiphenomenalists suppose it to be: see below), complete with particle-for-particle counterparts of us and all other organisms, yet different in that none of our counterparts had any raw feels. This is what I am calling the Zombie idea.

In spite of Stout's conviction that Common Sense is likely to be repelled by it, the idea can be alluring, especially when we realize that the possibility in question is of the barest logical or conceptual variety. There is no implication that the laws of nature would actually permit a Zombie world. Epiphenomenalists certainly have to concede that bare logical or conceptual possibility, since to deny it would be to admit that the facts of consciousness don't after all involve the existence of anything non-physical. But they need not also concede that a Zombie world is naturally or nomologically possible. Their view is that the laws of nature—for them, wider in scope than the laws of physics—guarantee that whenever the right physical conditions exist, the non-physical epiphenomena also occur. Common Sense tends to reject whatever cannot be

---

[2] Why not just define R as the set of all true statements ascribing raw feels to items in the universe specified by P? Because then you couldn't formulate (A) so as to rule out possible worlds where P was true but some different set of statements ascribing raw feels was true. Such worlds would not be Zombie worlds of the kind envisaged by Stout. Note that by 'possible' I mean something like logically or conceptually or barely possible. See 3.4 below.

fitted into familiar experience. So even when capitalized, it is not an appropriate tribunal for determining what is or isn't a genuine possibility.

You may find the full-blown Zombie possibility (A) intuitively less plausible than the following:

B. It is possible that *P* should have been true while some member of *R*, true in the world as it is, was false.

That is, the world might, logically, have been just as it is in all physically describable respects while one of our counterparts had a raw feel different from that of their original. This suggestion can seem perfectly obvious and unproblematic. On the face of it—even after lengthy consideration—there seems nothing that could bind the physical facts tightly enough to the facts about raw feeling to squeeze out (B). The slightest difference in the actual facts about raw feels, with *P* held constant, would be enough for (B). No matter how much detail might be added to our knowledge of the physical facts about colour vision, for example, it is hard to see how they could determine that we see colours exactly as we do, rather than in some slightly different way. At any rate there does *appear* to be a logical gulf between the physiological and other physical facts on the one side, and the facts about our subjective experience on the other.

So (B) tends to appeal to people's intuitions. But if you accept (B) it is hard to resist (A). If the totality of physical truths *P* doesn't logically or conceptually determine the character of our experiences, then when God had fixed on a complete physical specification for his creation, he had, in Kripke's phrase, 'further work' to do.[3] He had to decide upon the exact details of the raw feels that physical organisms should have. But now, if the totality of physical truths, including, of course, truths about the fine details of events in creatures' nervous systems, falls short of determining just which raw feels they have, it must fall short of determining that there is raw feeling at all. For how could the totality of physical facts determine *that* organisms had raw feels (contrary to (A)) without also determining *what* those raw feels were (contrary to (B))? Raw feeling without character wouldn't be

[3] S. Kripke, *Naming and Necessity*, 154.

raw feeling. So if you concede (B) it is hard to see how you could reject (A)—the full Zombie possibility.[4]

3.2   THE TWO-STAGE CREATION SCENARIO AND THE STRICT IMPLICATION THESIS

The Zombie possibility (A) entails that the links from the physical facts to the facts about raw feels are less than logically or conceptually necessary. If that possibility is genuine, the whole physical history of the universe could have been exactly as it actually will have been, while all terrestrial organisms, even though they were particle-for-particle replicas of ourselves, lacked raw feels. And if this universal Zombie idea seems too extravagant, the weaker suggestion (B), to the effect that the same total physical history would have permitted a somewhat different history of raw feeling, still seems plausible. But both are deeply depressing. For if even (B) were true there would be no prospect of solving our problems. Instead we should just have to accept it as one brute fact that we have raw feeling at all, and another brute fact that we have the raw feels we do have, given the total physical set-up. Attempts to explain either of these two facts in terms of facts about behaviour, dispositions, causal relations, or even brain processes would be doomed. Of course there have to be some brute facts. But I aim to show that we don't have to treat the facts of raw feeling as basic.

First I need to make it quite clear that (B) is incompatible with even minimal physicalism. We can start with an intuitively persuasive route to that conclusion. If (B) were true, then in

---

[4] This particular possibility must not be confused with the ones commonly discussed under the label 'absent qualia'. One difference is that the Zombie possibility as defined here covers all organisms, not just the odd one here or there. But the main difference is that the Zombies defined here are in all physically describable respects—not just functionally—exactly as physicalists suppose human beings actually are. Another important point is that the alleged Zombie possibility does not involve supposing that the physical facts about human beings might have been different from what physicalists think they actually are. Conceivably a Cartesian might concede that possibility; but it is beside the present point. In contrast, the usual claim about 'absent qualia' is only that there could be beings dispositionally and functionally equivalent to us, yet lacking sensations. In fact I think this is a genuine possibility, as I shall explain in the next chapter. The Zombie possibility entails the absent qualia possibility, but the converse is not true.

creating the world God could have done his work in two distinct stages. He could have started with the creation of a world that was in all physically describable respects exactly like the actual world. But if (B) is true, this stage of creation would leave further work to be done. God would still have to decide on at least some aspects of raw feeling and duly bring them into existence: the physical facts would have failed to bring these facts with them. So this two-stage creation scenario entails an ontological difference between the first and second stages.

But there is no need to appeal to intuition. The argument can be stated quite baldly. If there could have been a physical world just like the actual world—assuming this world is as physicalists suppose—where nevertheless the pattern of raw feeling differed from that of the actual world, then raw feeling is not wholly constituted by anything in the physical world. By definition what was introduced at the second stage would not be physical in any relevant sense.

Minimal physicalism therefore commits you to reject (B). That is, it commits you to deny that the members of P could have been true while some member of R, true in the world as it is, was false: P strictly implies R.[5] But of course physicalists hold that what goes for raw feels goes for all other kinds of mental states too. So by applying the reasoning in the last paragraph to mental states in general, we see that minimal physicalism commits you to a more general thesis. Suppose Q is the set of all actually true statements ascribing mental states to individuals in the universe physically specified by P. Then minimal physicalism commits you to the *Strict Implication* thesis:

P strictly implies Q: it is impossible that all the members of P should be true and some member of Q false.

Where P is the total history of the universe stated in the austere vocabulary of today's physics, together with statements of all physical laws, it is impossible that P should have been true while some actually true statement about people's mental states was

[5] It is usual to say that a statement A strictly implies a statement B if it is impossible that A should be true and B false. I will also say that a set of statements (such as P) strictly implies another set of statements if it is impossible that the conjunction of the members of the first set should be true and that of the second false.

false. Note the direction of the implication: from the physical to the mental.

The impossibility involved here is logical or 'absolute', not just nomological. You might suspect that a minimal physicalism doesn't call for anything so strong. Wouldn't a nomologically necessary link from the physical to the mental be enough, as is sometimes suggested by supervenience theorists?[6] In fact it would not be enough, and it is important to see why. Physicalism is intended to be a variety of monism. Whatever the details may be, the fundamental idea is that what actually exists involves nothing over and above the physical. So if you are a physicalist you are committed to the view that in any possible world which is in all physical respects an exact replica of this world, our counterparts in it have corresponding mental states to ours.

By saying 'corresponding mental states' we can avoid the complications of theories according to which an exact physical replica of the actual world would not necessarily be one in which the replica-Plato was Plato, the replica-London was London, and so on. According to such theories, my counterpart would not be me, nor would any thoughts he expressed by saying 'I'm thinking about Plato' be about Plato; they would be about counterpart-Plato. But these complications are clearly irrelevant: the physicalist has still got to say that our counterparts have mental states exactly similar to ours, even if their contents differ because they are about exactly similar things to the corresponding contents of our own thoughts and feelings, not about identically the same things. (Not that the mental states of our counterparts will necessarily be *all* the mental states in such a possible world. If angels are possible, then in some of those possible worlds there will be the non-physically constituted mental states of angels on top of the physically constituted ones of our counterparts.)

It is crucial that this holds not just for nomologically possible worlds. It holds for worlds that are possible in any sense. To suggest there is a nomologically possible world exactly like the actual one in all physically describable respects, yet different in some respect other than the problematic one mentioned in the last paragraph, is to imply that something beyond the physical is required for the existence of the mental states we actually have. So

[6] See e.g. J. Kim, 'Concepts of Supervenience'.

it is to commit yourself against physicalism—no doubt to some variety of dualism.

Physicalists might hope to escape being committed to the Strict Implication thesis by assertions of psychophysical identity. But there is no hiding place there. If the identities were supposed to hold in every possible world that was like the actual world in all physically specifiable respects, the Strict Implication thesis would thereby be conceded. So the idea would have to be that the identities hold in some but not all of those worlds. In that case two possible worlds, w_1 and w_2, are exactly like this world in all physical respects, yet while somebody's counterpart in w_1 has one type of experience or thought, the counterpart of that experience or thought is lacking in the w_2 counterpart; and this difference has no physical explanation because there is no physical difference. Clearly, then, something non-physical is responsible for the difference. So, whatever its exponents may have intended, that type of identity theory is not in fact physicalistic.

So any kind of physicalist is committed to the Strict Implication thesis. Like it or not, it is a necessary condition of physicalism; and that is the main point to bear in mind in what follows. However, it is worth noting that the Strict Implication thesis is not also sufficient even for minimal physicalism. Two further conditions are required. One is that the converse is not true: Q does not strictly imply P. This makes explicit the view, shared by all physicalists, that while the mental is fixed by the physical, the physical is not in turn fixed by the mental. The other condition is needed in order to rule out a certain peculiar kind of dualism. The Strict Implication thesis rules out dualism with respect to the mental states of physical organisms. But it doesn't rule out non-physical beings with their own non-physical kinds of thinking and feeling—assuming that there could be such beings. For that purpose physicalism needs a statement to the effect that there is nothing in the world except things whose existence is strictly implied by P. I mention these two additional conditions for the sake of completeness: we need not discuss them further. It is the Strict Implication thesis which seems to raise all the difficulties for physicalism.

3.3   MORE ON THE STRICT IMPLICATION THESIS

(a)   *Physical statements*

What are to be counted as 'physical' statements? I will be as vague as I can get away with. Physical and non-physical statements may be distinguished in terms of an austere *physical vocabulary*. This vocabulary is to be thought of as having been exhaustively listed, although there is no point in actually compiling such a list. It may be taken to comprise the special vocabularies of an idealized version of today's physics plus mathematics and logic. Just to be sure, we can explicitly exclude all expressions that would ordinarily be counted as mental or psychological, together with all words for 'secondary qualities' such as colours and tastes. Since there is plenty of room to vary the contents of this austere physical vocabulary, the Strict Implication thesis is more of a schema than a definite thesis. However, its significance does not depend on the precise demarcation of the physical vocabulary. It depends on whether any vocabulary (and theory) of the sort I have indicated could cover the phenomena of raw feeling. Physicalists have always had to grapple with the problem of showing how the facts of experience and intentionality can be squared with the view that the ultimate constituents of people are just the same as those of inanimate objects, and that the laws which suffice to explain the behaviour of the former are the same as, or at any rate reducible to or underlain by, those which govern the behaviour of the latter. So long as that is the focus of philosophical interest, the question of just what are to be counted as the fundamental constituents of the world, and just what are the fundamental laws, is barely relevant.

These considerations also make it unnecessary to go into the once much-discussed issue of defining the physical. One advantage that physicalism has over earlier varieties of materialism is that the role formerly allotted to matter is now allotted to whatever is posited by physics. Of course there are still problems. Physicalists seem to face a dilemma. If they define a priori what is to be counted as physics they risk being overtaken by historical change. But if they refuse to do so, and allow their position at any time to be determined by whatever may happen to be labelled 'physics', they risk hopeless vagueness at best, and at worst, triviality. Who can say what that label may eventually be applied to? However, if my earlier remarks are correct there is no serious problem here. It is enough for minimal physicalists to maintain that *on the assumption* that today's physics is adequate for describing and explaining those phenomena which are today normally counted as physical, the Strict Implication thesis holds—physical truths being explained in terms of the notions of today's physics. We can provisionally take a realistic attitude to the best physics we know in spite of our belief that it will eventually be superseded; and we can justify this attitude by pointing out that the philosophical problems which concern us here appear to be indifferent to the revisability of physics.

A *physical statement*, then, is one composed wholly of words from the physical vocabulary. *P*, the set of all true physical statements, will cover the whole history of the universe, past, present, and future. Bear in mind that it will also include, as well as all mathematics and logic, all physical laws. Of course it will not also include any *psycho*physical laws or generalizations, since these—assuming there are some—necessarily incorporate expressions from outside the physical vocabulary.[7]

(b)   Logical status of the Strict Implication thesis

Clearly the Strict Implication thesis is either necessarily true or necessarily false. For on the usual assumptions, given any pair of statements A and B, it is either necessarily true that A strictly implies B or necessarily true that it does not. However, it is contingent whether the world is one where a thesis *corresponding* to the Strict Implication thesis holds. Recall how it is stated:

It is impossible that all the members of *P* should be true and some member of *Q* false.

Let us label that sentence S. Just which thesis is stated by S evidently depends on the actual membership of the two sets

---

[7] Tim Crane argues that 'supervenience physicalists' have to show 'how there can be real mental properties, objective dependencies between them and physical properties, and yet no laws in which they figure' ('All God Has to Do', 250). But for reasons that I hope will emerge, I see no reason to deny that there are psychophysical laws—strictly implied by *P*.

denoted by '*P*' and '*Q*'. We know relatively little about which
sentences belong to those sets in the actual world. In some possible
worlds, exactly the same sentence S would state a different thesis
from the one I have stated by means of S—simply because '*P*' and
'*Q*' denote different sets in those other possible worlds. The Strict
Implication thesis is the one I have stated by using S. But in each
of those other possible worlds there is a corresponding thesis: the
one stated by using S in that possible world. And unless you think
Cartesian worlds, where non-physical items are involved in mental
life, are impossible, you must concede that in such worlds the
corresponding thesis is false. If our world is one where minimal
physicalism holds, then the actual membership of the two sets *P*
and *Q* is such that *P* does strictly imply *Q*, and S makes a true
statement. But if the dualists are right about our world, S makes a
different statement, which is false. So it is contingent whether our
world is one where a thesis corresponding to the Strict Implication
thesis holds.[8]

(c)   *Strict implication and supervenience*

The Strict Implication thesis is tailor-made for my purposes. It
provides a reasonably clear sense in which the physical can be said
to determine the mental—at any rate that particular aspect of
the mental which concerns us—without necessarily involving the
reducibility, definability, or translatability of mental statements by
physical ones. Others have used various notions of supervenience
for similar purposes. But I have reasons for sticking with the
notion I have defined. (Skip to the next section if you are content
with this assurance.) One is that there is no single generally accepted definition of supervenience. On the contrary, the availability
of a range of different concepts of supervenience is regarded
as something of a virtue. Not only are there various forms of
supervenience thesis. Writers on the subject tend to emphasize that
it leaves open what sort of necessity is involved. To add to the
potential confusion, several have suggested that, for the special
case of mental–physical relations, nomic necessity may be all that

---

[8] I missed some of the above points in my earlier attempts at clarifying the
relation in question (in 'Zombies v. Materialists' and 'Physicalism, Identity, and
Strict Implication').

is needed.[9] If what I said above is right, that is not so—or not unless you are some kind of dualist.

But the main reason why minimal physicalism should avoid supervenience theses is that the usual versions say either too much or too little. The two well-known versions discussed by Jaegwon Kim illustrate this point. His 'weak' version, applied to the case of mental and physical properties, may be paraphrased as follows:

> Necessarily, if something has a certain mental property, there is a certain physical property which it also has, and such that if anything has it, then in fact it also has that mental property.[10]

This is unsuitable for minimal physicalism because it entails that necessarily (that is, in any possible world) any given mental property is correlated with some physical property. The idea is that there *can* be no mental difference without a physical difference.[11] And that says too much for minimal physicalism because it rules out worlds where certain kinds of Cartesian dualism reign. I hold no brief for dualism, but I don't think minimal physicalism can rule out the possibility of dualism in that way. In contrast, the Strict Implication thesis leaves it open whether there might, logically, be such Cartesian worlds. Where supervenience implies that there *can* be no difference without a physical difference, Strict Implication says only that there actually *is* no difference without a physical difference. However, the weak supervenience thesis also says too little, since it is compatible with epiphenomenalism. For it requires only that the mental property be *in fact* correlated with the physical one.

Kim's 'strong' version of supervenience differs from the weak version by substituting 'necessarily' for 'in fact'. So far, then, it agrees with the Strict Implication thesis. But since it shares the same first part as the weak version, it is open to the same objection: it says too much for minimal physicalism. Kim's strong supervenience may perhaps be an appropriate relation if you intend to use it to ascribe a purely physical 'nature' to the mental.

[9] See J. Kim, 'Supervenience and Nomological Incommensurables', 152, and 'Concepts of Supervenience', 166.
[10] Adapted from J. Kim, ' "Strong" and "Global" Supervenience Revisited', 316.
[11] Cf. J. Bacon, 'Supervenience, Necessary Coextension, and Reducibility'.

But the Strict Implication thesis doesn't rule out the possibility that some minds should have been non-physical.

Strict implication is surely a more straightforward and readily intelligible relation than supervenience as it has been multifariously defined.[12] It lets us sidestep the marshy ground of supervenience and move on.

3.4   ABSOLUTE IMPOSSIBILITY AND THE EXAMPLE OF 'GNARLED'

According to the Strict Implication thesis it is absolutely impossible that all the members of P should be true while some member of Q was false—P being the totality of statements in the austere vocabulary of physics, Q the totality of true statements ascribing mental states, including raw feels, to the individuals physically picked out by P. But talk of absolute impossibility will raise hackles, and in this section I want to make clear that it is harmless. I also aim to make clear that, contrary to what might be supposed, establishing that one set of statements strictly implies another need not require translating the second into the first; nor finding logically necessary and sufficient conditions for the second in terms of the first; nor even knowing just which members of either set are actually true. Nor, finally, does it require us to be able somehow to derive the concepts needed for the second set from those introduced in the first.

To start from some simple cases. Consider:

1. Clara speaks French and Clara speaks Japanese.

2. Clara speaks French.

In the intended sense it is absolutely impossible that (1) should be true and (2) false; and of course it is also clear why. Nor does (2) introduce any concepts not already introduced by (1). But simple formal examples are remote from the case that concerns us, as are less simple ones such as:

3. ABC is a Euclidean triangle.

---

[12] See e.g. I. G. McFetridge, 'Supervenience, Realism, Necessity', and Bacon, 'Supervenience, Necessary Coextension, and Reducibility', for a variety of definitions of supervenience, and discussion of logical relations between them.

4. The sum of the internal angles of ABC is 180°.

Again it is absolutely impossible that (3) should be true and (4) false, and clear why; though there is no simple formal operation to transform the first statement into the second. These illustrations cover only a restricted range of cases. In both the implied statement is derivable from the first by means of logical and syntactic rules supplemented by definitions; while there are plenty of cases where that is not so. I will concentrate on one from an area remote from the mental.

The statement

5. Some hands are gnarled,

though true, is not a member of the set P of all true physical statements. For 'gnarled' is not in the austere physical vocabulary. (It is beside the point that (5) is a physical statement according to wider definitions than ours.) So suppose someone—perhaps a foreigner—were puzzled about the relations between a thing's being gnarled and the austere physical truths about it. The austerely described physical facts are unproblematic for this person; but oddly enough the facts about being gnarled are problematic. Now there is no doubt that the totality of facts statable in the austere physical vocabulary does completely determine that there are gnarled things. There is no possibility whatever that P should have been true while (5) was false (given that (5) is actually true)—no room for dualism with respect to gnarledness. But how might we set about convincing our benighted friend?

One preliminary point. As with the first two examples, it would be no use invoking natural law. There seems to be no lawlike connection, natural or other, between gnarledness and any physically definable class of physical truths (see below). Nor is this an impossibility like the impossibility (if Kripke is right) that certain identities, such as that between water and H_2O, should fail to hold. The impossibility that matters for the Strict Implication thesis can be loosely described as logical or conceptual. Since Quine, anyone using such expressions has to be wary. But his strictures have not rendered them altogether useless. It is consistent with his work to insist that the considerations we bring into play when we decide whether to assent to 'It is impossible that P should be true and (5) false' satisfy the following two conditions: (*a*) they are unlike the considerations we bring into play when we decide whether to assent to formally similar statements of (what we tend to call) merely natural or nomological impossibility, for example, 'It is impossible that "x is made of pure tin" should be true and "x will melt at around 232°C" false'; (*b*) these considerations are what would traditionally be called logical or conceptual. It is also consistent with Quine's work that those considerations should make us want to say that the impossibility in question is absolute rather than merely nomological. For in such cases there appears to be no room whatever for the truth of the first statement(s) to co-exist with the falsity of the second. Of course there are different views as to why this is so, but the points I want to make do not require us to pursue the further issues raised. What I have to say will be neutral between rival theories of necessity and impossibility.

A neat way of showing that (5) is strictly implied by *P* would be to define 'gnarled' in terms of the austere physical vocabulary, and then show that *P* contains the expanded version of (5). But that is a tall order. There is every reason to think that 'gnarled', together with a vast number of other words, for example 'smooth', 'hilly', 'mountain', 'lake', is not definable in austerely physical terms. To mention one reason, it is conceivable that there should have been hills, mountains, lakes, and smooth and gnarled things, even in a universe with a structure and laws significantly different from those in the actual universe. If that is right, it rules out the possibility not only of translations (meaning-equivalents) of the words in question by means of disjunctions of physical statements, but of definitions in those terms. So there can be strict implication from one set of truths to another without the conceptual scheme required for grasping the first set necessarily being capable of providing the concepts required for grasping the second.

Yet in spite of those difficulties we can easily see that there is strict implication here: that it's absolutely impossible that all the members of *P* should have been true while (5) was false. For it is unproblematic that 'gnarled' is applicable to things in virtue of their surface contours, or at any rate in virtue of the ways we are likely to be struck by features of their contours.[13] We call hands

---

[13] Since the applicability of 'gnarled' depends on how things strike us, anyone who wants to eliminate all such subject-dependent language will be an eliminativist about gnarledness. However, our imaginary worrier will presumably not be satisfied

gnarled when their shapes and surfaces show a sufficient amount of relatively abrupt, relatively prominent changes of gradient over and above those determined by their overall outline. We acquire this information, of course, by reflecting on our understanding of 'gnarled'. It is also unproblematic that the contours and shapes of things quite generally are wholly determined by the physically stable facts. Given a total description of old Dagwood's hands in terms of the positions of the molecules composing them, we could use that information to work out everything we wanted to know about their contours. There is no room here for lurking non-physical factors. So we know enough about the meaning of 'gnarled' to see that a thing's gnarledness is constituted by features of its contours, and enough about physics to see that the austerely physical truths are bound to determine its contours.

We know enough about gnarledness and contours, and *enough* about physical-language descriptions, to be confident not only that P strictly implies (5), but that there is nothing mysterious about that fact. But we need not know just which physical statements are true of this or that gnarled thing, nor even which statements ascribing gnarledness are true.[14] Nor do we have to be able to arrive at the concept of gnarledness on the basis of our grasp of the austerely physical concepts. I will argue that similar points apply to the particular case of the Strict Implication thesis. If so, it will be easier to understand how it could hold.

One more moral. We don't have to be embarrassed about using such a 'folk' word as 'gnarled'. It may not figure in the vocabularies of any developed science or correlate with any physically characterizable property. All the same it applies only to items with impeccable physical credentials. Analogously, we needn't be embarrassed about using folk-psychological notions when trying to pin down the right kinds of physical or functional items as candidates for what constitutes raw feeling.

Conceivably the Strict Implication thesis might be established by

by being told that if they spoke a different, purely physical, language they would worry no longer—any more than I can be satisfied by being told a similar story about raw feeling.

[14] This example seems to me to refute the claim made by Howard Robinson in *Matter and Sense*, 29, that we should not have an acceptable philosophical analysis unless we could find topic-neutral translations of statements supposedly ascribing states that supervene on physical states.

high-level conceptual considerations—perhaps by showing that the whole idea of non-physical items was incoherent. Hobbes argued that since 'all mutation is motion', all motion is of corporeal things, and experience is nothing but changes (mutations), 'mind will be nothing but the motions in certain parts of an organic body'.[15] Thus he argued for materialism a priori, incidentally ruling out possible counter-examples to the Strict Implication thesis. Another approach with the same result (if it worked) might be based on verificationism. Suppose there are no physical differences between a certain pair of possible worlds. Then it might be urged that there could be no meaningful statements true of either that were not also true of the other.

But such approaches smack of question-begging. The heavy language-philosophical artillery they depend on is among the apparatus whose reliability is put in doubt if the opponents of physicalism are right. In any case the two approaches just mentioned bring little promise of dispelling the mystery that surrounds raw feeling. The approach I favour is to provide an account of it which enables us to see how the Strict Implication thesis could be true (or more strictly, how a sentence stating the thesis could express a truth). For the reasons we have noted, the account need not provide translations or even logical equivalents to statements about raw feeling.[16] But it must make clear how a purely physical system could be a subject of raw feeling.

3.5   WHAT HAS TO BE DONE?

The majority of psychologists and other scientists, being minimal physicalists, assume that the facts of consciousness involve no more than physical processes. Showing they are right would involve showing that these facts are in principle capable of explaining all our capacities, free from significant causal gaps. To determine

---

[15] T. Hobbes, *De Corpore*, ch. 25, arts. 1 and 2.

[16] Compare David Armstrong's point that the question is 'whether it is possible to do full justice to the nature of these mental states by means of purely physical or neutral concepts. We therefore try to sketch an account of typical mental states in purely physical or neutral terms. The account might fall indefinitely short of giving translations of mental statements, yet it might still be plausible to say that the account had done justice to the phenomena' (*A Materialist Theory of the Mind*, 84–5).

how well justified that assumption is would not be a job for philosophers—unless, with Hobbes, they thought it could be done a priori. Even less can philosophers presume to explain how the brain actually works. But they can reasonably attempt to show how the Strict Implication thesis *could* be true. To do so will be to say enough about raw feeling for the claim that the thesis *is* true to leave us no longer puzzled. That is what I shall be attempting in the following chapters.

Ideally one would like to be able to spell out what it takes for something to be a subject of raw feeling in terms specific enough to remove all theoretical difficulties over how there could conceivably be mechanisms satisfying the characterization.[17] But that project seems at present to be a pipe-dream, although I shall assume it is at any rate theoretically feasible for beings with sufficient knowledge, intelligence, and other resources. However, I will suggest, in terms that I hope will eventually be agreed to be unproblematic, necessary and sufficient conditions for a system to be a subject of raw feeling. On that basis I shall try to make clear how the facts about raw feeling could satisfy the Strict Implication thesis in spite of the Transformation thesis and other apparent difficulties.

By this time, dualistically inclined readers will be close to mutiny. By what right am I putting so much weight on the Strict Implication thesis when our intuitions suggest that ours is one of those possible worlds where it (or rather, a thesis corresponding to it) is false? For there still seems to be a gap between the austere physical facts on the one hand and the facts about raw feeling on the other. Admittedly I am not insisting that the Strict Implication thesis is true. But I am assuming it *could* be true (strictly, that the sentence which states it could express a truth); and that may seem almost as bad. If there really is a logical gap between the physical facts and the facts about raw feeling, dualism is true after all: consciousness, or at any rate that aspect of it which I am calling raw feeling, is so special that it requires the presence of something non-physical.

Although dualism has almost died out among philosophers and psychologists, it still has supporters. Being anxious to deal fairly

[17] I am thinking of the kind of thing that Marr referred to as an algorithm (*Vision*, 23 ff.).

with honest doubt, I want to face this challenge squarely. However, I am not aiming to refute dualism, only to show that the ontological issue of dualism versus materialism can safely be left on one side. For this purpose I will devote the rest of this chapter to a defence of what I am calling the Swiss Cheese principle. Recognition of this principle will remove the nagging worry that an adequate account of raw feeling must invoke something over and above the physical. We shall be able to proceed on the assumption that it is constituted by something physical, whatever that something may be. So the Strict Implication thesis *could* be true. In this way the Swiss Cheese principle will help to explain how the 'inner' side of mental life could be constituted by purely physical processes.

Not only does the principle itself make this useful contribution. The argument for it will help to break down intuitive resistance to the idea that what appears to be a mere mechanism may constitute an experiencing subject. It will help to show how a structure describable objectively may amount to something with its own subjective point of view.[18] The argument centres on a piece of fiction.

3.6 NEURONE REPLACEMENT THERAPY: WILL IT WORK?

The old brain doesn't seem to be working quite as well as it used to. Perhaps I ought to eat more fish. But I've just been reading about something more exciting. It seems you can have your tired old brain cells replaced by new ones. Or rather, you can have them replaced by prosthetic neurones—by microminiaturized computers, in fact. They call it Neurone Replacement Therapy, or NRT.

It's known pretty well what a brain cell, or neurone, does in relation to the other neurones to which it is linked. So the NRT

---

[18] In 'Functionalism and Anomalous Monism' John McDowell insists (rightly, I think) that an understanding of the mental cannot be got from explanations based on considerations which ignore the content of mental states (see especially 195 f.). That is consistent with my claims about the Strict Implication thesis, which does not imply that an *understanding* of truths about mental states depends on an understanding of the austerely physical truths. That the mental depends on the physical does not imply that mental explanations depend on physical ones.

people say there's no reason why their ersatz neurones shouldn't work. Like full-sized computers, they are constructed from non-organic materials. Each has input and output units with vast numbers of electrical connections. It is programmed so that, whenever the inputs to the neurone it replaces would have caused it to fire, thereby transmitting an electrochemical impulse along its axon, it produces outputs which activate matching electrical firings along its connections to surrounding neurones. It's known that the states of the dendrites of neurones have a lot to do with long-term memory. The NRT people say their tiny prosthetic neurone computers are programmed to perform similar functions. As to the vital roles of neurotransmitters and neuroinhibitors, these too are taken care of by suitable interfaces between the biochemical environment and the ersatz neurones.

So I've decided to take a course of Neurone Replacement Therapy. Not being one for half-measures, I've opted for the Total Replacement Pack. Every one of my existing neurones will be replaced by a specially constructed microminiaturized computer, performing exactly the same input–output functions, and storage functions, as its original. However, since there are thousands of millions of neurones involved, and especially since I am rather anxious to make sure the prosthetic neurones work as advertised, the replacement is to be done in a succession of operations, taking many months.

Let's assume the prosthetic neurones, the tiny computers, really do perform all the input–output functions of the neurones they replace, together with their storage functions, and that the speeds of all electrical signals correspond to those in the original nerve fibres. The question that worries me is this. Is there any good reason to expect that when the whole replacement operation has been completed, my mental life will be in any respect significantly different from the way it is now?

3.7 THE SWISS CHEESE PRINCIPLE

I believe the answer to this question is No, because in common with many people I believe that the question of what materials something is made of has *in itself* no bearing on whether or not it has a mental life, or on just what its mental states are, or are like, if it has any. Whether it is wholly physical, wholly non-physical, or some kind of mixture, is irrelevant to these questions. What matters is not the materials, but how things constructed from whatever materials it might be interact—how they work, how they do their jobs. In Putnam's phrase, 'we could be made of Swiss Cheese and it wouldn't matter'.[19] This is what I am calling the Swiss Cheese principle. It is that a thing's composition—what materials it is made of—has no essential bearing on (*a*) whether or not it has a mental life; (*b*) what mental states it has, if any; (*c*) what, if anything, it is like to be it. This is not to say that any materials whatever could be put together to make a mind. It might indeed prove impossible to make a mind out of cheese. The point is that the materials don't matter provided they do the right things, whatever those things may be.

Probably most psychologists and philosophers accept the Swiss Cheese principle. Yet it is not immediately obvious. And it is extremely important when we are trying to get clear about what is involved in being a subject of mental states, and more particularly of raw feeling. If the principle is correct, two widely different schools of thought which have been very influential, and still have some adherents, are mistaken. One is dualism, which I will focus on here. The other, which I will call the bald psychophysical identity theory, will be dealt with in a later chapter. Before setting out my defence of the Swiss Cheese principle it will be useful to say a little more about dualistic opposition to it.

Dualism by itself need not set you in opposition to the Swiss Cheese principle. Conceivably someone might accept the principle, concede that there are possible worlds whose sentient and sapient inhabitants have mental states constituted by wholly physical items, yet for some reason insist that in the actual world mental states involve non-physical items. This position is after all only the dualistic image of the perfectly tenable physicalist view that although there could conceivably have been minds involving non-physical items, actually there are none. So to establish the Swiss Cheese principle will not call for the refutation of dualism. However, any dualists who accept the Swiss Cheese principle have a hard row to hoe. Evidence from detailed scientific work keeps coming in, and it becomes more and more difficult to see what

---

[19] H. Putnam, 'The Nature of Mental States', 191.

need there could be to invoke non-physical items to do what physical items seem quite capable of doing by themselves. (As we shall see, Putnam mentions telepathy as a conceivable ground for resistance to the principle. But even if there were overwhelming evidence for telepathy, and even if it couldn't be explained physically, still that would be no reason to maintain that all thinking, perceiving, and feeling involves non-physical items. Telepathy, even if it exists, is surely confined to a small proportion of the population.)

Historically the two most powerful considerations driving philosophers and others to endorse dualism have been (i) the *explanatory* difficulty of seeing how merely physical processes could generate the patterns of behaviour that human beings are capable of; (ii) the *conceptual* difficulty of seeing how the subjective aspects of mental life—the actual character of experience— could be plausibly understood to be constituted by merely physical processes.

The first type of consideration concerns only the question *how* what occurs could be explained—what can be done rather than what there is. One consideration that influenced Descartes, for example, is that he couldn't see how novel patterns of behaviour, such as we constantly display in our use of language, could be fully explained in terms of the workings of mechanisms. But the most that could be established by this sort of consideration would be that composition matters contingently. It clearly falls short of showing that composition matters necessarily. For it does nothing to show that no physical mechanisms whatever could generate the types of behaviour in question. Conceivably we might discover that those kinds of behaviour could not possibly be produced by purely physical means—or at least not in the right ways. For example, perhaps the mind operates at a faster rate than any possible physical system. But that would require a further argument, and one which there is no reason to anticipate. In any case the explanatory difficulty is philosophically insignificant, and recessive in defences of dualism. The dominant difficulty is conceptual. How can we make it intelligible that the 'inner' side of mental life could be constituted by the churnings of neurones? This has always been at the centre of the mind–body problem; and the Swiss Cheese principle contributes to getting over it.

Let us turn to Putnam's defence of the principle. In 'The Nature of Mental States' he invites us to imagine two possible worlds, one where people have 'good old-fashioned souls, operating through pineal glands, perhaps', the other where they have complicated brains. The souls in the soul world are functionally isomorphic to the brains in the brain world. He challenges dualists to explain how there could be any more sense to attaching importance to this difference than to the difference between copper wires and some other wires in a computer. 'Does it matter that the soul people have, so to speak, immaterial brains, and that the brain people have material souls? What matters is the common structure, the theory T of which we are, alas, in deep ignorance, and the hardware, be it ever so ethereal.'[20]

He goes on to discuss two possible objections. The first is that we are not interested in such automaton-like souls. His reply is that if the notions of functional organization and functional isomorphism don't apply to souls, then souls are things for which there can be no theory, which is 'pure obscurantism'.[21] The second objection is that the soul has powers that no mechanical system could have—telepathy, perhaps. His reply is, in effect, that this is extremely dubious, and can hardly be built into our notions of the soul. 'There cannot be a soul which is isomorphic to a brain, if the soul can read the future clairvoyantly, in a way that is not in any way explainable by physical law.' But he adds that telepathy might be handled by physical means, as might two other alleged difficulties: reincarnation and bodily resurrection.[22]

This defence of the Swiss Cheese principle is attractive. All that could be said to be lacking is an argument which actually shows that physical composition *couldn't* matter. Putnam's strategy is to challenge the dualist to explain how physical composition *could* matter; and I know of no adequate dualistic counter—apart from pointing out that 'obscurantism' is just a rude word. However, dualists are still likely to feel that it's simply inconceivable that anything merely physical could be such that it was 'like this' for the subject. If possible, then, we need a positive argument for the Swiss Cheese principle.

---

[20] Ibid. 292.
[21] Ibid. 294.
[22] Ibid. 294 f.

3.8 SOME GENERAL POINTS ABOUT THE NATURE OF MENTAL LIFE

First let us note one or two very general points about mental life. Most dualists and physicalists will accept the following assumption:

A. Whatever the details of mental life may be, it is constituted by a system of interacting processes, states and events.

The key word is 'interacting'. Clearly epiphenomenalists (of whom there are a few) and parallelists (of whom so far as I know there are none) will reject (A). But I have already rejected epiphenomenalism. Behaviourists too won't be happy about (A); but that doctrine has been rejected too and in any case behaviourists could hardly resist the Swiss Cheese principle. The vague word 'system' also bears some weight. I intend it to imply a certain degree of organization—enough, at any rate, to rule out something's counting as having a mind if the processes interacting in it do so by chance rather than as a result of some kind of organizational structure, however loose. I don't think it can be an objection to these remarks that they are vague, since the notions of mind and mental activity are themselves vague.

Mental life of any kind, it seems, must consist of interacting processes. As things are, these processes are typically linked not only among themselves but with the outside world. The typical possessor of a mind, I take it, at least collects information about its environment, stores such information, and initiates and controls its behaviour on the basis of incoming and stored information. But regardless of whether a mind's possessor is engaged with the outside world in these typical ways, having a mind involves a system of interacting processes. And these processes and their interactions are at least very important factors in determining just which mental states the subject has.

Now the question at issue is whether it can matter what kinds of items are involved in the internal interactions of a mind, provided they are capable of doing the right kinds of things (whatever those may be). To refute the Swiss Cheese principle it would be necessary to show that even if a certain system's internal processes *did* the right kinds of things, it wouldn't have a mind unless it *had* the right kinds of things: those processes must involve a certain special class of items—items with a certain composition. There is room for disagreement over the nature of those items. Dualists would say they must be 'spiritual'. Bald psychophysical identity theorists would say that, on the contrary, they must be physical—but they would agree with the dualists that the identity of each mental state depends essentially on its composition.

The only serious opposition to the Swiss Cheese principle has arisen from reflection on a certain subset of mental states: those involving consciousness. The reason is obvious. To the extent that you accept that the classification of mental states depends purely on behavioural dispositions or functions, there is no point in resisting the Swiss Cheese principle. It is only when you concede that certain mental states—states of consciousness—involve more than mere behaviour or the performance of functions, and indeed involve there being *something it is like to be* in those states, that you can feel compelled to suppose that composition matters. So if the Swiss Cheese principle can be shown to hold even for that subset of mental states, there will be no need to deal separately with those in whose classification behavioural dispositions or functions play a dominant role.

3.9   THE CORE ARGUMENT

Recall Leibniz's fantasy about walking into what is supposedly an enlarged mechanical mind, and finding nothing there to explain conscious perception. It is a measure of the strength of the intuitions which need to be dismantled that such a powerful thinker should have drawn support from that idea. Far from reinforcing his view that perception cannot be explained mechanically, it ought to prompt a very different reflection. *Whatever* it takes for something to be a conscious subject, viewing such a thing as mere observers—even though we are literally inside it—is bound to be vastly unlike sharing its own experiences. So if we investigate a brain, and find nothing but complicated patterns of electrochemical activity, that has no tendency to show that the processes we detect do not in fact constitute conscious perception. Viewing a system from the third-personal perspective, as an 'it', should not have been expected to give us any idea of what it would be like actually to be that system—to be 'I'. So our failure to acquire such an idea is no reason to suppose that there must be something hidden inside the system—something imperceptible—which supplies it with its first-personal perspective.

That reflection certainly undermines one of the lines of thought which incline people to dualism.[23] But it clearly falls short of an actual refutation. Indeed, it doesn't even amount to a demonstration of the Swiss Cheese principle. The dualist will still urge that there *must* be something else. The argument which follows is intended to meet that sort of resistance. In it, the idea of Neurone Replacement Therapy will serve two related purposes. It will enable us to focus on the factors which ensure that the Swiss Cheese principle holds, and it will make a start on the task of showing how descriptions of machinery can at the same time be specifications of something with its own conscious point of view. The argument works by exploiting our earlier points about causal relations. Specifically, it exploits the links between different mental states, and between conscious awareness and behaviour.

It all turns on a key question about the programme of Neurone Replacement Therapy. Is there *some* way of arranging the sequence of operations so that they make no relevant difference to the subjective character of my experience? (By a 'relevant' difference I mean one bearing on the Swiss Cheese principle, rather than one which results from things like my facing a huge hospital bill.) If there is some way of performing the change-over from standard organic neurones to microminiaturized computers which makes no relevant difference, then the Swiss Cheese principle is vindicated. For it is only in connection with states which have a subjective character that there is any pressure to resist the principle. If Neurone Replacement Therapy can be performed without affecting such states, the principle must be accepted. Even if there are other ways of performing the operation that would affect my experience, the existence of this one would show that composition, in itself, didn't matter.

---

[23] Bernard Williams, moving on from the platitude (as he rightly calls it) that 'there can be no third-personal perspective on the contents of consciousness', suggests that 'perhaps facts of the form *it is so for A* can, in some way or other, be included in the world just by including all the physical facts in it' (*Descartes: the Project of Pure Enquiry*, 297). He does not, however, claim that this reasoning is conclusive. (I am indebted to one of the OUP's anonymous referees for drawing my attention to Williams's discussion here.)

Let us therefore examine the other alternative: that there is *no* way of performing NRT which fails to affect the character of my experience: NRT always makes a difference. I will argue that, on the contrary, there will always be such a way. There are three cases to consider:

(*a*) NRT leaves me continuing to have experiences and aware of the difference in their character;

(*b*) NRT leaves me continuing to have experiences but unaware of the difference in their character;

(*c*) NRT leaves me unaware of a difference in the character of my experience because I am unaware of anything, perhaps because my whole mental life has been extinguished and I have turned into a kind of Zombie.

I will deal with each case in turn. (*a*) Since the operations have left me aware of the difference in the character of my experience, it seems reasonable to assume I could talk about it. I could say things like: 'Funny, that NRT salesperson told me I wouldn't notice any difference between my experiences before the treatment and after. Yet after this latest batch of operations I've noticed something very peculiar...' Not only could I say such things, I certainly would say them, and go on until I got my money back. However, if NRT had these effects, that could only be on account of differences between the *causal* properties of the prosthetic neurones and those of the ones they replaced. If both natural and prosthetic neurones shared exactly the same causal properties, then since nothing causes me to produce those complaints now, before I have even started the treatment, there is no way in which anything relevant could cause me to produce them after the treatment had begun. However, it was in the original contract that there were no such differences in causal properties. This is a vitally important feature of NRT: each individual computer is made to interact with other components of the brain in whatever ways the original neurone interacted. (In this sense each computer is 'functionally equivalent' to the neurone it replaces.) So this alternative—that NRT results in my becoming aware of the difference in the character of my experiences—is ruled out.

You might object that it is at any rate conceivable that the change-over should have effects that I was aware of but couldn't talk about. What if the operation left me paralysed? But that possibility is ruled out by the point we just noticed: NRT has no significant effects on my behavioural capacities or dispositions. So there is a genuine objection here only if on the one hand the operation results in my becoming aware of a relevant difference in the character of my experience, while on the other hand I retain all my abilities and tendencies to speak and write. But does this suggestion even make sense? I don't see how it can. Try to imagine the situation. I am aware of a change in the character of my experience. For example, the colour of pillar-boxes and other objects I know to be bright red strikes me now as more like a dull greyish brown. I am aware of this change, yet I can't talk or write about it. So what happens when I try to describe it? Do I become absolutely tongue-tied, or do I perhaps find my mouth still tending to produce the kinds of description I should have applied if there had been no change in the way I saw red things? If I become tongue-tied, can I later say something about *that*? If so, we have just the kind of behavioural difference that the NRT package precludes. But in any case, my becoming tongue-tied in every such situation is itself a significant behavioural difference. So the first alternative is ruled out. However, the second alternative is no help either. For if I find my mouth producing utterances I believe to be false, how can I fail to want to comment in turn on this distressing state of affairs? Do I become tongue-tied now? No, for the reason just given. But can it leave all my verbal and other behavioural capacities and dispositions completely undisturbed? Again the answer must be No. Evidently there is no *necessary* link from a change in the character of our experience to the loss of a hitherto present ability to describe it. If there are any doubts about this answer, recall that we have plenty of empirical evidence that our capacities to talk about our experiences are perfectly capable of surviving impairments in our capacities to have certain kinds of experiences. Sudden blindness is one obvious example. So if there is a way of managing the NRT operations which results in a difference in the character of my experiences that I am aware of, there must also, given this empirical evidence, be a way which does not impair my ability to talk about that difference. (This is empirical evidence to support a conceptual point. The conceptual point is that there is a necessary connection between states of awareness and the ability of their subjects, given suitable linguistic resources, to talk about those states.) So the objection fails. Case (*a*) is ruled out.

(*b*) The second case is that the difference in the character of my experience is so subtle that I am unaware of it. One possible explanation might be that there have been compensating changes. I might perhaps come to instantiate the Transformation thesis, for example, provided there were compensating alterations to the structures responsible for my memories of how I had perceived things before the changes. Another explanation might be that the changes were too gradual for me to notice them. There are two distinct reasons why this case can be ruled out. The first is that opponents of the Swiss Cheese principle are committed to the view that at any rate some substitutions of components in my mental machinery would necessarily, by themselves, result in relevant differences in the character of my experience—even though the substitutes were functionally equivalent to their originals. They are committed to this view by their insistence that composition matters. So even though they might concede that some ways of managing NRT would go unnoticed by the subject because of things like subtle compensating changes, they could hardly maintain that this would necessarily be so in every case. It makes no sense to say that the only possible changes in subjective experience producible by NRT would be ones that the subject could not possibly be aware of. *Ad hominem*, then, if case (*b*) is possible, so is (*a*). But (*a*) is impossible, so (*b*) is impossible too.

The other reason is more interesting. It is that if NRT could produce imperceptible differences in the character of my experience, it could produce perceptible ones too. For there seem to be only two ways in which the present case could obtain. One is if the changes were too gradual for me to notice them; the other is if they were compensated for by other changes. The latter possibility clearly implies that the changes would have been perceptible if there had been no compensation, which proves the point. For then there could not be type (*b*) cases unless there could also be type (*a*) cases. But the first possibility equally clearly implies that if the changes in question had been quicker, their cumulative effect would have been noticeable. So we may conclude quite generally that if NRT could produce *imperceptible* differences in the character of my experience, it could produce perceptible ones too. There is some way of managing the operations so as to produce a relevant, noticeable change in the character of my experience. This is another reason why the impossibility of case (*a*) brings case (*b*) down with it.

(*c*) The third possibility is that the operations might result in blotting out awareness altogether. Then my failure to notice the resultant change would have no tendency to vindicate the Swiss Cheese principle. On the contrary, the unpleasant truth would be that NRT produced a highly relevant and significant change in my mental life—total annihilation of awareness—yet there would be no way in which I could tell that this had happened. However, this possibility, like the last, may be ignored unless it is supposed to apply to all possible ways of performing the NRT operations. The idea would have to be that in any possible programme of substitution there would come a point where awareness suddenly stopped. Up to that point no change in the character of my mental life would be noticeable; beyond it I should be like a Zombie.

Now I think the world could conceivably have been such that this suggestion was correct. There seems no way to demonstrate a priori that the situation with regard to awareness and its substrate could not possibly be as described. However, there is certainly no way to demonstrate a priori that the situation *must* be like that. More to the point, we have empirical evidence pointing decisively in the opposite direction, evidence which shows that not all ways of managing NRT would necessarily involve a sudden switch from full awareness to total loss of conscious life. First, our own experience shows us that awareness comes in degrees. We get drowsy, semi-conscious and so on, without losing awareness altogether—and sometimes we can know we are in such states of less than full awareness. So it is easy to conceive that some ways of managing the NRT operations might result in our noticing that they were producing such alterations. Second, and consonantly with the last point, we know that awareness involves very many neurones working together. That being so, even total destruction of some of the neurones involved in awareness would not inevitably result in the sudden total loss of awareness envisaged above. A fortiori, substituting miniature computers for some of the relevant neurones would not have that result. It follows that the present suggestion conflicts with known facts. In the world as it is, even if some ways of managing NRT could result in total loss of awareness, there must be others that would produce relevant and significant changes in the character of my experience. We can therefore ignore this case.

Case (*a*) has been ruled out, and cases (*b*) and (*c*) have turned out to entail case (*a*). But these are the only possible ways in which NRT could result in a relevant difference in the character of my experience. So it cannot have that result. We are left with the first alternative. NRT, in itself, has no relevant effects on the character of my mental life, or states of awareness, or what it is like to have my experiences.

To summarize. We raise the question whether there is any way of performing NRT that would leave the character of my experience relevantly unaffected. If there is such a way, the Swiss Cheese principle is true for that reason. But if there is no such way, in which case NRT would inevitably result in a change in the character of my experience, the operations could be managed so as to leave me able to talk about the change. Even if some ways of performing NRT would result in differences I was unaware of, or altogether deprived me of awareness, there must be others that would produce a difference I could talk about. And that is inconsistent with the definition of NRT as having no effects on behaviour.

The argument confronts us with a case where we know that the end result is essentially just a very complicated Leibnizian 'mill', while we also come to realize that the consciousness involved does not depend on anything over and above that very mill. After the operation, a sufficiently small person could step inside my head and experience the Leibniz effect: the assemblies of microminiaturized computers would be whirring away, and apparently there would be nothing to provide for conscious experience. Yet we have seen that nevertheless the whole system continues to constitute a conscious subject.

You might wonder what, if anything, turns on the choice of neurones as the candidates for replacement. Why not smaller items, such as molecules or atoms? Or why not larger constellations of things? In the direction of smaller scale items there is no problem. Clearly the core argument would work just as well for smaller items as for neurones. But the question of whether it would work for larger complexes is trickier. Since it does work for neurones, however, I will not pursue that question. You might also wonder what turns on the choice of computers as candidates for replacing neurones. But the argument doesn't depend on the fact that the ersatz neurones are computers. It depends solely on the assumption that whatever items occupy that role perform the relevant functions of the neurones they replace. So the argument shows that states of awareness, at any rate, don't depend on the composition of what constitutes the subject's mind, provided the relevant functions are performed.

So the Swiss Cheese principle is vindicated. Or rather it is vindicated if we overlook certain dualistic objections. But we must do no such thing. The argument needs certain modifications.

3.10   CARTESIAN RESISTANCE

Objection: 'You have still ignored the possibility that the central work of the mind is done by something non-physical, which interacts with physical things such as neurones. If this Cartesian doctrine is so much as consistent—it doesn't have to be true—the argument fails. For in that case it fails to show generally that it doesn't matter what minds are made of. All it shows is that a mind's "peripherals" don't have to be made from any particular kind of stuff.'

Reply: In common with all tenable theories of mind, Cartesian dualism has it that mental events, states and processes interact with physical ones. Unlike many people I see no insuperable difficulty over the very idea of such interaction. So I won't reply that dualism is unintelligible or involves some contradiction. My reply turns on the point that if interaction is held to occur, no objection in principle can be raised to *physical* items taking over those causal roles of *non*-physical items that are relevant to the subject's behaviour. Of course dualists may still insist that in fact certain sorts of things can be done only by non-physical items—by psychic rays, for example. If true, that would be interesting. But I know of no reason to suppose it is true. More to the point, it wouldn't support the philosophically relevant claim that non-physical items are conceptually necessary for the existence of mental states. I need not attempt to refute the kind of dualism according to which physicalism could be true but happens not to be. Clearly such a dualism would implicitly accept the Swiss Cheese principle.

Now recall Descartes's suggestion that the soul interacts with the pineal gland. This organ is supposed to function as a transducer from the mental to the physical, and from the physical to the mental. In particular it is supposed to impart motion to the animal spirits and thence to the limbs. It has certain 'behaviour-relevant' causal functions: certain functions in the production and control of behaviour and in the production, maintenance, and modification of behavioural capacities and dispositions. But evidently there can be no a priori reason why the particular behaviour-relevant functions which Descartes supposed were performed by the pineal gland should necessarily have been performed by that organ. Indeed, he could not have ruled out a priori the possibility that something *non*-physical performed those functions. But by the same token, and quite generally, he could not have offered any a priori reason why *physical* items should not have performed the behaviour-relevant causal functions allegedly performed by events, states, or processes in what he maintained was the non-physical soul. Of course you may have independent reasons for maintaining that in fact such-and-such functions are performed by non-physical items rather than by physical ones. (For example, you might insist that only a non-physical soul could survive death.) But so far as concerns the behaviour-relevant causal powers of events, states, and processes in the soul, once you have conceded that there is interaction between the non-physical and the physical, you have no a priori basis for denying that there could have been physical items with the same behaviour-relevant causal powers as you claim certain non-physical items actually have.

These points enable us to meet the present objection. Suppose *e* is any arbitrary non-physical event which, according to the Cartesian, constitutes a certain happening in my mind. *e* consists of some change in my mental substance. (For that is the assumption on which the present objection is based.) By the last paragraph, the Cartesian must concede that an event *f* in some physical substance—in a suitably constructed brain, for example—could have had all the behaviour-relevant causal links with the rest of my mental substance, and hence with my body and limbs, that in fact, on the Cartesian view, *e* actually has. So suppose that instead of *e* (an event in my soul) there had occurred *f*, a purely physical item which nevertheless had all the behaviour-relevant causal relations with the rest of my soul and body that *e* has. Since the substitution leaves all existing behaviour-relevant causal connections intact, it leaves my behavioural dispositions and capacities intact as well. Now, either this substitution makes a difference to the subjective character of my mental life, or it does not.

If it makes no difference, so much the better for the Swiss Cheese principle. Suppose, then, that all possible further substitutions of that kind have been made. That is, suppose all Cartesian mental events, states, and processes which allegedly occur in my mental substance have been replaced as far as possible by corresponding physical items with the same behaviour-relevant causal functions, provided none of these substitutions makes any difference to the subjective character of my mental life. If the result is that no non-physical items are left, the Swiss Cheese principle is vindicated as before. We must therefore consider the other alternative: that beyond a certain point this programme of substitution does make a difference to the subjective character of my mental life.

As before there are three cases, (*d*), (*e*), and (*f*).

In case (*d*), as in case (*a*) in the last section, I am aware of the difference made by further substitutions. This possibility can be rejected for similar reasons to those given for rejecting the corresponding possibility (*a*). Case (*e*) also falls to reasons parallel to those which ruled out (*b*). In the last possible case, (*f*), there is a point in the programme where any further substitution of behaviour-relevant functionally equivalent physical items for non-physical ones would suddenly blot out all conscious mental life. Perhaps some minor initial substitutions might have no effect on experience. But anything further would result in total obliteration of the mind, even though it would leave a Zombie-like husk still going through the usual motions. Presumably Descartes would claim that this point came early in the programme. Indeed he might insist that there could be no substitutions at all of the kind I have been talking about without total loss of the soul. After all, the soul is supposed to be the subject's essential spiritual core, not a mere locus of the causal transactions that occur within it. It is what ensures that there is something it is like to be the subject. It is all-or-nothing: either the soul is connected to the body and functioning fully, or it is out of the way altogether. So Descartes would probably regard the programme of gradual substitution as misconceived.

Recall, however, that we don't have to show that Cartesian dualism could not possibly have been true. It is enough to show that it is not necessarily true, so that there *could* have been subjects of conscious experience who were made from purely physical constituents. Moreover, even if Cartesian dualism is true of the actual world, it must be consistent with the known empirical facts. When we take account of the empirical facts, we can see that the 'all-or-nothing' objection cannot be sustained. For, as we noticed when discussing case (*c*) in the last section, mental life is not 'all-or-nothing'. Various factors, including drugs, brain damage, and diseases such as Alzheimer's, can bring about gradual and partial alterations to the character of our experience, and indeed to the character of our minds (as we may put it), without suddenly blotting out mental life altogether. Nor can Descartes claim that these changes leave the soul unaffected, that they merely occlude our powers of self-expression. There is abundant evidence that intelligence, sensitivity, emotional responses, and pretty well any other component of personhood you care to name can be more or less permanently impaired by those factors. It follows that even if some ways of carrying out the hypothetical programme of substitution might remove all mental life at a blow, Descartes must concede that there are others where the effects would be gradual. In that case, if (*f*) is a possible case, (*d*) must be possible too. But (*d*) has been ruled out; so (*f*) too must be rejected.

Cartesian resistance to the Swiss Cheese principle has now been seen to fall to an argument similar to the core argument of the last section. I conclude that the Swiss Cheese principle is correct.

3.11 WE MAY ASSUME THE STRICT IMPLICATION THESIS IS TRUE

If the Swiss Cheese principle is correct, dualism is irrelevant to the philosophy of mind. Given the principle, and given that both epiphenomenalism and behaviourism are to be rejected, any philosophical account of the mind can afford to be indifferent to the question of what minds are made of. Throughout, the arguments have illustrated and emphasized the significance of behaviour-relevant *causal* functions in our understanding of the nature of mental states. This point will become even more prominent later.

An immediate consequence of the Swiss Cheese principle is that the Strict Implication thesis might be true. For even if it turned out that in the actual world certain non-physical items were involved in mental interactions, the Swiss Cheese principle assures us that those same causal roles could have been performed by physical items instead. From the point of view of our interest in the phenomena of raw feeling, therefore, it doesn't matter whether mental interactions happen to involve non-physical items. There will be no loss if we make the simplifying assumption that the Strict Implication thesis is true.

That is the chief conclusion of this chapter. Let me emphasize that it doesn't solve our problems, since it goes no way towards explaining *how* the Strict Implication thesis could be true.

To return briefly to the Zombie idea. As defined, that possibility has now been ruled out. If it doesn't matter what minds are made of, then even if some non-physical items are involved in raw feeling in the actual world, there is a possible world where those items are replaced by physical ones while raw feeling is left unchanged. So in any possible world that is in all physical respects as physicalists suppose the actual world to be, our counterparts have exactly the same raw feels as we have. No possible world is a Zombie world in the sense defined.[24] However, that still leaves us with some way to go. We want to understand how the physical facts *could* determine the facts about raw feeling.

[24] See n. 4 above.

4

Perceptual Information

Raw feeling is heterogeneous. It is involved not only in all varieties of sensation and conscious perceptual experience but in dreaming, after-imaging, hallucinating, and such oddities as phosphenes. Still, there is a unifying principle. We noticed earlier that there is no sense in the suggestion that there could be 'wild' raw feels floating about. Raw feeling is unified by the fact that it requires a subject: if it exists at all there is something which has it. But what does it take to be such a subject?

That remains the fundamental question—and it remains daunting. But two considerations help to make it tractable. One is that the most pervasive variety of raw feeling is associated with perception. So we can focus on the slightly less general question of what it takes for something to be a subject of conscious *perceptual* experience. The other is that the terms in which the question is to be answered don't have to be the most basic or detailed that could be conceived. As with the example of 'gnarled', we need only enough explanation to remove the philosophical perplexities. In particular, we need only enough to enable us to understand how the Strict Implication thesis could hold.

For this purpose the notion of information will be crucial. Conscious perception at any rate involves acquiring information about the surrounding world, even if it also involves something else. In this chapter I will try to make the appropriate conception of information clear enough for our purposes, and also convey some idea of how it helps towards the solution of our problems.

4.1 PURE STIMULUS-RESPONSE SYSTEMS

We can start by considering systems which, although they might at first appear to be subjects of conscious experience, turn out on investigation to be too simple to have it. Consider the tick:

After mating, the female climbs to the tip of a twig on some bush. There she clings at such a height that she can drop upon small mammals that may run under her, or be brushed off by larger animals. The eyeless tick is directed to this watchtower by a general photosensitivity of her skin. The approaching prey is revealed to the blind and deaf highwaywoman by her sense of smell. The odour of butyric acid, that emanates from the skin glands of all mammals, acts on the tick as a signal to leave her watchtower and hurl herself downwards. If, in doing so, she lands on something warm—a fine sense of temperature betrays this to her—she has reached her prey, the warm-blooded creature. It only remains for her to find a hairless spot. There she burrows deep into the skin of her prey and slowly pumps herself full of warm blood. Experiments with artificial membranes and fluids other than blood have proved that the tick lacks all sense of taste. Once the membrane is perforated, she will drink any fluid of the right temperature.[1]

At first sight this creature might strike us as a conscious perceiver, a subject of conscious experience. Through its experience of the world, we might think, it discovers how things are, and acts in the light of that information. Certainly its behaviour seems quite complex. But we are told it is triggered by just three stimuli: light, butyric acid, heat. Each causes a particular pattern of behaviour. Now, if the tick's entire behavioural repertoire turned out to be produced by similar mechanisms it would illustrate a very simple scheme. There is a fixed set of patterns of sensory input, a fixed set of patterns of behavioural output, and a straight functional relation from stimulus to response. Stimulus S_0 always causes response R_0, stimulus S_1 always causes response R_1, and so on. The application of this scheme to a given system obviously depends on decisions about which types of events to count as stimuli and which patterns of behaviour to count as responses. Events don't come labelled 'stimulus' or 'response'. Given perverse enough decisions, any concrete object whatever, animate or inanimate, could be made to fit the pattern. But I am assuming the decisions are taken with a view to arriving at non-trivial explanations of the behaviour of the systems investigated, as the tick example illustrates. If a system's entire behavioural repertoire fits the

[1] Jakob von Uexküll, *Umwelt und Innenwelt der Tiere* (1909), quoted in *The Oxford Companion to Animal Behaviour*, ed. D. McFarland, 449 f.—a delightful and instructive work to which I am indebted.

scheme on that assumption, I count it as a pure stimulus-response system.[2]

It seems to make sense to describe some pure stimulus-response systems as capable of perceiving things. Perhaps the tick may be said to perceive the light and the approaching mammal.[3] But that is a very attenuated sort of perception. Perception in the full sense, the kind we ourselves enjoy, involves learning about the environment—acquiring information.[4] Again you might suggest that the tick acquires information about the direction of the light or the presence of a mammal. But here we must respect the crucial distinction between information that is there to be gathered by some subject or other, and information that is for the perceiver.[5] Things like litmus paper or cameras may be said to collect information. But it is for us, not for them. The litmus paper can't do anything about its colour; the camera can't do anything with the exposed film inside it. Similarly, if we needed a butyric acid detector, we could use a tick. But the tick itself (still assuming it is a pure stimulus-response system) acquires no information about butyric acid that is for it. We ourselves sweat in high temperatures. But although we learn to connect sweating with high temperatures, it happens regardless of what we may know. So in itself, my sweating doesn't count as my acquiring or using information. Similarly, the tick's reactions to stimuli don't count as its acquiring or using information.

Essentially there is no difference between such creatures and things like typewriters or pianos. No matter how many times you hit middle C when the cat walks in, the piano won't learn to produce that note when the cat walks in again. Quite generally, with pure stimulus-response systems, what comes in leaves no significant traces and produces no significant modifications to their patterns of behaviour. They are incapable of any kind of

---

[2] Note that this simple functional scheme provides no role for the system's internal states. Note too that a response will not be triggered until the whole of the (relevant) stimulus-pattern has been put into the system.

[3] According to *The Oxford Companion to Animal Behaviour*, 'it is a nice illustration of what can be done with a simple perceptual apparatus' (450).

[4] This is so even during periods when the external scene remains unchanged. Then the subject learns something to the effect that such-and-such features are still present, unchanged. See D. M. Armstrong, *A Materialist Theory of the Mind*, 214 f.

[5] D. C. Dennett uses this phrase in *Content and Consciousness*, 46 f.

learning. They can't learn because they can't store information that is for them. Since perception is at least a matter of learning about one's environment, pure stimulus-response systems cannot perceive in the full sense, and a fortiori cannot be subjects of perceptual experience.

I have been arguing only that a creature whose entire behavioural repertoire consisted of stimulus-response mechanisms could not be a subject of perceptual experience. There is no reason why a creature which is in fact a subject of experience should not also have some stimulus-response mechanisms, and be capable of experiencing the stimuli involved. Heat makes us sweat; but we also feel the heat. This additional capacity has obvious uses. A creature which can experience a given type of stimulus, even if the latter always causes an automatic response, would seem better off from the point of view of survival than one which cannot experience the stimulus at all.

4.2 THE BASIC PACKAGE

If a system is a subject of conscious perceptual experience, it must at least be able to acquire information that is for it. But what does this involve? Obviously the information-theoretic notion of information, explained in terms of probabilities, is not appropriate here. It provides no way to explain differences of content among things or states of affairs that are equally probable.[6] Nor, at the other extreme, must our notion of information require the subject to be a full-blown psychological subject, wielding concepts and having beliefs as we do. (That will become clear soon if it is not so already.) However, there is no need to attempt an account of the relevant notion from scratch. I will outline what I hope will be an uncontroversial framework for the jobs I intend to put it to. A key consideration is that it comes in a package with other notions such as *decision-making* and *goal*.

Recall the tick. Assuming it is a pure stimulus-response system, it cannot sensibly be described as assessing its situation or deciding how to behave, even in a rudimentary sense. There is no

---

[6] See F. I. Dretske, *Knowledge and the Flow of Information*, for discussion. Ch. 1 provides a very useful exposition of information theory.

more question of its deciding how it will behave than there is of a typewriter's deciding which letter it will print when you strike the 'A' key. If an event qualifying as a stimulus strikes a pure stimulus-response system, its response is automatic. That is why it cannot acquire or store information that it could use. For clearly, if a system is to be able to acquire and use information about its surroundings it must be capable of being changed by the impact of those surroundings in ways that can result in its producing non-automatic behaviour. The changes must be capable of making certain kinds of difference to what it does, when what it does is to some extent under its own control, to some extent guided by its own goals or purposes, hence by a kind of assessment and decision-making. Only then can what occurs be described as its own behaviour. I imagine there will be fairly wide agreement that such changes, in such a system, constitute its acquisition of information that is for it in the relevant sense.

We started from the idea that the system has to be able to make use of information, when that is not just a matter of reacting to a stimulus. And it seems clear that in order to be able to use information it must be able to initiate some kind of behaviour, and guide that behaviour on the basis of its stored and incoming information, given whatever goals it may have. So a system cannot acquire information that is for it unless it can initiate and control its behaviour, which of course involves its having goals. And it must retain information about what its goals are, and acquire information about the scene of action. So we have arrived at the idea of an unbreakable complex of three main capacities, centred on the use of information. The system must be able to (i) collect information from the environment, (ii) store that and other information, and (iii) initiate and control its behaviour on the basis of incoming and stored information, given whatever goals it may have. This constitutes a Basic Package of capacities. Possession of any one of them necessarily involves possession of the other two.[7]

---

[7] Aristotle initiated this kind of reasoning, which seeks to establish that certain psychological features come in packages. He remarked that 'whatever has sense-perception also has both pleasure and pain and both the pleasant and the unpleasant; and whatever has these also has desire. For this is a reaching out for the pleasant' (*De Anima*, 414b4–6). See also Armstrong, *A Materialist Theory of the Mind*, 253, and D. C. Dennett, *Content and Consciousness*, ch. 3.

Pure stimulus-response systems lack the Basic Package. They don't acquire or store information that is for them because nothing that happens inside them amounts to the storage of information they can use. Connectedly, nothing that happens inside them amounts to their assessing their situation or deciding what to do. Consider, for example, a thermostat. Given a fixed temperature setting it responds to any temperature below that setting by putting or keeping the switch on, and to any other temperature by putting or keeping the switch off. That qualifies it as a pure stimulus-response system. Contrary to what some people have suggested, it doesn't store the information (for it) that 'It's hot enough here now', for example, because it simply reacts to its inputs in a fixed way—even though its internal state counts as information for us.

We have at least a preliminary answer to the question of what it is for the system to acquire information which is for it. It is a matter of its undergoing whatever internal changes are both caused by stimulation from outside, and equip it with capacities for modifying its behaviour in ways which improve its chances of achieving its goals—when whether or not it actually does anything in connection with a given set of these changes depends partly on what I am calling its assessment and decision-making processes, however primitive those may be. If that is right, there need be no great mystery about these notions of acquiring information, having goals, assessing the situation, making decisions. They apply to any system whose structure ensures that stimulation, internal changes, and output are related in the ways sketched. I suggest that these remarks entitle us to use the notion of information without embarrassment, in spite of the considerable problems that are raised by questions about content (just what does it take for a system to have this or that belief, for example?). I don't think we need go into those problems. It is not as if we were required to *define* the acquisition of information in purely physical terms. For our purposes it will be enough to see that the notion of information required for explaining the Basic Package can be elucidated in a way which makes it unproblematic that a purely physical system should acquire and use information.

The Basic Package seems necessary for being a subject of conscious perceptual experience, since without it the system could not sensibly be said to acquire information. But is it also sufficient?

4.3   THE MACHINE TABLE ROBOT

As a step on the way to dealing with that rather tricky question I will describe a kind of robot which at first appears to possess the Basic Package, but lacks conscious perceptual experience. Consideration of this and other cases will help me to clarify further how the Basic Package must be understood.

Imagine that a horde of scientists has somehow managed to produce a machine table for my brain, treating it as a finite state machine.[8] They quantize time into very short instants so as to be able to treat the brain as capable of only a finite number of possible states and only a finite number of possible inputs and outputs. Each possible input is a single total pattern of stimulation, embracing all the separate patterns of stimulation to each sense organ at an instant. Each possible output is a similar total possible pattern of efferent output at an instant. The scientists construct a super-robot whose body—with the notable exception of its brain—matches mine in all respects relevant to those aspects of sense-perception and motor control which are reflected in the machine table for my brain. However, instead of constructing an artificial brain they install an enormously powerful computer inside the robot's head and load it with the machine table for my brain—which is just a vast set of ordered quadruples (quadruples of numbers, in the present case).

The robot works as follows. Each 'afferent' wire leading from the 'nerves' at the robot's sense receptors is connected to a single array. The terminals of this array are connected to the computer's input unit. At each instant the total pattern of sensory input will be represented by a binary number, since each afferent 'nerve' will be either firing or not firing. Similarly the computer's output unit

---

[8] A finite state machine is an abstract object defined by a certain finite set of possible inputs, a finite set of possible states, a finite set of possible outputs, and a machine table. The machine table is a function which, for each pair consisting of one of the given inputs and one of the given possible states, specifies its next state and output. It can be conveniently represented as a finite set of quadruples:

I_1 S_1 S_2 O_3
I_2 S_1 S_3 O_4
. . .
I_p S_q S_r O_s

The first line is to the effect that when the machine is in state S_1 and receives input I_1, it moves into state S_2 and produces output O_3.

is connected to its motor 'nerves'. Here too the total pattern of output at any instant is represented by a binary number. The scientists start the robot off with a number—the 'state index'—which corresponds to some selected possible state represented by a number in the machine table. Each instantaneous pattern of input feeds in to the stored machine table and state index, and is matched up with the initial pair of numbers in one of the ordered quadruples. This causes the new state index given in the machine table to be registered, and at the same time causes the defined output pattern to initiate a brief burst of excitation at the efferent 'nerves'. So (if you can put up with the simplifications) the robot will be disposed to behave, in any possible sequence of circumstances, just as I myself would have behaved in those circumstances, given that history.

The Machine Table robot is obviously nothing like a practical possibility. But I am making a theoretical point and don't regard that as an objection. Again, my description presupposes that the workings of a purely physical brain are all that is involved in the production of behaviour. Dualists won't like that; but we saw in the last chapter that even if dualism is actually true, it could have been false without any effects on our mental lives. So from the theoretical point of view there is no significant objection here. A more serious objection might be that the workings of the brain could not be represented by a finite state machine at all because, like the earth's atmosphere, it is a chaotic system. No matter how finely you divided up the time intervals and no matter how minutely you specified the different possible instantaneous total states of the brain, you wouldn't be able to capture the ways the brain would behave any more than you could do the same for the weather. That seems quite possible. But it is pure speculation—though less implausible, I would say, than speculation to the effect that *quantum* phenomena have some significant bearing on the mind–body problem.[9] And even if it is correct in general, who is to say that my own brain isn't an exception? All my argument

---

[9] See M. Lockwood, *Mind, Brain and the Quantum*, and R. Penrose, *The Emperor's New Mind*. I hope it will become clear in the course of the book why I see no reason to introduce the special peculiarities of quantum mechanics into explanations of consciousness. Even if they turn out to play some significant part in the functioning of our own brains (a big 'if'), that will be—if I am right—at best merely a contingent fact about ourselves, not a necessary condition of any possible consciousness.

requires is one exception; and proving a priori that there could be no exceptions at all would be a very substantial task indeed. Still, I cannot claim that the Machine Table robot is an absolutely genuine possibility. It just helps to make certain points vivid.

Is the Machine Table robot a subject of conscious perceptual experiences? For two distinct reasons I think it is not. One is that it does not have the Basic Package. This will become clear later, when we have looked more closely at the idea of information being 'for' the system. The other reason is that having conscious perceptual experiences involves being a subject of raw feeling. And raw feeling, as I argued in the last chapter, cannot be adequately construed either behaviouristically or ultra-externalistically; it must be construed realistically. But no processes in the Machine Table robot could constitute its own processes of raw feeling, realistically construed.

Of course we could associate various features of this robot's internal processes with different raw feels. We could devise 'logical constructions' for them. But my contention is that logical constructions would not supply what it lacks. The workings of its machine table merely *simulate* real mental processes. On my realistic view they simulate the evolution through time of a lot of more or less separate processes, which (in the real thing) endow the individual with distinct systems of behavioural capacities. Just now I am looking at the characters displayed on my word-processor screen. Accordingly I am in the associated state of visual raw feeling. But at the same time I hear a passing car, feel the pressure of my elbow on the table, and smell freshly ground coffee. So I am also in the diverse states of raw feeling associated with those other perceptual states. Now, each of these states of raw feeling equips me with a distinct system of behavioural capacities. For example, the one caused by the word-processor screen enables me, among many other things, to point to occurrences of the letter 'F'. The state caused by hearing the car enables me to look in the direction of the car. On my account these are distinct real states which result in my acquiring distinct systems of capacities. Being distinct real states they must be constituted by distinct real components of my current brain processes—patterns of excitation of different complexes of neurones, perhaps. But there are no such distinct real components of the processes in the Machine Table robot. Its behaviour, including any behaviour

relating to its apparent raw feeling, is all caused by the workings
of the stored machine table, where each *total* instantaneous state
is represented by an arbitrarily correlated binary number—a
sequence of binary digits. That sequence obviously has no components which could be made to correspond with components of
the relevant distinct processes in my own brain. So on my account
the Machine Table robot lacks raw feeling, and perceptual consciousness generally.[10]

The Machine Table robot at any rate appears to possess the
Basic Package of capacities. However, the situation is still not
clear. The central notion of information being for a system needs
further explanation. Eventually we shall see that in fact the
Machine Table robot does not have the Basic Package.

4.4 THE REALISTIC CONSTRUAL OF INFORMATION BEING FOR THE SYSTEM

Recall the imitation giant which briefly entered the discussion of
behaviourism in Chapter 1. There is a whole range of such cases.
They vary in the number of operators, the nature of the machinery
under their control, and, crucially, in the operators' role in the
system. Some of these systems will resemble the pantomime
horse. They are essentially puppets, whose only difference from
the standard variety is that their puppeteers are inside them. Let us
pause over the pantomime horse.

Anyone who maintains that the pantomime horse itself has
perceptual experiences must have a pretty blunt axe to grind. But
if it doesn't have experiences, why is that? One simple answer is
that, given realism about raw feeling and experiences, there are no
processes which could constitute its own experiences. There are
the experiences of its two operators, Front Legs and Back Legs,

---

[10] See R. Kirk, 'Sentience, Causation, and Some Robots', for more on the
Machine Table robot, which is a variant of a device described by Ned Block. The
above paragraph revises the idea of 'causally independent' processes discussed in
that article. The Machine Table robot is not offered here as a straight counter-
example to behaviourism and ultra-externalism. It illustrates the point of the
notion of raw feeling, and how our knowledge of a system's internal processing
could lead us to deny that it was a genuine subject of raw feeling even though it
had the right dispositions. I claim that when my full position has been set out,
there will be no good reason to insist on behaviourism or ultra-externalism.

but nothing to integrate them in anything like the way they would need to be integrated to constitute the experiences of the system as a whole. The absence of plausible candidates for its own perceptual processes points to the conclusion that in a sense there is no such thing as the pantomime horse at all. What we have is just a couple of people dressed up in a funny costume and acting a part. They are acting the part of a fictional character, as the actor plays the part of Hamlet, or the person inside the gorilla suit acts like a gorilla. Since such fictional characters don't really exist, it's not surprising that they don't really have experiences either. Experiences certainly occur within the system. But they are not of the right sort to constitute the experiences of the system itself.

Those remarks are correct as far as they go, I think, but they need supplementation. We can start by considering whether the pantomime horse has the Basic Package. It certainly appears to. It appears to collect information about what is happening; it appears to remember things and to control its behaviour on the basis of that information. But is the information for the pantomime horse itself? Well, information certainly gets into it and contributes to determining how it behaves. If that is all it takes for information to be for the system, then the pantomime horse has the Basic Package. However, that construal of the key notion is essentially behaviouristic. It disregards the nature of the internal processing and requires only that whatever processing there may be relates inputs and outputs in suitable ways. For that reason it is inconsistent with the realistic approach I have been defending. On a realistic view of the processing involved in perception, incoming information is for the system only if there are internal processes which constitute the system's own sorting, conceptualizing, assessment, and use of that information. It is not enough for there to be some processes or other which suitably relate inputs to outputs, as with the pantomime horse—even though these processes might serve as a basis for logical constructions to be counted as sorting, conceptualizing, and the like. These latter must be real processes which stand in appropriate causal relations to the incoming information.

Suppose the pantomime horse's two operators make it behave as if it were suffering from a headache, although neither of them has a headache. Perhaps it behaves as if it understands what is said to it in English. As far as its behaviour is concerned, we have a system which seems to have a headache, seems to possess the concept *headache*, and seems to count itself as instantiating that concept. On a behaviouristic approach it must be counted as really having a headache and really wielding that concept in the way its behaviour suggests. But on that approach its having the headache and wielding the concept are mere logical constructions out of its behaviour and dispositions. On a realistic approach things are very different. There are no internal processes so related to the pantomime horse's behaviour that they could be regarded realistically as constituting either its actually having a headache, or its wielding that concept. Since the horse costume is quite inert, the only relevant processes would be those going on inside the two human operators. But neither of them has a headache. And when Front Legs makes the thing nod its head in response to the question 'Have you got a headache?', neither Front Legs nor Back Legs believes that anything really has a headache. Nor does either of them regard the gesture of assent as conveying any individual's belief. Where the headache ought to be, if the pantomime horse were a system which really had a headache, there is a void. And where there ought to be processes constituting the system's bringing itself under the concept *headache*, if it were really wielding that concept, there are only other individuals making it behave *as if* it were wielding it. In fact the pantomime horse differs only superficially from glove puppets like Punch and Judy, where it is glaringly obvious that no information at all is being received by the puppets themselves.

Since there are no real internal processes which constitute the pantomime horse's having a headache, or its own sorting, conceptualization, assessment, and use of incoming information, that information cannot be described as being for it on my realistic approach to these matters. The Basic Package must be understood in terms of that realistic construal. This means that the pantomime horse doesn't have the Basic Package. For similar reasons the Machine Table robot doesn't have the Basic Package either.

4.5 THE GIANT

A different example will help us to clarify the relevant notions further. Let us consider a special kind of imitation giant. It is big enough to house a lot of machinery and a lot of people. From the outside it looks to us much as Gulliver looked to the Lilliputians. Its operators ensure that it not only behaves like a gigantic human being but has all the behavioural dispositions of a human being— for they are fanatics. Each of the main folk-psychologically defined departments of the mind—whatever these might be: perceptual analysis, memory, planning, speech, control of action, say—has a special team assigned to it. In all cases but one the members of these teams need not know the overall purpose of their activities, which is to keep the GIANT (Gigantic Information Acquisitor and Non-wheeled Transporter) behaving in ways that would have been appropriate for a real giant. Some of the teams on board monitor television screens and loudspeakers whose inputs come from its 'eyes' and 'ears', and pass on information to the memory team, the planning team and others. The role of the planning team is crucial. They are the only people on board who have to know what the system is doing, for they assess the incoming information and decide how it will behave. They pass on information and instructions to the executive team, who press the buttons which initiate and control the movements of the GIANT's limbs and vocal apparatus.

Now the GIANT differs from the pantomime horse in at least this respect: there are processes which have some claim to be the whole system's perceptual processes. These are the ones which start off with the workings of the television cameras in its eyes, for example, and take in both the monitoring which is carried out by the people watching the screens and also the transmission by these people of messages to the memory and planning teams. Since there are separate teams for the visual system, the auditory system, and the other sensory systems, they are distinct real processes too.

The GIANT may seem to have the Basic Package. The processes described in the last paragraph but one are at least plausible candidates for being processes which constitute the total system's acquiring, storing, and using information about its environment. And it looks at first as if this information is genuinely for the GIANT, if only because the memory team stores information which is used for controlling the system's behaviour. However, on re-flection we can see that the GIANT does not actually have the Basic Package, realistically construed. It is still essentially a puppet. The members of the planning team control it much as Front Legs and

Back Legs control the pantomime horse. An illustration will help
to show why this is such a decisive consideration. Suppose the
planning team makes the GIANT behave as if it is a believer in
phlogiston. When people shout questions like 'How do you explain
combustion?', the GIANT replies with chunks of the phlogistic
theory. Now, the members of the planning team are not themselves encumbered with that extinct theory. So the following
question arises. Are there any processes inside the GIANT which
could constitute its own processing of information in terms of the
phlogistic theory—its own use, in its assessment and decision-
making, of the beliefs and concepts of that theory? The critical
consideration here is that all the GIANT's utterances result from the
planning team's assessments, deliberations, and decisions, based
on their general policy of making the system both behave and
be disposed to behave as if it believed in phlogiston. And the
planning team's assessments, deliberations, and decisions have
altogether the wrong character to constitute the GIANT's own. Yet
those processes are the causes of the GIANT's behaviour. So there
is nothing which could be realistically construed as its own assessment, deliberation, or decision-making. This means that the
incoming information is not after all for the GIANT in the relevant
sense.

It is important not to confuse this point with a different one.
You might suspect that I have fallen into the same elephant trap as
John Searle with his Chinese Room argument. Searle assumed that
if the operator in the Chinese Room didn't understand Chinese,
then the system as a whole didn't understand Chinese either. The
'Systems Reply' to this argument is that what matters is whether
the system as a whole understands Chinese. Whether any of its
components also understands Chinese is beside the point.[11] I think
the Systems Reply to the Chinese Room argument is entirely
correct, and demolishes that argument. However, I may seem to
have assumed that just because the members of the planning team
don't share the GIANT's supposed beliefs and concepts, it follows
that the GIANT doesn't really have those beliefs or concepts. But
that is not my argument.

Bear in mind how the GIANT is actually controlled. As I am

[11] See J. Searle, 'Minds, Brains and Programs', and, for more discussion, D. C.
Dennett, *Consciousness Explained*, 435–40.

telling the story, its behaviour is determined by decisions made by the planning team. And these decisions are made on the basis of their views about what behaviour would be appropriate for the GIANT in its current situation. I don't say that the points I am making would apply to every system working on superficially the same lines as the GIANT. There might be an otherwise similar system whose behaviour was not determined by what the members of its planning team thought appropriate. They might all be ignorant of what the system as a whole was doing. Like Searle's Chinese Room operator, they might simply be manipulating patterns according to a book of rules, with no idea of what it was all for. Perhaps a system controlled in that way could be a genuine subject of perceptual experience. My claim is only that a system controlled as I have said the GIANT is controlled could not be such a subject. That claim avoids anti-Searle arguments because it doesn't rest on the assumption that any beliefs held by the system as a whole must be shared by members of the planning team. It rests on the quite different point that nothing going on inside the GIANT could constitute its own assessment or decision-making processes, realistically construed.

We noticed earlier that information for the system has to be such that the system as a whole can use it. So the system must have its own processes of assessment and decision-making, however rudimentary, and the information must be potentially capable, via these processes, of influencing its behaviour. In order for processes going on inside a system to constitute its own assessment and decision-making, then, it would not be enough for them to cause its behaviour *in some way or other*. They would also have to be integrated both with the processing of information coming into and stored by the system, and with the initiation and control of its behaviour. It seems safe to assert this much on the basis of reflection on our ordinary folk-psychological scheme of description and explanation. Of course that scheme is rough and vague. We can hardly hope to reach any very sharp conclusions about just what connections would amount to 'integration', nor will I attempt to do so. No doubt there is an enormous range of possibilities. What has been said may be summarized as follows.

In order for the information coming into and stored by a system to be for it in the required sense, (*a*) there must be processes which can be realistically construed as its own assessment and decision-making on the basis of that information;

(*b*) the processes which constitute the sorting and conceptualizing of incoming and stored information must be integrated with those which constitute its assessment and decision-making;

(*c*) its assessment and decision-making must be integrated with the initiation and control of its behaviour.

Now, in the case of the GIANT the phlogiston example shows that none of these conditions is satisfied. For the assessment and decision-making processes which control its behaviour include thoughts such as 'What would a phlogistic theorist do now?', or 'We'd better make it say "There's dephlogisticated air in that bottle"'. The contents of these thoughts are *incompatible* with what the GIANT's own thoughts would have to be. This incompatibility marks a hiatus in the processing. In no sense could those thoughts be said to be integrated with what passes for the GIANT's *own* sorting and conceptualizing of incoming and stored information. So condition (*b*) is not satisfied. Of course people's thoughts are often inconsistent. But the planners' thoughts are not internally inconsistent. They are inconsistent with what the GIANT's thoughts would have to be—if it had any. So it has none. Hence conditions (*a*) and (*c*) are not satisfied either. (I am assuming that in general it is a matter of objective fact what the contents of people's thoughts are.[12])

You might be willing to concede that the planning team's thoughts are incompatible with what the GIANT's own thoughts would have to be, yet still object. Why shouldn't the very same processes that we interpret as the planners saying things like 'What would a phlogistic theorist do now?' *also* constitute the GIANT's having different thoughts—ones entirely appropriate to itself? If so, why shouldn't the incoming information be for the whole system after all?

This type of objection has in effect been anticipated. Keep in mind that behaviouristic or other non-realistic interpretations have been ruled out. If the GIANT has its own decision-making processes and its own raw feel processes, they must be real processes, more

---

[12] See R. Kirk, *Translation Determined*, for a defence of that assumption.

or less distinct from one another, as we saw when discussing the Machine Table robot. And they must be appropriately integrated with the various other processes. Now, the only possible candidates for its own decision-making processes would be the activities of the planning team and of the executive teams under its control. But the point of the preceding discussion has been that nothing about these activities licenses the claim that they constitute decision-making processes which could be those of the GIANT itself, construed realistically. We know quite enough about what is going on to rule out that possibility. It is the planners' own answers to such questions as 'What would a phlogistic theorist do now?' which lead to the GIANT's behaving as it does, and there is simply a blank if we search for processes which could constitute the GIANT's having *its* own thoughts on the matter.

Another apparent objection may have occurred to you. We can suppose that some members of the planning team use the information stored by the memory team to maintain an up-to-date record of the GIANT's putative current beliefs and desires. Of course the teams who monitor and report its sensory input are constantly transmitting information to the memory team about what events it has 'seen', 'heard', and so on. But we can take it that this information is conceptualized fairly neutrally. The reporters say things like 'The candle in the bottle has just gone out'. But the planners will want to record the system's putative beliefs and desires in terms of its own putative concepts. So they will insert in the current 'belief' list sentences like 'There's dephlogisticated air in that bottle'. Similarly they might put sentences such as 'I want some dephlogisticated air' on to the 'desire' list. Now, Language of Thought enthusiasts[13] may be tempted to think that no more would be needed to make this system a genuine psychological subject. The presence of token sentences on the belief or desire 'blackboards', given the planning team's commitment to producing the right behaviour, might be supposed to do more than ensure that the system just behaves appropriately. It might also be supposed to ensure that it really has beliefs and desires with the same contents as the stored sentences. A further suggestion might then be that no matter what other processes may actually result in the GIANT's behaviour, they

---

[13] See J. A. Fodor, *The Language of Thought*.

must constitute its own decision-making, contrary to what I have
been arguing.

But the suggestion is mistaken. The use of blackboards, computers, or whatever, to keep track of the GIANT's putative beliefs
and desires, cannot make a significant difference to the situation.
They might help the planners to avoid confusion, but they can be
no more than a useful aid. For the planners might have unusually
powerful memories, which would obviously serve the same purposes as lists. A further consideration is that all the mechanisms
inside the GIANT, together with all the other teams, are in effect
merely the planning team's instruments. If the structure had been
smaller they would have been unnecessary. The planners would
have been able to see and hear for themselves what was going
on outside, and make the system move about unaided. So from
our point of view the GIANT isn't essentially different from the
pantomime horse, or even from the man in the gorilla suit. In a
way the GIANT is a fictional being. Again, then, the conclusion
must be that there are no processes which could constitute the
GIANT's own assessment and decision-making. If there were, they
would have to be the causes of its behaviour. But the sole causes
of its behaviour are the assessment and decision-making processes
of the planning team. And, as we have seen, their processes of
decision-making don't have the right contents to be counted as the
GIANT's own. So the GIANT has no such processes of its own. By
now that should not surprise us. We can see that it is merely a
complicated puppet. None of the incoming or stored information
is for it in the relevant sense. So it doesn't even have the Basic
Package.[14]

4.6 THE RICHNESS OF
PERCEPTUAL INFORMATION

When the members of the GIANT's 'visual perception' team monitor
the television screens they pass on descriptions of what they see. It

---

[14] What about large organizations such as the United States? They can be said
to receive information, sort, conceptualize, and assess it, store it, and use it to
initiate and control their political behaviour. Is the information for them in the
relevant sense? I am inclined to say it is. But so far as I can see, that is beside the
point. For such systems lack the sorts of capacities that would be necessary for
them to be counted as subjects of perception. See below.

is only through these descriptions that the memory and planning teams are able to store information about how things are outside. If the visual team doesn't say just how the candle's flame is flickering, for example, the planners don't know about it. But we have seen that any information is only for a system if the system can use it. And the only information the GIANT can use is what reaches its memory and planning teams. Evidently, then, there is a wealth of information which is available to the members of the visual perception team inside the GIANT, but not to the GIANT itself. Now, we have seen that in any case the GIANT is not a genuine subject of experience because it lacks its own assessment and decision-making processes. But even if we ignore that deficiency, we can now see another reason why it would still not be a subject of the kind of perceptual experience we enjoy, the kind which raises the philosophical perplexities that concern us. For in our case, if we are looking at a lighted candle, finely detailed information about how the flame flickers is constantly present to us. And that isn't true of the GIANT. So even if it had some kind of perceptual experience, it wouldn't be like ours.[15] Our kind of perceptual information has a certain richness. I will explain what I mean by this.

We can start with a familiar manifestation of richness. Perceptual information often defeats our attempts to specify it. We seem to receive more than we can characterize, at any rate in ordinary language. As I look out of the window I could describe my experiences as of crumbling brick walls, a red car, trees in leaf. But the details overflow these characterizations. The exact subtle variations of colour and texture in the bricks, the shapes and motions of the leaves, just don't get conveyed. Of course I could expand the descriptions. In special cases I might be able to describe a brief experience fully and without ambiguity—total darkness, perhaps. We might even devise a special scheme for assigning hue, saturation, and lightness to each point in the visual field at a given instant. But we lack such a scheme. And the striking thing about perception is that we acquire all this abundant information in spite of not being able to specify it at all fully.

---

[15] A further deficiency is that the GIANT would not be able to understand many of its own utterances even if it had the Basic Package, which it doesn't. For some of its utterances appear to describe its experiences, and they wouldn't actually do so if it had no such experiences (see 6.5 below).

That is at any rate a manifestation of what I am calling the richness of perceptual information. But it appears to make the notion rather mysterious. For what is the acquisition of information if not the acquisition of beliefs? In that case, how can the beliefs whose acquisition is involved in perception fail to be specifiable? How is richness possible?

4.7 PERCEPTUAL INFORMATION AND CONSCIOUSNESS

I will approach this apparent difficulty indirectly, via two influential accounts of perceptual consciousness. The first is Armstrong's. He maintains that perception is 'nothing but the acquiring of true or false beliefs concerning the current state of the organism's body and environment'.[16] The acquisition of beliefs in turn is the acquisition of capacities for discriminatory behaviour. Beliefs about our environment are broadly 'mental states apt for selective behaviour towards the environment'. Particular perceptual beliefs involve a capacity 'for selective behaviour towards a particular object on a particular occasion'; and possession of such capacities, he holds, entails possession of concepts, which are 'higher-order capacities: capacities for acquiring capacities for selective behaviour towards particular objects on particular occasions'.[17]

These suggestions are attractive. But notice that they seem to allow the GIANT to be a perceiver. The GIANT acquires states apt for selective behaviour towards the environment as a result of the co-operation of the various teams inside it: that is why they are there. And these states require nothing additional in order to be counted as 'mental' states on Armstrong's account, since he characterizes mental states simply as states apt for the production of certain kinds of behaviour. The GIANT has both the two classes of capacities mentioned: capacities for selective behaviour and higher-order capacities to acquire such lower-order capacities. So it qualifies as an Armstrongian perceiver. But in fact it has nothing like our sort of perception because it lacks the Basic Package; and it lacks that because it has no assessment or decision-making

---

[16] Armstrong, *A Materialist Theory of the Mind*, 209.
[17] This and the last two quotations are from *A Materialist Theory of the Mind*, 339 f.

processes of its own. Even if it did have the Basic Package, its perceptual information would lack richness. So it is a counter-example to Armstrong's excessively behaviouristic account of perception.

Armstrong does not maintain that all perception is conscious. So he needs to distinguish conscious from non-conscious perception. On his account conscious perceptual experience involves a kind of 'inner sense'. It is perception by the organism not of external things, but of its own mental states. Perception of external things is a matter of the acquisition of beliefs or information: here he is surely right. But on his account conscious perception, which he calls 'introspection', is similar. 'It is the getting of information or misinformation about the current state of our mind.'[18]

I will return to that account in the next chapter. But now let us consider another account that has been influential: Dennett's in 'Toward a Cognitive Theory of Consciousness'. In that article—which has been superseded by his account in *Consciousness Explained*, to be discussed later—he tentatively offered an outline flow-chart. The main components are Control, a short-term buffer memory (M), a Perceptual Analysis component, and a speech or 'public relations' component (PR).

Suppose Control 'decides' ... to 'introspect': (1) it goes into its 'introspective subroutine', in which (2) it directs a question to M; (3) when an answer comes back (and none may) it assesses the answer: it may (a) censor the answer; (b) 'interpret' the answer in the light of other information; (c) 'draw inferences' from the answer, or (d) relay the answer as retrieved direct to PR.[19]

So his suggestion was that introspection (hence consciousness) is just a matter of these processes occurring in a system of this general kind. In his words: 'Having an inner life—being something it is like something to be—is on this account a matter of having a certain sort of functional organization.'[20]

There are obvious contrasts between the two accounts. Armstrong is concerned to explain how our folk-psychological concepts can be applied to a purely physical system, so his picture of the operations of the mind is especially congenial to folk psy-

---

[18] Ibid. 326.
[19] D. C. Dennett, *Brainstorms*, 156.
[20] Ibid. 171.

chology. Dennett's approach is orientated more towards the ways in which a possible scientific psychology might deal with the phenomena in question. Still, the two accounts are consistent in their broad outlines. But both are too behaviouristic. Dennett's, like Armstrong's, is undermined by the GIANT, which could surely be organized on the lines of his flow-chart. As with Armstrong's story, the trouble is not so much with these broad outlines. It is that nothing seems to guarantee that the internal processing is of the right kind: that it satisfies the conditions for realism about mental processes, including those summarized by (*a*), (*b*), and (*c*) in the last section.

There is a further difficulty with Dennett's account of 'introspection'. It centres on the role of the short-term buffer memory, *M*. For Dennett, 'introspection' is a matter of Control's sending questions to, and receiving and assessing answers from, *M*. But it looks as if that could be done even if the information in *M* were not, and never had been, conscious. Think of 'preconscious' information—everything we know or believe but don't currently have before our minds (as we say). We can bring it to mind when we want to, but that often takes a special decision. There seems no reason why a system should not conform to Dennett's scheme even though its perceptual information were normally received and retained preconsciously, and didn't become conscious unless specially called up by Control. In fact, of course, conscious perceptual experience equips us with information instantly, without any need for special calls on memory. It acts directly on our assessment processes—a point I will amplify and discuss shortly. If we bear in mind this defect of Dennett's 1978 scheme—which was, after all, offered only tentatively—we shall be better placed to work out something better.

Back now to the apparent difficulty of understanding how information could be acquired without necessarily being fully specifiable in ordinary terms. We can now see that there is no real problem. Consider languageless creatures. It clearly makes sense to describe some of them—babies, cats, and dogs, for example, even some insects—as acquiring information about their environment, information which we may loosely say is about such things as other animals, their home territory, doors, even colours. Yet we may be reluctant to say they have concepts or even beliefs. Certainly they don't have our own concepts *animal, door, colour*.

Still, we can surely say they acquire perceptual information because we know they acquire capacities for relevantly distinctive kinds of behaviour: they tend to return to their home territory; they know how to deal with doors; they can learn to behave differently to things of different colours, and so on. It looks as if the acquisition of such capacities, provided the internal processing is right, counts as the acquisition of information (for them). Nor does there seem any reason to deny that such creatures have the Basic Package, realistically construed, in spite of the fact that the capacities in question do not seem to involve what we should ordinarily count as full-blown concepts or beliefs. Possession of ordinary concepts involves a whole range of capacities, such as the ability to recognize, to treat appropriately, and to apply suitable verbal descriptions to instances. But there is plenty of information acquisition which involves less than that whole range. So the richness of perceptual experience, manifested in our often being unable to give full specifications of the information we acquire, raises no special problem. Much of that information is sorted and classified at subconceptual levels. It gives us masses of fleeting capacities to deal with the fine structure of the passing scene; but many of those capacities don't correspond to any of our ordinary concepts. The information comes in packets which slip through the mesh of those concepts.

We noticed that richness shows up in our often finding it hard to describe the passing scene. Yet we can often recognize pictures of the things we see, even though we cannot describe them fully or accurately in ordinary terms. That we nevertheless have the detailed information is proved by our recognizing the pictures (sometimes we can actually draw or paint them). But it is one thing to have the information at that low level; something else to have brought it under the higher-level schemes of classification involved in ordinary concepts.

Our perceptual information is rich, and any adequate account of conscious perceptual experience must do justice to this feature. But is it just a contingent feature, or could there be non-rich perceptual information? Pausing over this question will improve our grasp of the nature of conscious experience in general, even though what I have to say will be sketchy and tentative.

Recall that a system capable of using the perceptual information it acquires must be capable of what I am calling assessment and decision-making. Assessment and decision-making of a kind—and it may be very primitive—is necessary if the system is to be capable of using information rather than merely reacting to inputs. I don't mean it must be capable of self-consciously presenting possible alternative courses of behaviour as options for itself, or of what we would call deliberation. That would presumably require it to have some concept of itself, and the systems I have in mind need not all have such a concept. There seems no reason why humble organisms should not in some sense contemplate various possible states of the world from their own point of view, without actually using concepts of *themselves*. (I will return to this topic later.) But something of that kind, with the organism eventually selecting one of those possible states of the world and initiating appropriate behaviour, would be sufficient for assessment and decision-making in the attenuated sense appropriate here.

In order for the system to be capable of contemplating possible states of the world, it must conceptualize to *some* extent. It must at least have something like concepts in terms of which possible states of the world are in some sense considered. But—this is the critical point—those concepts will have to be at a higher level of generality than the simpler quasi-concepts in terms of which its immediately present perceptual information is packaged. The features of the world that interest us tend not to be immediately apparent: it's not as if everything were clearly labelled. Even if mice did wear labels, cats would still have to make decisions on the basis of partially visible ones. In some sense the cat wants a world where it is eating the mouse. But it has to assess and interpret much of the incoming information. (It sees the grass moving: is that the wind or the mouse?) So there is a gap between its acquiring low-level information, and its interpreting and assessing that information in terms of higher-level schemes of classification. (The cat can move towards the twitching grasses even when it hasn't classified the movements as mouse-caused.) If that is right, we have an explanation of why the richness of perceptual information is not just contingent.[21] It is an inextricable component of the Basic Package. Having the Basic Package turns

[21] Presumably this gap helps to explain such phenomena as seeing different aspects of the Necker cube and the duck-rabbit. It also helps to explain how we can fail to identify the thing we have our eyes on—as in the case of hunt-the-thimble, discussed by Dennett in *Consciousness Explained*, 333–6.

out to require the possibility of information being acquired at relatively low levels of conceptualization without having to be brought immediately under the system's higher-level classifications. And that *is* the richness of perceptual information. Now, we know that terrestrial organisms of any complexity can as a matter of fact be usefully described as classifying information at a number of different levels. The above considerations, sketchy though they are, may help to explain that fact. At any rate I will assume from now on that for any system with the Basic Package, when the latter is construed realistically and subject to the conditions (*a*), (*b*), and (*c*) which were listed in section 4.5 above, its incoming perceptual information is sorted and assessed at different levels, and is in fact rich in the sense explained.

4.8   HELP FROM CONNECTIONIST MODELS

But how *can* perceptual information be both rich and for the system? This looks like a considerable difficulty, especially because until recently it appeared that the only way to explain how the second requirement might be satisfied was at the cost of the first. For the assumption of classical Artificial Intelligence and cognitive science has been that information must be capable of being stored and processed in the form of sentences or sentence-parts. It has been assumed that the brain is like a computer in the narrow sense that it has programs resembling the sorts of programs that Artificial Intelligence workers themselves use—programs in which the information stored and processed satisfies syntactic rules not unlike those of programming languages such as LISP. One result has been that philosophers sympathetic to that assumption have felt driven to defend a perverse account of the nature of experience. Some have suggested it is analogous to acquiring beliefs, when the latter are regarded as analogous to sentences processed in the head. On Armstrong's account, perceptual experience is the organism's acquiring beliefs about its environment, a view which, even if not influenced by the classical Artificial Intelligence assumption, is tailor-made to suit it. And Dennett may have been influenced by the assumption when he suggested that seeing was 'like reading a novel at breakneck speed'.[22] But it is at any rate

---

[22] Dennett, *Content and Consciousness*, 139.

hard to see how the perceptual processes of a system working on these lines could have the feature of richness.

To reject the sentence-based approach of classical Artificial Intelligence is not of course to deny that perception involves the acquisition of information. But, as we noticed in the last section, the difficulty is that it seems possible for information to be acquired without feeding straight into the organism's assessment and decision-making processes and instantly equipping it with a swarm of fleeting capacities. A sentence-based approach can handle the acquisition of information of some sorts. But it is embarrassed by the problem of the acquisition of low-level, rich perceptual information, when that information doesn't just get into the system, but instantly feeds into its controlling processes. An ideal way to get over the difficulty would be by giving an account of the detailed mechanisms of perception. Unfortunately that is still lacking: we must await further scientific developments.[23] In any case it isn't necessary for my purposes. I am not attempting to do the scientific work a priori. Still, it would be good if we could form some conception of what such mechanisms might conceivably be like. And in fact we can gain illumination from recent work on models of cognitive processing variously referred to in terms of 'neural networks', 'parallel distributed processing' (PDP), or 'connectionism'.[24]

Connectionist models are inspired by the thought that the brain consists of a vast number of interconnected cells. So the basic conception is that of a large number of relatively simple units sending signals to one another along one-way channels. The signals may be excitatory or inhibitory. The units are idealized versions of neurones, and the network as a whole is thought of as receiving and sending out signals analogously to the ways the brain receives signals from the sense organs and sends out signals which activate the motor neurones. At any moment each unit in a connectionist model has a certain 'activation value', determined by its inputs and its value just prior to that moment. Typically, like a

---

[23] See Dennett, *Consciousness Explained*, for an illuminating account of the current state of empirical investigations.

[24] I owe the following sketch of the connectionist approach mainly to the two volumes of *Parallel Distributed Processing*, by D. Rumelhart, J. McClelland, and the PDP research group. Their first chapter, 'The Appeal of Parallel Distributed Processing', is an excellent introduction.

neurone, it will transmit signals only when its activation value reaches a certain threshold. So at any moment there is a certain total pattern of activation values among the individual units of the network. As time passes this total pattern changes, depending on five main factors: the original pattern of activation values, the successive patterns of inputs received by the system from its environment, the strengths of the connections among the units, the rules according to which the activation value of each unit is modified by its inputs and in turn affects its outputs, and the rules according to which the connection strengths are modified.

Actual connectionist models tend to be of relatively small components of a complete cognitive system. But there can be such models of the entire central nervous system of an organism capable of acquiring and storing information. In such a model, the organism's information is represented by the *distribution of connection strengths* throughout the system. Two main considerations give sense to this crucial claim. First, at any moment it is the strengths of the connections from unit to unit which determine how a particular pattern of sensory input modifies the activity of units in the system, and contributes to producing its behaviour. In this way the system's behaviour depends partly on its current total pattern of connection strengths. Second, just what that total pattern is at any moment is determined by the inputs it has received in the past, in accordance with whatever rules have been fixed by the investigator. So changes in the total pattern of connectivity exhibit the system's sensitivity to features of the world outside. They make it intelligible to describe the system as acquiring and storing information about its environment.

There will normally be no clear-cut answer to the question of just which internal feature of a system of this kind constitutes its having a given item of information. Consider first that it only makes sense to say that the system 'has information' if it has certain kinds of connections with the outside world. As Wittgenstein has taught us, nothing is intrinsically representational. Even some object that would strike us as an exact likeness of a certain well-known person is not for that reason a representation, since it might have no other connection whatever with that person.[25] So an internal feature of a system of the kind we are

[25] See H. Putnam, *Reason, Truth and History*, ch. 1, for exposition and discussion of this point.

discussing can be said to carry information about a feature of the external world only if it stands in certain suitable relations to the system's interactions with the world: to its behavioural capacities. In general, though, the system's behavioural capacities will depend on the working of the whole of its network of interconnected units, not on that of some subset. This general consideration alone ensures that there will be some arbitrariness in assigning particular items of information to particular internal features of the system. That general point is powerfully reinforced by the distinctive feature of connectionist models noted in the last paragraph. Information is stored by means of the distribution of connection strengths among the units of the system; and typically the same set of units is involved in the storage of many different items of information. So by the nature of the system we are not likely to be able to provide any very sharp indication of which particular feature carries a given item of information. Contrast the kind of organization envisaged by classical Artificial Intelligence, which involves the explicit storage of sentences corresponding to definite items of information. (Notice, however, that the difficulty of pinpointing which features constitute storage of which pieces of information doesn't prevent the processes in a connectionist system from having the sort of separateness that was mentioned earlier, in connection with the Machine Table robot. The actual *processes* constituting this or that experience can perfectly well be distinct. The fact that different processes may involve activating the same neurones doesn't make them less distinct.)

This is not to deny that the connection strengths among one particular subsystem of units might well have much more to do with certain particular behavioural capacities, and hence with certain particular items of information, than those among other subsystems. Indeed it seems likely that this will often be so. A certain particular constellation of units, interconnected in certain ways, might well be activated when and only when the system was in some way dealing with rabbits, for example. In such cases we might say that information about rabbits was stored in such-and-such a region of the system. We might even say that the system's possessing a constellation of units with these interconnections amounted to something like its having the concept *rabbit*.

An important characteristic of connectionist systems is that each unit's behaviour is determined entirely by the inputs it receives from whichever other units are directly connected to it. There is no central control monitoring the state of each unit. So the behaviour of the total system typically results from the way in which a large number of relatively small constraints, exerted by each unit over its neighbours, eventually produce significant large-scale changes in the whole. In this process the role of mutually excitatory and mutually inhibitory connections is crucial. Consider, for example, a connectionist model of reading. Consistently with the points made in the last section, it might embody a number of levels of processing. At the lowest level there might be subsystems geared to detect those features which combine to make letters of the alphabet—vertical, horizontal and slanting bars, curves, and so on. Units activated by a vertical bar will tend to inhibit those activated by a curve or a horizontal bar. At the next level there might be subsystems designed to detect individual letters, using as inputs the outputs from the first subsystem. Here an individual unit might be assigned to each letter, in which case there will be mutually inhibitory connections between them. On the other hand the connections between the unit corresponding to the letter 'E', for example, might have mutually excitatory connections with the lower-level detectors of horizontal bars.[26]

So much by way of summarizing some of the main general features of connectionist (or PDP or neural network) models of cognitive processing. I need not emphasize the promise of this approach as a path to understanding the actual mechanisms of cognition. All sorts of psychological facts seem susceptible to explanation in its terms, including numerous features of memory, pattern recognition, associative learning, detection of regularities, generalization, seeing 'aspects' (as with the Necker cube), retrieving information from incomplete or defective data, and much more.[27] Of course there are difficulties and unsolved problems, but for our present purposes they are relatively unimportant. For, to repeat, I am not attempting empirical science, but trying to see how there could conceivably be a route from the purely physical facts to the facts of consciousness. And the connectionist approach makes at least a very plausible contribution to this project. For our

---

[26] See e.g. Rumelhart, McClelland, *et al.*, i.20–3.
[27] For illustrations, see the volumes by Rumelhart, McClelland, *et al.*, chs. 1, 3, 14, 15, 16, 17, and 18.

purposes there are three areas where it promises insights which are particularly relevant.

One is pattern-recognition. Once a certain pattern of activation has been stored (as a pattern of connection strengths), a system can activate that pattern in response to a pattern of inputs even when the latter is incomplete or otherwise imperfect.[28]

Another is all aspects of learning, including associative learning, where the task is to learn to produce a given arbitrary pattern of activation as output when presented with another arbitrary pattern as input.[29]

The third area is concept-possession. If anything has concepts in a full-blooded sense, we do. But the ease with which we talk of concepts must not lure us into assuming that concept-possession is an all-or-nothing matter. As we have already noticed, it involves a range of different capacities. Notably it often involves the capacity to recognize instances of the concept in question. It involves the capacity to form beliefs and make inferences in terms of the concept. We also tend to include in concept-possession the ability to use appropriate words. However, what I have to say later will relate mainly to the first ability: recognition of instances.

It is now possible to form some conception—admittedly sketchy—of how there could be mechanisms by means of which perceptual information could be not just for a system, but act directly on its main assessment processes in the sense indicated: so that the system instantly acquires the multitude of fleeting capacities associated with rich perceptual information.

---

[28] See e.g. Rumelhart, McClelland, *et al.*, i, ch. 1.
[29] See ibid., chs. 1, 5, 8, 17, and 18.

5

Conscious Subjects

To be a subject of conscious perceptual experience a system must have the Basic Package, understood realistically. And some incoming perceptual information must act directly on its main assessment processes in a sense I need to explain more fully. But contrary to what many theorists maintain, no further cognitive sophistication is required. Having the Basic Package, with some perceptual information directly active, is sufficient as well as necessary for having conscious perceptual experience. In this chapter I will defend that claim, focusing chiefly on perceptual experience. As a preliminary to my explanation of information being 'directly active', and in order to stress the relatively low level of cognitive sophistication that is needed, I will start by considering a rather humble creature.

5.1   THE STICKLEBACK

The stickleback or tiddler is a common little freshwater fish. In the breeding season the female acquires a silvery colour instead of her usual dull grey-green, while the male's belly turns bright red and he sets about constructing a nest on the floor of the pond. He aggressively repels intruders from his territory but entices any ripe females into the nest, where they lay their eggs. Having fertilized the eggs he protects them, and at intervals fans them (which in fact keeps them well oxygenated, though we could hardly ascribe that intention to the fish).[1] Although much of his mating behaviour is known to be 'hard-wired', there are features which seem to rule out his being a pure stimulus-response system in my sense. For example, in order to be able to drive intruders away from the nest or to court females and entice them to enter it,

---

[1] For much more about sticklebacks, see R. J. Wootton, *The Biology of the Sticklebacks*.

he needs somehow to remain aware of both nest and visitors, continuously acquiring information about their respective positions. Given reasonable assumptions about the workings of such systems, this implies that the stickleback has the Basic Package. More to the point, as I will eventually explain, it also implies that he is a subject of conscious perceptual experience.

Perhaps a convincing connectionist model of the workings of the stickleback could in time be produced. But even if that turns out to be impossible, a crude outline of such a model will help us to get clearer about the nature of the Basic Package, about how perceptual information could both be rich and act directly on the system's main assessment processes, and so about what it takes for something to be a subject of conscious perceptual experience. I will suppose that, apart from whatever else may be necessary for the Basic Package, the model also has these four features:

(*a*) *Perceptual analysis* operating at a number of levels, as envisaged earlier. The low levels will no doubt consist of a lot of feature detectors, on the lines of the famous edge detectors noted by Hubel and Wiesel.[2] The higher levels would consist of subsystems able to detect a wide range of more complicated kinds of things, and in turn would be geared to activate:

(*b*) *Ideas*, that is, subsystems of units, each with its own pattern of connectivity, each variously linked with other Ideas and with the different input systems, and providing among other things the system's capacity to recognize patterns. In this sense Ideas roughly correspond to one aspect of concept-possession. Thanks to connectionist work on recognition and associative learning, we have some understanding of how there could be such subsystems and how they could implement that ancient notion, the association of ideas. The Ideas stored in our model stickleback would include ones that we might call *Food*, *Mate*, *Rival*, and *Pondweed*. Because of the contexts in which these Ideas were originally set up, the activation of any one of them tends to activate others, related causally or by context (or perhaps innately) to the first. And these other complexes might set off others in turn, which might be quite remote from the source of the original sensory stimulation. Not all

---

[2] See D. H. Hubel and T. N. Wiesel, 'Receptive Fields of Single Neurons in the Cat's Striate Cortex'. For some difficulties and discussion, see G. W. Humphreys and V. Bruce, *Visual Cognition*, esp. chs. 2 and 3.

stimulation will come from outside the system, of course. Hunger and sexual urges, for example, will be generated internally.

(*c*) What I will call an *Approach* unit and a *Retreat* unit. Any given Idea may be permanently or temporarily connected to one or other of these units, which I suppose should be mutually inhibitory. When an Idea is associated with the Approach unit, and when both units are activated to a sufficient level, there are mechanisms that tend to result in the organism's initiating behaviour which tends to bring it closer to a thing or situation instantiating that Idea. (See below.) The Idea in question need not have been activated by an actual external instance. For example, things could be so arranged that hormone levels alone are enough to raise the activation level of the Idea *Mate*. Similarly, *mutatis mutandis*, the joint activation of the Retreat unit and an associated Idea tends to result in behaviour tending to take the organism away from things instantiating that Idea. Evidently these suggestions are a gross oversimplification.[3] Yet they may still serve our purposes. Working in conjunction with the feature to be mentioned below, then, the Approach and Retreat units help to provide machinery that will generate and control behaviour.

(*d*) Two *Method-sorting* subsystems, one linked to the Approach unit, one to the Retreat unit. Joint high activation of the Approach unit and an associated Idea brings that unit's own method-sorting subsystem into play. It is the operation of this subsystem which tends to ensure that appropriate behaviour is initiated. Similarly, activation of the Retreat unit's method-sorting subsystem tends to result in behaviour which takes the organism away from whatever matches the co-activated Idea.

The method-sorting subsystems exploit the association of Ideas. In some situations very little 'sorting' will be needed because a particular pattern of behavioural response may be innate. That seems to be so for much of the stickleback's elaborate courtship and mating behaviour. In such cases we may suppose there is a direct causal link from the activation of an Idea by some behaviour pattern manifested by the female to the male's next move.

---

[3] Of course there could be an ordering of the strengths with which different stimuli affected behaviour, so that courtship, for example, would always be overridden by imminent danger without benefit of Approach or Retreat units. But I am assuming that the stickleback is not a pure stimulus-response system, and is capable of processing the outputs from its perceptual analysis subsystems.

Indeed, you might think that in such cases there would be no role for the Approach unit. However, to the extent that the organism can be diverted from pursuit of its stereotyped courtship behaviour by stimuli such as urgent hunger or threat, there must be a mechanism whereby the innate links can be overruled. The Approach and Retreat units provide such a mechanism because they are independent of any particular Ideas, and initiation of behaviour depends on joint activation of one of them and an Idea, not on any Idea alone.[4]

In cases where the organism's current situation is relatively remote from an instance of the operative Idea—the one initially co-activated with the Approach (or Retreat) unit—I envisage that the method-sorting subsystem activates a number of Idea-sequences. In the Approach case each sequence starts off from the given Idea and leads to others which correspond to possible paths by which the stickleback can move closer to an instance of the operative Idea. With luck, some of these are close to the Ideas being activated by the stickleback's current situation. In that case their connections with the latter are reinforced and they acquire their own links with the Approach unit. This linkage in turn causes behaviour appropriate for approaching something instantiating these same closer Ideas. The Approach unit is then linked with the next Idea in the sequence, and a sequence of appropriate behaviour is under way. Similarly, *mutatis mutandis*, for the Retreat case. Let me emphasize that there is no implication that any of the processes involving the activation of Ideas will *themselves* be conscious ones. I am concerned to explain conscious perceptual experience, not conscious thought in general. It is beside the point whether the processes which result in more or less appropriate behaviour are themselves conscious.

Bear in mind that the present aim is not to produce an account of actual mechanisms. It is to help to make intelligible how there could be mechanisms which instantiated the processing of rich, directly active perceptual information. We need some conception of how there *could* be a system in which such processes took place. For that purpose I hope the above remarks, gappy though they are, may be adequate. Filling the gaps would obviously call for imaginative engineering. But I suggest it would not call for

---

[4] See again the Aristotle quotation in n. 7 to the last chapter.

anything we should find it impossible to conceive—it would not call for some magical intervention. The actual machinery is remarkable, but it is not miraculous.

As the stickleback swims about, then, its eyes, ears, nose, and other sense-receptors are bombarded with stimulations. In terms of our model, these stimulations are analysed at low levels and then, if they fit certain patterns, they activate various Ideas such as those of *Food* and *Pondweed*. The Ideas immediately activated by sensory stimulation may activate others, and these in turn will interact with the Approach and Retreat units, so that as time passes various more or less elaborate courses of behaviour are initiated. For example, the fish swims towards the pondweed, catches sight of a larva and eats it, swims on, and then, because its hormones are activating *Mate*, becomes sensitized to the presence of ripe females (or rather, as we know, to the presence of anything roughly like a ripe female in respect of silvery colour and large belly). After a period during which the various activated Ideas interact, it might start courtship behaviour; or, if its blood sugars are low (if hunger still presses), it might go in search of more food. Much of the stickleback's behaviour will qualify as goal-seeking because of the nature of its causation and control. Typically it will be modified on receipt of sensory information which updates stored information about relevant features of the environment, and typically a given sequence of behaviour will be terminated when the initiating stimulation pattern ceases.

The interaction of the Ideas and the Approach and Retreat units amounts to a primitive kind of interpretation, assessment, decision-making, and control. And these processes are surely integrated in ways which satisfy the requirement stated in the last chapter. So a creature working on the lines of the model stickleback has the Basic Package. But notice that the functions of interpretation, assessment, decision-making, and control are not performed by a special unitary subsystem, an internal Control, as in some models. The connectionist approach enables us to grasp how, instead, those functions can be diffused throughout much of the whole system.[5] (Only through *much* of the system because

[5] In this way our model avoids the gross error of what Dennett calls 'Cartesian materialism'. See his *Consciousness Explained, passim*, and 5.3 below. In an earlier paper, 'Consciousness and Concepts', I used the phrase 'decision-making processes' where I now use 'assessment processes'. Assessment involves a kind of decision-making, but it is perhaps misleading to suggest that the converse is also true.

there may be plenty of subsystems whose internal workings are more or less closed off from the rest of the system. They are connected with it only through input and output units: the rest is 'hidden'.)

A highly important feature of the system's operation is that, although it is relatively primitive, there is nevertheless a considerable amount of interpretation and assessment going on. We could perhaps describe the lower-level perceptual analysis as already a kind of interpretation. However, in itself it doesn't constitute interpretation *by the system as a whole*. The presence of elaborate analytical processes of that kind is consistent with the system as a whole being unaware of the features being analysed. A very complicated process of analysis might result in no more than the activation of a single neurone, which in turn immediately triggered a set pattern of behaviour. That seems to be how the frog, for example, manages to catch flies. Analytical processes which add up to something like the message (in our terms, not the frog's) 'fly-sized thing moving in fly-like way' cause the frog's tongue to flick out in the correct direction quite automatically.[6] As our earlier considerations on pure stimulus-response systems showed, this doesn't mean that the frog itself is aware of the features analysed by its subsystems. In fact a frog, being a relatively sophisticated animal, may have experiences of flies. But the point is that a creature with a sophisticated method for *detecting* flies need not have *experiences* of them. Their presence might just automatically trigger the appropriate pattern of response without any conscious process being involved. In our stickleback, in contrast, there is interpretation and assessment by the system as a whole. This occurs whenever the outputs from perceptual analysis cause different Ideas to interact with one another and with the Approach and Retreat units. I describe these processes as interpretation and assessment because they constitute, in effect, the organism's assessment of the significance to it of whatever items have activated those processes. But it is vital to keep in mind that processes qualify as the acquisition of information, interpretation, or assessment only because they occur in a whole system of the right kind.

Again, the contrast with pure stimulus-response systems is instructive. In their case significance-for-the-organism is built into the genes. For example, evolution has decided that butyric acid

---

[6] See J. Y. Lettvin *et al.*, 'What the Frog's Eye Tells the Frog's Brain'.

and warm fluid are significant items for the tick. So the tick is hard-wired to respond to these stimuli by pre-set response patterns, unburdened by the need to assess its total situation or exercise even the most rudimentary judgement. But for certain kinds of creatures there are obvious advantages in flexibility of response. For them, a number of different items of incoming information have to be assessed before any action is initiated. In such cases the question of what is significant for the organism is to a large extent left to the organism itself to determine, perhaps by processes like those in our model stickleback.

I hope it is clear that, and how, the perceptual information acquired by our stickleback is *for* it. Those patterns of stimulation which constitute the acquisition of information feed into the central regions of the whole system where the processes of assessment and decision-making take place—those processes which initiate and control the whole system's behaviour. The stickleback model also illustrates what I mean by saying that information acts directly on the main assessment processes. Broadly, it is a matter of sensory inputs causing changing patterns of activation of various subsystems of units, these changing patterns causing still further changes, and so on, until there are changes which constitute the acquisition of certain kinds of discriminatory capacities—changes which therefore constitute the acquisition of information by the system as a whole because potentially, though not necessarily, they have effects on its behaviour.

5.2   MORE ON 'DIRECTLY ACTIVE' INFORMATION

Incoming information may act directly on the system's assessment processes or it may act indirectly. The distinction is intended to coincide with, and explain, the difference between conscious and unconscious perceptual information.[7] There is no difficulty in conceiving of situations where someone has information that can

---

[7] In 'Consciousness and Concepts' I wrote of information being 'present to the system's main decision-making processes'. The expression 'acting directly on' here does essentially the same job, but brings out the fact that those physical events which constitute the acquisition of the information cause changes in the assessment (and decision-making) processes. The information is still 'present to' those processes.

only have come from perception, yet has had no conscious experience which could have yielded it. We don't have to exercise our
imaginations: there are examples in the psychological literature.
'Subliminal' perception is a familiar case. For example, one series
of experiments seems to show that subliminal stimuli may be
semantically analysed unconsciously. 'Emotional words, presented
below threshold to the eye, have been found to change auditory
sensitivity, and vice versa.'[8] There seems no reason why we should
reject this interpretation of the experiments. It is hardly con-
troversial that some perceptual information is acquired unconsciously. In that case it does not act directly on the system's main
assessment processes. Of course, if the information is for the
system, it is already in one sense *available* to its main assessment
processes. It is only because it potentially influences those processes that it can be said to be information for the system at all.
But the point is that perceptual information can be available
without being directly active. In that case, I suggest, it is not
conscious. The difference shows up in the subject's behavioural
capacities. (I need hardly add that the distinction is not sharp.)

In the psychological experiments just alluded to, the fact that
the subliminal information in question was not conscious showed
up in subjects' inability to give any indication, straight off, of
what it actually was. That is consistent with its not acting directly
on their main assessment processes. Note that verbal behaviour is
not the only indicator. The fact that subjects could not say what
the information was is not, by itself, very good evidence that the
information was not directly active. Rich perceptual information
is not easily brought under ordinary descriptions. What is good
evidence is a subject's inability to represent the information in any
way at all, or even to recognize it when it is presented again, this
time above the threshold. Accordingly, evidence of the capacity to
represent or at least to recognize the information is evidence that
it was directly active, and so was conscious. However, although
those capacities to represent and recognize are important, the
most directly relevant and easily identified capacities are the com-
monplace ones of producing appropriate non-verbal behaviour.
You show you have conscious perceptual information about the
coin among the pebbles by actually picking the coin up; you show

---

[8] *The Oxford Companion to the Mind*, ed. R. L. Gregory, 753.

you have consciously heard your name called by answering; and so on. Acquisition of such capacities is typically instantaneous and requires no special acts of recall, which is why I say that information which instantly endows you with such capacities acts directly on your main assessment processes. You can control your behaviour on the basis of such information immediately it comes in. Unconsciously acquired information, in contrast, seems to manifest itself only in response to special calls on memory (if then) or in other indirect ways.

Another example will help to bring out the main points. I see a film which includes subliminally exposed images of a certain book: next time I'm in the bookshop I buy it. So the subliminal message got through and influenced my behaviour. In a way, the information was available to my main assessment processes—it affected my actual behaviour. However, we can suppose that I had no conscious recollection of the subliminal images, nor was I conscious of them at the time they were being projected on to the screen. This shows up in the fact that if you were to run the same film twice, once with and once without the subliminal messages, I should claim they were exactly the same. The messages didn't affect my recognitional capacities. This illustrates the way in which the two classes of incoming perceptual information—that which is for the system but not directly active, and that which is also directly active—can be distinguished on the basis of the different capacities they produce in the system.

The idea of unconscious perception may still seem puzzling. How *can* perceptual information be available to the system without being directly active? I don't have to describe actual mechanisms, but I can offer suggestions which may remove the appearance of mystery. One way that the information may work indirectly is through the fairly permanent changes involved in memory. The information—in the shape of physical modifications in appropriate places in the brain—might lie dormant until triggered by some stimulus; or it might quietly produce subtle changes in the system's total pattern of information, hence in its total pattern of dispositions. After all, we are very familiar with the idea of information which is on the one hand available to us, but on the other hand not currently producing the sorts of large-scale, constantly changing, more or less fleeting capacities that we have been considering. Most of the ordinary factual information we have falls under that description: we have it, but it is not in my sense active. Yet to make the information available to our main assessment processes, we have only to search our memories. So it should not raise insuperable problems if some perceptual information is similarly available but not directly active.

Our earlier consideration of the richness of conscious perceptual information also helps to throw light on these matters. Incoming information is typically subjected to a whole variety of interpretation, and that at different levels. In the early stages it is just a matter of feature-detection. Later there are other kinds of classification, some of them more or less like classification under concepts. It is important to bear in mind that if certain perceptual information is acting directly on the system's main assessment processes, the features detected in the early stages are not somehow lost. Those detections continue to affect the main processes as well as the results of classifications made deeper in the network— otherwise the information would not be rich.[9] It is the vast number, range, and variety of these early-detected features, continuing to act directly on the main processes, that constitute the richness of perceptual consciousness. Now, although early feature-detections continue to influence our capacities in ordinary conscious perception, it is easy to imagine that in certain cases they might fail to do so, even though some of the later discriminatory processes, triggered by those earlier ones, are still active. In such cases some relevant information is acquired, but because the only surviving discriminatory processes are at relatively high levels of generality, that information lacks richness. In such cases the higher-level information would still be acting directly on the main assessment processes in my sense. But because the earlier feature-detections were no longer active, the information would not be rich, and so would not amount to ordinary conscious perception.

It is necessary to distinguish a system's 'main' assessment processes because processes in a subsystem may well be involved in something like the subsystem's own assessment. If that is so, then since we are concerned with what it is for the whole system to have conscious experiences, the main assessment processes of the

---

[9] Compare Dennett's insistence that 'feature detections or discriminations' only have to occur once: 'the information content thus fixed does not have to be sent somewhere else to be rediscriminated by some "master" discriminator' (*Consciousness Explained*, 113).

whole system must be those involved in the acquisition of information relevant to the whole system's assessment of its situation,
and control of its behaviour.[10]

5.3 HOW THE STICKLEBACK'S INTERNAL PROCESSES HAVE CHARACTERS FOR IT

We can suppose that the perceptual information acquired by the
stickleback does act directly on its main assessment processes, at
least some of the time. And clearly that information is also rich.
For at any moment when the system is functioning fully there is a
complex input pattern from each of its sense organs, and most of
that pattern acts directly on the processes of interpretation and
assessment. So low-level perceptual information may be acting
directly on the main assessment processes even though it has not
yet been sorted or interpreted in terms of the schemes involved in
the actual assessment. In general there is no point between sensory
input and assessment at which a certain particular classification is
imposed, and downstream from which details not thereby classified
are lost to further interpretation. On the contrary, the detailed
input patterns are constantly available for further interpretation,
and the higher-level interpretative processes are, as we have seen,
components of the assessment, decision-making, and controlling
processes. In this way the whole of the passing scene, as detectable
by the stickleback, reverberates richly through the system via the
mechanisms of perceptual analysis and Ideas. This entails that the
stickleback has conscious perceptual experiences; at any rate I will
try to show that it does.

Information from different components of the passing scene
impinges on the stickleback without any of them entirely blotting
out the information it is simultaneously receiving from others. The
different components may be events registered in different sensory

[10] Could information act directly on a *subsystem's* assessment processes? The
case of cerebral hemispheres might provide an illustration. But on my account, a
subsystem will not be capable of conscious *perceptual* experience unless it also has
the Basic Package. Conceivably that might be so in some commissurotomy cases;
but I will not pursue the issue here. Note that my position is not that 'mere height
in a hierarchy of control' (P. Carruthers, 'Consciousness and Concepts', 44) makes
the difference between whether or not there is conscious experience. I don't see
why there should not be conscious subsystems in a conscious system.

systems, for example the movement of pondweed and the sound of voices from people on the bank; or they may be different events captured by the same sensory system, for example a floating larva and the plump silvery body of a potential mate. These external events do not in general automatically cause any particular pattern of behaviour. There are processes of assessment, however unsophisticated they may be. And the point I want to emphasize now is that the stickleback's assessment of different but simultaneous events implies that its processing of those events has, in a sense, different *characters for it*. Suppose it has sight simultaneously of both a plump silvery female and a red-bellied rival male, at distances and in circumstances where no particular reaction is immediately evoked. A kind of assessment takes place, and depends on the difference in the character (for it) of two sets of *internal* processes: those caused by the colour of the male, and those caused by the colour of the female. For although these internal processes are typically caused by the impact of external things, they are strictly independent of their external causes: they could have been produced by other means. It is because these internal processes are not mere links in a stimulus–response chain, and are involved in processes of assessment, that they can be said to have different characters for the stickleback.

There is no mystery about how such differences in character (for the system) could exist. They consist in different patterns of activation of various complexes of units in the system—one pattern distally caused by the rival male, the other by the ripe female—which have different effects on the processes of assessment, decision-making, and action initiation. These differences depend on the different feature-detections arising in the early stages of perceptual analysis and still active. Without those differences in character, there would be no differences in how those processes could affect behaviour. It is only because of those differences in character that the system can decide to behave differently towards their different external causes. But note: talking in these terms does not introduce anything new into the story. It is just a redescription of what is involved in the direct action of perceptual information on the system's main assessment processes. Simply because different kinds of rich perceptual information are directly active, certain internal processes have different characters for the system.

5.4 THE STICKLEBACK AS CONSCIOUS SUBJECT

That, I maintain, is sufficient for there to be conscious perceptual experience and raw feeling. Recall the six statements which gave a rough fix on raw feeling in Chapter 1:

I. Whenever we use any of our senses something is caused to occur—raw feeling, or . . . the having of raw feels—which has a general character associated with that sense and a specific character partly but not entirely determined by the things acting on that sense at the time.

II. To be a subject of raw feeling involves having at least minimal consciousness, hence being something it is like something to be.

III. The various kinds of raw feeling could occur independently of any external items which might actually cause instances of them to occur, and also of any behaviour or behavioural dispositions which those instances may cause.

IV. There is also raw feeling outside perception. It is a constituent of dreaming, of hallucinations, and of mental imagery of all kinds.

V. A subject of raw feeling can detect its occurrence in ways that others cannot, except perhaps in special cases—for example as a result of connections between brains.

VI. Raw feeling is not to be construed on the relational model, as a matter of there being particulars to which the subject is related; nor as a matter of such particulars being somehow bundled together.

These six statements are of course to be understood in the light of discussions in earlier chapters, especially Chapter 2. I maintain that the explanation of how certain internal processes can have 'characters for the system' constitutes an explanation of how there can be raw feeling—how it is that the notion roughly fixed by those statements has application. Statement I is at least consistent with this claim, and II will also hold if I am right. As to III, we have already noticed that although those internal processes which constitute the direct action of rich perceptual information are typically caused by certain kinds of external things, they are logically independent of them. Indeed, that appears to be necessary if the internal process is to constitute the system's acquisition of information. The system is so constructed that *internal* changes of these special kinds can be caused by external things; and these internal changes carry the different information they do carry partly, if not entirely, on account of differences between the different external things they are causally linked with. Similarly, the occurrence of such processes does not necessarily imply that any particular sort of behaviour ensues. (The creature might even be paralysed.) Statement IV will be dealt with later in this chapter. Statement V surely holds for our stickleback's relations with the information that is directly active, and so for its raw feeling if I am right. The creature doesn't have to observe its own behaviour, for example, in order for various internal processes to have different characters for it. Finally, the vital statement VI holds if raw feeling is constituted by processes having characters for the system. For what I have been saying carries no implication that the processes which consist of information acting directly on the system's main assessment processes stand as objects to a subject constituted by something else. However, this central idea needs to be made clearer.

The fundamental point is this. What we have been discussing is a model of something which is a subject *as a whole*. It is the stickleback, not one of its components, which is a subject of experience.[11] So there is no basis for marking off two broad constituents of the stickleback's internal life: on the one hand sensory inputs, and on the other a Cartesian subject taking those inputs in. If anyone offered such an account they would owe us a further account of that Cartesian subject itself, which must not in turn involve its own mini-subject, on pain of a vicious infinite regress related to the one noted by Ryle in his attack on sense data. Clearly, no adequate account of consciousness may include a mini-subject or homunculus as an irreducible component. In my story of the stickleback, the main assessment processes in no way amount to such a homunculus. They are just component processes in a total system which constitutes a subject as a whole. However, you might suspect that, in spite of my protests, my talk of

[11] There may be a case for saying that if you extracted the stickleback's brain and kept it alive and appropriately stimulated in a vat, then it would be a subject of conscious experiences. But that does not affect my point, which is that there is no mini-subject somehow inhabiting the stickleback (or its brain) to which the 'directly active' processes are related as objects.

'characters for the system' somehow insinuates the treacherous Cartesian split into the story. But here I can refer back to the model of the stickleback. What we have is a system in which processes of feature-detection, interpretation, assessment, decision-making, and action-initiation take place without any sharp dividing lines between them. There is nothing there that can be regarded as constituting an internal mini-subject. It is convenient for us to have these different concepts when we are describing what is going on. But the actual processes are an inextricable swirl involving complexes of units all over the system. There are no sharp distinctions to be drawn between inputs on the one hand, and the processes of feature-detection, classification, interpretation, and assessment on the other. Recall, too, that it is only because all these processes work together that those individual descriptions apply. If there were no processes of interpretation and assessment, the incoming patterns of activity would not constitute the acquisition of information: the situation would resemble that of the camera, where no information is for the system. Similarly, if there were no incoming patterns, the later processes would not constitute interpretation or assessment. All of this entails that my talk of characters for the system has to be understood in a way that does not imply an internal mini-subject faced with an ethereal television screen whose images are coloured with what Dennett felicitously calls 'figment'—a sort of spiritual paint.[12] What still makes it legitimate to talk of characters for the system is the fact that when different sorts of perceptual information come in, and act directly on its assessment processes, it is differences among the *internal* processes which affect the system's assessments, not necessarily any differences among their external causes.

It will be useful to compare this position with Dennett's in *Consciousness Explained*. One of his main targets is what he calls 'Cartesian materialism'. This is 'the view you arrive at when you discard Descartes's dualism but fail to discard the imagery of a central (but material) Theatre where "it all comes together"'.[13] Aiming to substitute more useful metaphors, he offers that of 'multiple drafts'. The analogy is with academic publishing, where different people see rather different drafts of a paper and there is no easy answer to the question of just which is *the* paper. The

[12] Dennett, *Consciousness Explained*, 346–68.
[13] Ibid. 106.

metaphor is cashed on the basis of the widely accepted view that mental activity consists of vast numbers of parallel processes, to be thought of as the simultaneous workings of numerous sub-systems in the brain. In perception, notably, sensory inputs are elaborated, modified, and interpreted simultaneously by special-ized subsystems along many parallel tracks in various parts of the brain. On his account, these events of 'content-fixation' are not sufficient for consciousness. Now, so far my own position is consistent with Dennett's. However, I find his further development of the metaphor of multiple drafts problematic. He maintains that consciousness requires what he calls 'probing': 'Just what we are conscious of within any particular time duration is not defined independently of the probes we use to precipitate a narrative about that period.'[14] So he appears to offer *narrative-precipitation* as what distinguishes conscious from unconscious events. Of course the distinction is not supposed to be sharp. But since he assumes—surely correctly—that not all content-fixations and narratives are conscious, he does need to provide some account of the difference between conscious and unconscious ones. But narrative-precipitation cannot, I think, do the work he wants.

If the 'narratives' in question were only what I have been calling interpretations—the sortings and classifications which take place as the system processes inputs from the sense organs—then they would not serve his purpose because they include many which are not conscious. So presumably he is talking about narratives at the personal level, expressed in the sorts of linguistically anchored concepts we use to make statements about our experiences. But narratives of this kind are not adequate for making the judge-ments involved in actually receiving rich perceptual information, as we saw in the last chapter. The richness of the perceptual information we receive tends to defeat our capacity to specify it fully. So the suggestion that narrative-precipitation is necessary for conscious experience puts the cart before the horse. It is only because we are already receiving rich perceptual information—consciously—that any question of 'probing' arises. Conscious ex-perience may prompt us to formulate its content in terms of our linguistically anchored concepts. Hence its being conscious cannot be explained by our producing such formulations. (This is not to

[14] Ibid. 136. For the view that not all content-fixations and 'narratives' are conscious, see e.g. 113, 457.

deny that the linguistically expressible *content* of experiences may in some cases depend on that kind of probing. But I am making a point about the occurrence of conscious experience, not about assigning content to it in terms of linguistically anchored concepts.)

Dennett warns against the temptation to suppose that in perception there is a real distinction between judging as a result of things seeming to be a certain way, and things seeming to be a certain way as a result of judging.[15] I have no quarrel with that point—provided 'judging' is allowed to cover what I am calling interpretations. But if it is fixed more narrowly, to cover only linguistically anchored formulations, then there is in general no problem about the existence of a genuine distinction, as we have seen. Altogether, Dennett's attempt to mark off the conscious from the non-conscious in terms of probing and narrative-fixation seems not to work. On the other hand, the notion of perceptual information acting directly on the system's main assessment processes seems to do the job adequately for our purposes.

That it does so emerges particularly clearly when we reflect on the way it entails that internal processes have characters for the system in the sense explained. If I am right, the occurrence of processes with characters for the system is the occurrence of raw feeling. I suggest that it is here that what is literally internal is also the locus of something 'inner' in the special sense which interests us—where descriptions in 'topic-neutral' or objective terms entail that there is scope for descriptions from the subjective point of view as well. I am not saying that humble creatures like sticklebacks engage in Joycean monologues. The point is that if there are processes which have characters for such systems, then the systems have experiences which they could describe *if* they had language.

You might suspect that fish and perhaps even cats and dogs lack conscious perceptual experience. You might think there is more to it than my account provides for. Some philosophers and psychologists will object that further cognitive sophistication is required—perhaps the ability to introspect, perhaps even language: a 'Joycean machine', in Dennett's phrase.[16] According to Armstrong the ability to introspect is required in order to provide for cases of absent-mindedness, sleepwalking, blindsight, and the like. Carruthers has offered similar arguments. According to the

---

[15] See ibid. 133 f.
[16] Ibid. 281.

psychologist Nicholas Humphrey this ability has evolutionary value for social animals because it enables them to arrive at psychological interpretations of one another on the basis of their introspective knowledge of their own states. These views have to be taken seriously. They are mostly defended by argument, not mere intuition. (If anything they seem rather counter-intuitive.) In order to resist my claim that our stickleback has conscious perceptual experiences, it would be necessary to show that it could acquire, as it does, all the kinds of information it does acquire, and use them as it does, without having conscious experiences. I don't see how that could be done. But let us examine the likely objections.

5.5 NO FURTHER COGNITIVE SOPHISTICATION IS REQUIRED

We noticed that according to Armstrong conscious experience is a kind of perception, when perception is just the acquisition of information. However, on his account conscious experience involves a kind of 'inner sense'. It is perception by the organism not of external things but of its own mental states. He uses the word 'introspection' to cover not only cases where we self-consciously consider our own mental states, but also what I am calling conscious experience.[17]

He urges that there must be introspection in this sense if there are to be purposive trains of mental activity: unless we could be aware of our current mental activity we should not be able to adjust it to take account of how it was proceeding.[18] But this, though important, fails to explain why ordinary perception should be the object of this sort of introspective awareness. At any rate it fails to explain it if, as appears, Armstrong counts most of our perceptual experience as conscious in that sense. Much of the time when we are enjoying ordinary conscious perceptual experience, what interests us is the things out there that we can see, hear, smell, and so on. To carry on our ordinary activities we certainly

---

[17] D. M. Armstrong, *A Materialist Theory of the Mind*, 93–5, 323–38. In the following pages I draw on material from my 'Consciousness and Concepts'.
[18] Armstrong, *A Materialist Theory of the Mind*, 327.

need perception of what is happening. But we don't at the same time need to know about the internal states that constitute such perception. Yet if that perception is mostly conscious, it ought to fall under Armstrong's explanation; and apparently it doesn't. There is a further difficulty. Why should the perception of *internal* events necessarily involve conscious experience when, on Armstrong's account, the perception of *external* events doesn't?

Humphrey argues that there must be introspection if an animal is to be able to operate as one of 'nature's psychologists'. It must be able to interpret the behaviour of other members of its species on the basis of its introspective access to the sources of its own behaviour. And in his view, 'apart from this role in helping a social animal to do psychology, consciousness has, as I see it, no value whatever'.[19] This is an interesting evolutionary explanation of the role of introspection in the narrow sense. It would also help to explain *self*-consciousness. But like Armstrong's suggestion, it doesn't seem to explain cases of conscious experience where we are not introspecting in that narrow sense. Presumably Humphrey would reject the idea that we are introspecting all the time we are awake. Yet surely there is an important distinction between introspection in the sense of being aware of one's own mental states, and that wider phenomenon which both Armstrong and Humphrey include under the same heading and which I am calling conscious experience.[20] (In any case there is no difficulty over the latter's survival value. If incoming information is acting directly on an organism's main assessment processes in the sense I have explained, the organism has the best possible basis for working out how it will behave. A stickleback faced at the same time with

[19] N. Humphrey, *Consciousness Regained*, 44. See also chs. 1, 2, 3, and 5 of the same work. In that work Humphrey tends to treat consciousness and self-consciousness as identical: see below, this section. In his more recent work, *A History of the Mind*, his position appears significantly different. For example he claims that 'before there were any other kinds of phenomena there were "raw sensations"—tastes, smells, tickles, pains, sensations of warmth, of light, of sound and so on' (21). He then sees it as a problem to explain how these 'subjective sensory states' could come to be 'used to represent the outside world' (22). It should be clear that I see no special problem here.

[20] Humphrey might reply that it was impossible for what I am calling conscious experience to have entered the evolutionary story unaccompanied by introspection in the narrow sense. He appears to suggest as much at p. 53 of *Consciousness Regained*. But if I am right it is possible, in which case his explanation doesn't after all apply to conscious experience in general.

a piece of food and a predator can arrive at behaviour tailored to fit its own assessment of the situation. Contrast the position of an otherwise similar creature which acquired perceptual information not acting directly on its main assessment processes. Not having the information forced upon it—not instantly acquiring the relevant capacities—it would presumably acquire no motive for reconsidering its position, and stand a greater risk of being caught and eaten.)

Carruthers has offered an account of conscious experience which requires its subjects to have even more cognitive sophistication than Armstrong's. He notes what he regards as two varieties of 'non-conscious' experience. One is the familiar example of the car driver who appears to see the lorry double parked by the side of the road and steers round it, yet claims not to have been aware of it. The other is blindsight (to which I will return). To enable conscious experience to be properly distinguished from such cases, Carruthers proposes that 'a conscious, as opposed to a non-conscious, mental state is one that is available to conscious thought—where a conscious act of thinking is itself an event that is available to be thought about in turn'; and 'a conscious experience is a state whose content is available to be consciously thought about'.[21] So on his account conscious experience requires at least three levels of mental activity. One is that of simply having experiences. The next is that of thinking about those experiences. The third is that of thinking about the thinking which goes on at the second level. (Not that thinking at the second and third levels must actually occur in order for experiences to be conscious. All he requires is that the content of experiences be available to thought which is in turn available to further thought.) Armstrong had earlier given similar reasons for bringing conscious experience under the heading of 'inner sense'. In *A Materialist Theory of the Mind* he aimed to deal with objections to his general view that mental states are 'states of the person apt for the production of certain sorts of behaviour'. One is that consciousness is something more than the occurrence of such a state. He agrees, citing the case of the absent-minded driver, and immediately suggests that

---

[21] P. Carruthers, 'Brute Experience', 262 and 263 respectively. He defends the same position in his 'Consciousness and Concepts'. I have replied to his arguments there in 'Conscious Experience and the Concept of Experience'.

'consciousness is ... *awareness* (perception) of inner mental states by the person whose states they are'.[22]

Yet such reasoning provides at best weak support for the view in question. Absent-minded driving, sleepwalking, and other examples such as behaviour under hypnotic suggestion and blind-sight, are all capable of being dealt with just as well, if not better, in other ways. They leave my position unaffected.

First, the absent-minded driver. Carruthers appears to see the double-parked lorry but claims he was not 'aware of seeing' it.[23] But in what sense was he not 'aware' of it? It could mean only that he didn't think about his experience of seeing the lorry, or conceptualize it to any great extent. But evidently that is beside the point. The question is whether he altogether lacked conscious visual experiences of the lorry. And that is at best problematic. It is just not clear that he paid no attention whatever to what he was seeing. We might say, compatibly with my account of conscious experiences, that when he was driving along he was certainly paying little attention to what he was seeing, yet all the same did have conscious visual experiences. Most of his mental resources were employed elsewhere, so the experiences were not much analysed or conceptualized, or given any significant place in his memory. That would seem enough to account for the feature he describes as not being aware of seeing the lorry. (Certain drugs blot out memories of events of which the subject was indisputably conscious. Subsequent failure to recall such events is hardly compelling evidence that they were never consciously experienced.)

But suppose he really did lack all conscious visual experiences when he was driving on that occasion. Then his situation would relevantly resemble the sleepwalker's. But in that case it could not be maintained that the incoming information was acting directly on his main assessment processes. Like the sleepwalker, he would be on automatic pilot. Information would be getting in all right, but his behaviour would not be mediated by those processes (and so would not strictly be the behaviour of the whole system).[24]

So if the perceptual information in question really was acting

---

[22] Armstrong, *A Materialist Theory of the Mind*, 94. He takes a similar line in *Consciousness and Causality*, with sleepwalking as an example.

[23] Carruthers, 'Brute Experience', 258.

[24] It follows, I think, that although certain capacities would be acquired, they too would not be those of the system as a whole: he wouldn't be 'all there'.

directly on the driver's main assessment processes, there seems no reason why the episode should not have been one of mere forget-fulness. If, however, the information didn't get through to those processes, that would account for both the apparent lack of con-sciousness at the time and the subsequent absence of memories. Either way, neither absent-minded drivers nor sleepwalkers give us reasons to analyse ordinary conscious experience as involving 'inner sense', or the tiers of thought envisaged by Carruthers.

Humphrey apparently equates consciousness with self-consciousness.[25] And there may seem to be a simple line of argu-ment to that position—straight from my own, in fact. On my account the Basic Package, understood in the realistic manner explained in the last chapter, is both necessary and sufficient for perceptual consciousness. But it involves what I am calling 'assess-ment processes'. Now in our case, at any rate, assessment typically involves considering our *own* situation. So assessment in general may seem to require the subject to have a concept of *self*. You consider your situation, so you must have some idea of yourself, and you must be able to distinguish yourself from others.[26] The implied level of conceptual sophistication may seem considerably higher than I have recognized. So isn't it implausible to suggest that the humble stickleback may have conscious experiences?

If the Basic Package does indeed necessarily involve having a concept of *self*, then no doubt I am wrong about sticklebacks. However, I think the reasoning just outlined is unsound. Only very rudimentary processes of assessment are needed for the Basic Package. And the above reasoning provides no explanation of why an organism's processes of assessment, even though they presumably involve some kind of consideration of alternative pos-sible courses of action, require it to have a full-blown concept of itself. Recall our earlier discussion of concepts and capacities. We may be reluctant to ascribe even very ordinary concepts like those of *animal, door, colour*, to creatures without language. Yet many such creatures display quite sophisticated capacities which we find it natural to describe in terms of such concepts. Having a full-blown 'ordinary' concept is by no means something unitary. A

[25] 'What other kind of consciousness there is I do not know': Humphrey, *Consciousness Regained*, 48. See also n. 18 above.
[26] Julian Jaynes offers a similar argument in his *The Origins of Consciousness in the Breakdown of the Bicameral Mind*, 63.

range of different sorts of capacities and processes is typically involved, including, but not exhausted by, recognitional capacities and capacities to treat instances in relevantly similar ways. It seems that a creature may easily have some of them without others. So there seems no particular reason why the assessment processes in a languageless creature—even quite a humble one—should not be able to (as we put it) represent possible states of affairs in which it is in fact involved in activities such as eating, mating, or swimming, without actually having a concept of *itself* engaged in those activities. Certainly it must distinguish between itself and others (though a cat chasing its tail may make you wonder even about that). But that seems to be enough. If so, there may be perceptual consciousness without *self*-consciousness except in the attenuated sense just indicated.

5.6 LANGUAGE IS NOT NECESSARY

It is often urged that language is necessary for consciousness. An arresting variant of this view is Julian Jaynes's contention that it was only after human beings had been using language for some time that their brains acquired those capacities that make for consciousness. He argues that even the Greeks of Mycenean times, who had not only language but writing, lacked consciousness. Their decision-making depended on their 'hallucinating the voices of authorities over them, and those authorities hallucinating yet higher ones, and so on to the kings and their peers hallucinating gods'.[27] However, hallucination is surely impossible for beings who lack conscious perceptual experience in my sense. And in fact Jaynes's other remarks make clear that he understands consciousness in a much richer sense, and that what I am calling raw feeling would not be sufficient for it. For example, when he illustrates his claim that consciousness is not necessary for learning, he means only consciousness *that* certain things have been learned.[28] But I

[27] Ibid. 79.
[28] e.g. he says: 'simple associative learning can be shown to go on without any consciousness that it has occurred' (*Origins of Consciousness*, 32). I think consciousness *that* something is the case is very different from conscious experience. So, contrary to what Carruthers has suggested ('Consciousness and Concepts', 43 f.), I think it is a mistake to look for a single account of both conscious

am not at all maintaining that conscious beliefs, desires, and other full-blown intentional states are possible without language. So Jaynes's position is not necessarily opposed to mine. However, Dennett, in *Consciousness Explained*, may at first appear to make a stronger claim.

At one point it seems that Dennett's main account of consciousness necessarily involves language in the shape of what he calls a 'Joycean machine'. The idea is that human consciousness consists of culturally evolved software of a 'serial' kind, installed in the hard-wired 'parallel' architecture we largely share with our languageless primate cousins. We are born with brains equipped with a lot of specialized subsystems and much plasticity. We then acquire 'an already invented and largely "debugged" *system* of habits',[29] the dominant ones being those involved in possession of language. The flow of spoken and unspoken monologues is analogous to the flow of instructions and data through a standard sequential computer. He explains his suggestion with the aid of the notion of a 'virtual machine': a program (for example an operating system) which can be run on any of an indefinitely wide range of hardware, yet presents the same appearance to the user regardless of differences in the underlying hardware.

In our brains there is a cobbled-together collection of specialist brain circuits, which, thanks to a family of habits inculcated partly by culture and partly by individual self-exploration, conspire together to produce a more or less orderly, more or less effective, more or less well-designed virtual machine, the *Joycean machine*. By yoking these independently evolved specialist organs together in common cause, and thereby giving their union vastly enhanced powers, this virtual machine, this software of the brain, performs a sort of internal political miracle: it creates a *virtual captain* of the crew, without elevating any one of them to long-term dictatorial power.[30]

It certainly looks as if Dennett is committed to the view that possession of a Joycean virtual machine is not only sufficient, but necessary, for consciousness, for he writes: 'I hereby declare that YES, my theory is a theory of consciousness. Anyone or anything

experiences and what he calls 'conscious beliefs and desires'. I take it that the latter are beliefs and desires which we know we have. Conscious experiences, in contrast, need not be experiences which we know we have.

[29] Dennett, *Consciousness Explained*, 193.
[30] Ibid. 228.

that has such a virtual machine as its control system is conscious in the fullest sense, and is conscious *because* it has such a virtual machine.'[31] However, he also insists that consciousness is not 'a special all-or-nothing property that sunders the universe into two vastly different categories'. Language—the dominant component of the Joycean machine—does mark 'a particularly dramatic increase in imaginative range, versatility, and self-control', but these powers 'do not have the *further* power of turning on some special inner light that would otherwise be off'.[32] That last remark is surely correct. The metaphor of the inner light makes sense only if there is also an inner spectator, and we must all join him and Ryle in rejecting those metaphors. But now it is clear that our original impression was mistaken. In supposing that he maintained that possession of a Joycean machine was necessary for consciousness, we overlooked the crucial phrase 'in the fullest sense'. In fact he seems to be committed only to the view that language is necessary for consciousness of a *human* kind. Since it is undeniable that language makes a colossal difference to our experience and ways of thinking, and seems necessary for many of the kinds of beliefs and desires we express, that view would be hard to challenge. Certainly it poses no threat to my own. However, one or two further comments will be useful.

Consider first the question of cognitive architecture. Dennett's Joycean machine consists of a serial virtual machine imposed on hardware with a parallel architecture. But anything a parallel machine can do can in principle be done by a serial machine, as he himself points out.[33] So that feature cannot be definitive of a human type of consciousness, even though it is a matter of great interest from the scientific point of view. Again, any virtual machinery can be hard-wired, as Dennett also points out. So the Joycean machine's being virtual cannot be definitive of a human type of consciousness either. In short, the architecture of the Joycean machine is beside the point if the aim is to do useful work on the philosophical problems of consciousness.

Now let us consider how serious is the claim that human consciousness involves possession of a Joycean *machine*. Merely to describe it as a 'system of habits' is to make no commitment to

---

[31] Ibid. 281.
[32] Ibid. 447.
[33] See ibid. 217 f.

its being a machine in any tight sense. But without such a commitment, what is offered as a theory of consciousness boils down
to the claim that it consists in *behaving* like a language-user. And
I have already explained, with the aid of the examples of the
pantomime horse, the GIANT, and the Machine Table robot, why I
think that position fails. Producing the right patterns of behaviour
is not enough: the nature of the internal processing matters.[34] If
on the other hand a system has the right patterns of internal
processing, so that it has the Basic Package in the realistic sense,
and some perceptual information acts directly on its assessment
processes, then even if it has no language, some of its internal
processes have characters for it. I have explained why I think this
entails it has conscious perceptual experience.

Dennett anticipates an objection: 'After all, a von Neumann
machine is entirely unconscious; why should implementing it—or
something like it: a Joycean machine—be any more conscious?'
His reply is that 'the von Neumann machine, by being wired up
from the outset that way, . . . didn't have to become the object of
its own elaborate perceptual systems. The workings of the Joycean
machine, on the other hand, are just as "visible" and "audible" to
it as any of the things in the external world that it is designed to
perceive—for the simple reason that they have much of the same
perceptual machinery focused on them'.[35] This is puzzling. Certainly we language-users see and hear our own verbal behaviour
(though not of course the internal 'workings' that give rise to it).
But seeing and hearing our verbal behaviour is just a special case
of seeing and hearing our behaviour in general. So it cannot
possibly produce conscious perceptual experience in a subject

---

[34] Would Dennett agree? Does he accept what Block calls 'psychologism', or is
he a behaviourist after all? In *Consciousness Explained* he briefly considers that
question and replies that he is 'happy to endorse the answer that Wittgenstein gave
to it' (462). But Wittgenstein hardly made his position crystal clear. Several of
Dennett's remarks appear to commit him to a form of behaviourism e.g. 'When
you say "*This* is my quale," what you are singling out, or referring to, *whether you
realize it or not*, is your idiosyncratic complex of dispositions' (ibid. 389. See also
311, 398). However, two factors seem to have made the question marginal for
him: his strong concern to discover the way human minds actually work, and his
recognition of the overwhelming likelihood that any other actually conscious
beings are likely to be organized in ways that would compel us to count them as
genuinely intelligent (ibid. cf. 438). I think his stern rejection of anything like the
notion of raw feeling deprives him of a basis for a satisfactory treatment of the
issue.

[35] Dennett, *Consciousness Explained*, 225 f.

which lacks it. At any rate I know of no reason to suppose it could. On my account infants who are just starting to acquire language have the Basic Package, and so have conscious perceptual experiences. It surely calls for some gritting of teeth to maintain that they lack conscious experience until after they have learnt to talk. Of course language transforms our lives, and indeed our consciousness. But I know of no plausible argument to show that it actually produces consciousness in the sense that concerns us.

5.7 BLINDSIGHT

Now for the puzzling case of blindsight. Damage to the visual cortex causes blindness, the size and shape of the area of blindness corresponding to the area damaged. Usually the victims report no visual sensation in the affected areas. However, a small number can within limits detect and discriminate things presented there. For example, they can tell when a light is shining, point to a spot of light, distinguish between differently orientated stripes, and tell the difference between 'O' and 'X'. Yet they still deny that they can actually see things presented inside their blind areas. Weiskrantz coined the term 'blindsight' for this phenomenon. He writes:

D.B. was questioned repeatedly about his vision in his left half-field. Most commonly he said that he saw nothing at all. If pressed, he might say in some tests, but by no means all, that he perhaps had a 'feeling' that a stimulus was approaching or receding, or was 'smooth' (the O) or 'jagged' (the X). But always he stressed that he saw nothing in the sense of 'seeing', that typically he was guessing, and was at a loss for words to describe any conscious perception.[36]

Such cases may at first appear to be a counter-example to my position. A closer look shows that they are either neutral or actually support it. Evidently blindsight subjects acquire *information* about things in the affected area, in spite of their denials that they *see* things there. But it is also evident that they do not acquire as much information as normally sighted subjects do. Nor, it seems, does this information generally act directly on their main

[36] L. Weiskrantz, *Blindsight*, 31.

assessment processes as it does in the case of normally sighted people.

All the blindsight subjects discussed by Weiskrantz display markedly limited powers to detect and discriminate things presented in their blind fields, compared with people with normal vision, or with themselves as regards the unaffected areas of their visual fields. (If this were not so, it is hard to see why damage to the striate cortex should have been supposed to have any effect on vision at all.) They respond only to relatively gross stimuli: bright lights and bold, strongly contrasting shapes (though perhaps detection of movement is an exception). Indeed, it is suggested that all they are actually sensitive to in their blind fields is the location and movement of things. If that is so, their insistence that they have no visual experiences of things in the affected areas seems quite compatible with my position. For information about location, movement, and some other features would fall quite a lot short of the mass of information that is provided by normal vision. It would not be like normal vision, or indeed like any other kind of sensory experience. So for that reason alone, perhaps, it might not be recognizable as sensory experience at all—even if it was.

However, this suggestion is not altogether satisfying. The trouble is that Weiskrantz's subject D.B., although he occasionally reports some rather puzzling kinds of experience in his blind field, very often reports absolutely no experience of any sort whatever. He just 'guesses'. Moreover, Weiskrantz reports, 'performance in the absence of any subjective experience can be superior to that resulting from stimuli placed in a "live" part of the field'.[37] To do justice to these reports it seems we need to recall the second striking feature of blindsight subjects. In order to bring out the information they have, they need to be prompted, often quite insistently. Typically they have to be asked to 'guess' whether such-and-such a kind of thing is present; and often they are given only a 'forced choice' between just two or three specified alternatives. In this respect the situation resembles that of unconscious perception, or of people who don't trust their memory yet still remember quite a lot. They have to be prompted, even told

---

[37] Ibid. 97. He explains that by 'live' part of the field he is referring to parts of the blind field where the subject reports some kind of experience.

just to guess. The information is there, but it is stored away, not available for immediate use. In this way blindsight subjects fall short of satisfying the conditions I have laid down for conscious perceptual experience. The information is *not* in my sense acting directly on their main assessment processes. Either way, then, blindsight is not after all a counter-example to my position.

5.8 WHY THERE COULDN'T BE ZOMBIES

Yet since perceptual information can be collected without conscious awareness, as the cases of subliminal perception and blindsight demonstrate, what guarantees that my stickleback is conscious? Why shouldn't something with the Basic Package still lack raw feeling, even if some of its perceptual information acted directly on its main assessment processes? I have already set out my main reasons against that suggestion: if those conditions are satisfied, then there are internal processes which have characters for the system, in which case the system has raw feeling. Shortly I will offer an argument which highlights the key considerations. Notice first, though, that in any case blindsight hardly yields a plausible model. It is true that the blindsight subject acquires some information about things in the affected area. But as we saw, it is markedly less than a person with normal vision would have acquired. In order to look like a serious counter-example, therefore, the suggestion would have to be that there might be a sort of generalized blindsight: a condition *like* blindsight but applying to the whole of the system's perception, when the subject acquired exactly the same information as a normally sighted person— information which was acting on its main assessment processes just as it is for the normally sighted person. But I have been arguing that satisfaction of those conditions would be sufficient for perceptual consciousness. So the claim that the suggested possibility was genuine would amount to no more than a blank denial of my position.

Of course there may be types of processing which are necessary for perceptual consciousness and not covered by my description, broad though that is. If so, I shall be glad to learn what they are. But at any rate the generalized quasi-blindsight suggestion merely begs the question. In fact it looks like a variant of our old friend, the Zombie idea. I now set out an argument to show that the alleged possibility is not genuine.

The Zombie idea was that there could be organisms exactly like ourselves in all physically describable respects, including the minutest details of their internal processing, yet for which, in Iris Murdoch's telling phrase, all was 'silent and dark within'.[38] I will argue that this description involves a contradiction. To start with, it is clear that Zombies would have the Basic Package even when that is construed in the realistic way explained in the last chapter. They would acquire, store, and use information about their surroundings. Also, incoming perceptual information would be acting directly on their main assessment processes. For by definition their internal processing, under its purely physical description, is exactly as physicalists suppose our own to be. (Remember that if perceptual information were *not* acting directly on their main assessment processes, that would show up in their behaviour.) So if Zombies still lacked something necessary for perceptual consciousness, that non-physical thing, *x*, would have to have the following properties:

(i) Adding *x* to a Zombie's constitution would transform it from something without raw feeling into something with raw feeling, and in particular into a subject of perceptual consciousness.

(ii) Adding *x* to a Zombie's constitution would make no difference to its actual behaviour or to its capacities to interact with its surroundings and control its behaviour as effectively as we do. Indeed it would have no effects at all on the physical processes inside it.

[38] Iris Murdoch, arguing against behaviourism in *The Sovereignty of Good*, 13. (Remember that Zombies are defined to be *as physicalists suppose we are*, not as Cartesians suppose we are. See 3.1 and 3.2.) Humphrey tells a story about our ancestors who were 'not conscious.... They were no doubt percipient, intelligent, complexly motivated creatures, whose internal control mechanisms were in many respects the equals of our own. But... they had no way of looking in upon the mechanism.... Their brains would receive and process information from their sense-organs without their minds being conscious of any accompanying sensation...' (*Consciousness Regained*, 48 f.). Even though he entitles this piece a 'Just-So Story', he seems to regard this as plausible factual speculation: see ibid. 53. If the following argument works at all, it shows that such creatures are impossible. (In his later work, *A History of the Mind*, he seems to agree: see 207–16.)

Now, as I use the word 'information'—and surely I am not being
eccentric about it—in any given situation a Zombie would receive
absolutely all the information it would have received if it had had
x. *The presence or absence of* x *would make no difference to its
acquisition of information.* This is a crucial point, and some
readers may feel that it begs the question. They might insist
that only organisms with *x* really receive information, really
are subjects. After all, on their view *x* makes all the difference.
However, information is for a system only if the system can *use* it.
That is surely indisputable. In that case *x* could have no bearing
on whether or not a Zombie received information which was for
it. This is guaranteed by property (ii): the presence of *x* would
make no difference to what a Zombie could do, to its capacities.
Being inert with respect to physical processes, *x* could not affect
behaviour and hence could not endow a Zombie with usable
information it didn't have already. Since we human beings—
who must be supposed to possess *x* on the present suggestion—
certainly do acquire and use information, it follows that *x* has
nothing to do with our acquisition of information. Hence Zombies
also acquire and use all the information we do—all the information they would have acquired if they had had *x*, since *x* has no
bearing on the matter.

In sharp contrast to *x*, raw feeling has a highly important
bearing on the information we acquire, at any rate on the information we acquire through conscious perception. It plays a
decisive role in the causal network. The occurrence of raw feeling
ensures that we get information about various perceptible features
of the things we encounter. For example, one particular type of
raw feeling, the sort which typically occurs when I see a ripe
tomato, has a great deal to do with my ability to distinguish
visually between ripe and unripe tomatoes. Since *x* could have
nothing to do with the acquisition of information, and raw feeling
has a great deal to do with it, *x* could not possibly have both
property (i) and property (ii). Each excludes the other. But *x* must
have both properties if Zombies are possible. Therefore Zombies
are not possible.

In this argument I have of course assumed that the notion of
raw feeling is acceptable, and that if Zombies had it, they would
have full perceptual consciousness. To that extent the argument
is *ad hominem*. However, if that assumption is challenged by

those who maintain that Zombies are possible, they owe us an explanation of what it is that Zombies might be lacking, if not raw feeling. They must make sense of a *rival* notion. But we have already noted two devastating objections to any such rival notions. First, unlike the notion of raw feeling, any notion which permits even the bare possibility of Zombies entails dualism, hence absolute privacy, and is therefore vulnerable to Wittgenstein's private language argument. Second, the Zombie possibility entails epiphenomenalism (or parallelism) and is therefore vulnerable to the arguments of section 1.8. I suggest that such a notion affords nothing of value which is not afforded by the notion of raw feeling. However, sceptics are invited to suspend judgement until they have considered the discussions in the following two chapters.

5.9   IS CONSCIOUSNESS ALL-OR-NOTHING?

In nature there must be a vast number of species as to which it is indeterminate whether or not they have the Basic Package. No doubt our nearest animal relatives, the primates, have it. No doubt whales and dolphins have it too; and the drift of my argument is to the effect that humbler creatures also have it—cats and dogs, birds and fish. For some people the idea that such creatures are conscious may be hard to take. In any case, it seems unlikely that the question whether something has the Basic Package always has a determinate answer. The definition is vague, and there is a vast number of species which behave in all kinds of ways, so there must be many borderline cases.

On the other hand, consciousness may seem to be all-or-nothing. Certainly it is often assumed to be so. So if my position implies that there are many indeterminate cases, it conflicts with this widespread assumption. Indeed, the idea of indeterminate cases may seem problematic. If you confine yourself to the 'objective' or topic-neutral approach, studying animals as an outside observer, there may be no problem. The trouble arises when you face up to the implications of ascribing consciousness. If a creature is conscious, there is something it is like to be it. It has its own point of view, however limited. And when you think in those 'subjective' terms, it is hard to see how consciousness could be anything but either all there, or completely absent. How could there be *neither* determinately something it's like to be this creature, *nor*, determinately, anything of the sort?

Three considerations help to mitigate the apparent harshness of this position. The first is that the objection draws heavily on our intuitions of what is possible, when we know how misleading intuitions can be. But perhaps that consideration is too moralistic. The second is more to the point.

If creatures very different from ourselves are conscious, their consciousness can be expected to be very different from our own. Two factors are relevant: the types of stimulations they are sensitive to, and the richness of the information they receive. For example, fish have 'lateral lines' which give them information about water pressure, bats have echolocation, some snakes have directionally sensitive infra-red detectors, while the octopus appears to be colour-blind. If we are normal human perceivers, a wealth of information reaches us via several senses, each conveying information in several dimensions. In particular, of course, the volume and variety of the visual information we can take in at an instant is amazing. But a smaller set of senses, each conveying a range of information much more restricted than our own, can also provide perceptual consciousness and the informational basis for a possible life. (The example of deaf and blind people shows this: no need to think of non-human animals.) For some species, there also seems no reason why perceptual consciousness should not be both restricted in quality when compared with ours, and also intermittent. What it is like to be a creature of that kind would evidently be very different from what it is like to be someone with normal human perception. Their dim lights may not be vastly different from the total absence of consciousness.

The third consideration, which I think reinforces and extends the second, is that the reported experiences of Weiskrantz's blindsight subject suggest that he himself, D.B., had some difficulty in telling whether or not he was having experiences in the 'blind' portion of his visual field. As we noticed, he said he 'perhaps had a "feeling" that a stimulus was approaching or receding'.[39] Such a difficulty suggests that the idea of it being indeterminate whether or not a creature has perceptual consciousness is, after all, not

[39] Weiskrantz, *Blindsight*, 31.

absurd. At any rate, I suggest that this and the other two points show that the case for perceptual consciousness as an all-or-nothing property is less than compelling.[40]

5.10 SUBJECTS OF RAW FEELING

I have been trying to make clear what it takes for something to be a subject of conscious perceptual experience—clear *enough*, since we saw in Chapter 3 that we need only enough explanation to remove the philosophical perplexities associated with consciousness. In particular we need only enough to let us understand how the Strict Implication thesis could hold. I have argued that being a conscious subject takes less than it would need on some accounts, more than it would on others. It does not need the capacity to bring one's mental states under the sorts of concepts we associate with ordinary human language. There is no reason why many kinds of non-human animal should not be subjects of conscious experience. But it does require the subject to have the Basic Package understood in the realistic way explained earlier. So some varieties of robot, together with systems like the pantomime horse and the GIANT, are also ruled out. And since organizations, such as the United States, seem to have nothing which could constitute information acting directly on their main assessment processes, rather than going to the equivalent of memory, they too fail—for that reason alone—to qualify as conscious subjects. That rules out one otherwise promising series of apparent counter-examples. On the other hand, nothing I have said rules out the possibility of conscious computer-controlled robots, whether language-using or not.

Although all subjects of conscious perceptual experience are also subjects of raw feeling, I suggested in Chapter 2 that the converse does not hold. There is little chance of encountering actual examples; but in principle it seemed there could be systems which were subjects of raw feeling but not of perceptual experience. Brains in vats were one example. If the account of perceptual consciousness offered in this chapter is satisfactory, that suggestion was correct. For what lies at the heart of per-

---

[40] Dennett takes a similar line. See *Consciousness Explained*, 447 f.

ceptual consciousness—raw feeling, or the occurrence of processes with a certain character for the system—is not *necessarily* linked with its typical external causes or effects. In normal perceivers, raw feeling has a vital role in the causal network. But conceivably it could occur independently of its typical causes and effects. Nor, in that case, would a neuroanatomical description convey all that was going on. Such descriptions would omit the highly interesting fact that the firings of neurones also constituted episodes of raw feeling, of a subject it is like something to be. Recall the particular case of Boris, introduced in Chapter 2. If in the period of time in question I had the raw feels I usually have when I see a ripe tomato, then Boris would have those raw feels too. So in such favourable circumstances as those, we could start from purely physiological information about an isolated vat-brain and, knowing what it takes to be a subject of raw feeling, arrive at the justified conclusion that it was the brain of such a subject.

Even in normal subjects, raw feeling is not exhausted by its occurrence in perceptual experience. Dream imagery involves raw feeling, and so does much waking imagery, voluntary or involuntary. I will not attempt to provide sharp boundaries for the application of an essentially vague concept. I introduced it in order to identify an area of continuing philosophical perplexity. The classification of varieties of inner states need not concern us except as far as it helps to remove that perplexity. Still, I will say a little about what it is for something to be a subject of raw feeling in general—but only a little, since I think that, with one or two exceptions to be examined in the next two chapters, the main sources of philosophical trouble have already been dealt with.

In general I suggest that a system is a subject of raw feeling if it is either a subject of conscious perceptual experience or its internal processes are in certain ways similar to those of a subject of conscious perceptual experience. The question of what it is to be such a subject has been dealt with already, so we need to decide what are the relevant kinds of similarity. There seem to be two ways in which the internal processes may be relevantly similar.

The first is if they are the internal processes of a system which needs only to be suitably connected to a body under its control, and to stand in the right relations to the outside world, in order to constitute the controlling component of a subject of conscious perceptual experience. Suitably stimulated brains in vats would satisfy this condition, as would stand-alone computers programmed (if possible) to provide the 'brains' of robots with the Basic Package and directly active perceptual information. Evidently this definition works only on the assumption that we have a clear enough conception of what can be counted as the 'controlling component' of a subject of conscious perceptual experience. The brain is a paradigm case, and so is the robot's controlling computer system. No doubt there are hard cases too; but we know we are dealing with vague concepts.

The second way the internal processes may be relevantly similar is if, while not actually caused by external objects as in the case of genuine conscious perceptual experience, they act directly on the system's assessment processes as they would have done if they had been so caused. Something like this idea has been with us at least since the time of Aristotle.[41] Recall the vital point about the relevant sorts of directly active processes in a system with the Basic Package. They constitute the acquisition of rich perceptual information because they immediately put the system in a position to produce certain sorts of behaviour (recognitional behaviour, for example, or behaviour such as picking coins out from among pebbles). Now, the capacity to produce such behaviour in turn depends on the system's having its own special schemes of classification, interpretation, and assessment. The incoming information is not independent of the sorts of classification, interpretation, and assessment which the system operates with. (Remember the frog.) But given a system with a particular scheme of that general sort, the way the incoming directly active processes are themselves caused cannot make a difference. So if they are non-standardly caused, it will be for the subject, other things being equal, as if they had been standardly caused. In this way there can be raw feeling outside perception. Hallucinatory experiences and some kinds of illusions are examples. There can also be raw feeling in systems which altogether lack perception, such as brains in vats.

Sensations, for example pains, feelings of nausea, of heat and of cold, involve raw feeling. This too seems to raise no special problems from our point of view. It seems that sensation can be construed as a variety of perception in some cases, and as

---

[41] Aristotle remarks: 'imagination [will be] a movement occurring as a result of sense-perception.... imaginations persist and are similar to perception...' (*De Anima*, 428b30 ff.).

resembling perception in the rest. Pain, for example, can be regarded as a kind of perception of (typically) harmful bodily states, such as those resulting from injury. Rather as the rich information coming from arrays of retinal cells enables us to direct our attention to parts of the external world, and behave appropriately, so the information coming from arrays of pain receptors over the body enables us to direct our attention to the affected parts, and take appropriate action towards them. But again, as with external perception, there is scope for the normally informative processes to be activated in some non-standard way. Then they create misinformation, as with 'phantom limbs'.[42] But there is no necessity to construe all sensation on the model of perception. You might perhaps regard some cases of nausea as a kind of perception of, for example, the state of the subject's digestive system. But other cases are not easily seen as perception. Nausea resulting from sickening thoughts is one example; yet it resembles perception because it resembles the first kind of nausea.

The possibility that processes associated with interpretation may themselves creatively originate something like the activity that would normally have been caused by what I am calling the 'directly active' processes provides for a whole range of illusions, more or less resembling actual experiences. But since I am chiefly concerned only to explain how there can be raw feeling in general, not to explore all its varieties, I will not pursue that particular question. There is, however, one more variety which I want to mention: dreaming. It may seem to pose a special problem. How can the raw feeling involved in dreaming fit my account, when it seems extremely dubious that the dreamer's 'main assessment processes' are brought into play? The irrationality of dreams suggests that not much assessment is involved, if any. My tentative suggestion is that although the main assessment processes do not generally function to their full capacity in dreams, they are still in action. After all, we are capable of pretty crazy assessments when tired or drugged, so the irrationality of our dream-thoughts is not decisive. Clearly they can operate with different degrees of efficiency. More could be said; but I see no insuperable difficulty here.

---

[42] See e.g. R. Melzack, 'Phantom Limbs'. He emphasizes the role of what I am calling the processes of interpretation and assessment, where activity may arise even in the absence of external stimulation.

That completes my account of what it is for something to be a subject of raw feeling. A system is a subject of raw feeling if it is either a subject of conscious perceptual experience or its internal processes are similar to those of a subject of conscious perceptual experience in the ways I have explained. Varieties of raw feeling other than those involved in perception have also been found to be explicable in terms of my account.

The approach taken in this chapter has been broadly 'functionalist'. Since that word is more of a banner than a name for a specific theory, I will say a little more about what I understand by it. A minimal statement of functionalism might go as follows:

> To be a subject of mental states is to be capable of being in any of a range of internal states of certain kinds, which are sensitive to inputs from the environment, interact among themselves, and cause behaviour. What characterizes a particular mental state is its functional role: its relative position in this system of possible inputs, possible other states, and possible outputs. Given that a system satisfies these conditions, and assuming the details can be filled in satisfactorily, any other features it may have are irrelevant to whether it has mental states.

Of course, that is hardly informative except for indicating the general form of functionalist accounts of the mind. Much depends on what the 'certain kinds' are and in what terms they are to be specified. And further specifications must be filled in as well, otherwise almost any object would be counted as having mental states—pebbles, stars, turnips, what have you. Evidently the different ways of completing the functionalist account provide one basis for distinguishing varieties of functionalism. Is the account rooted in the conceptual scheme of science or is it content to use folk-psychological concepts? What are the functions in question, and how are they to be specified? In terms of typical causes and effects? (These in turn may be remote from, or close to, the sense-receptors. Are they to be rabbits or leporiform images?) In terms of evolutionary role? In information processing terms? The sense in which my own approach is broadly functionalist is that I have followed Armstrong, Dennett, and many others in attempting to make the nature of conscious experience intelligible by means of such notions as cause and, especially, information. Not that the relevant notion of information has been taken for granted—a familiar sort of complaint against functionalist accounts of the mind. On the contrary, it has been explained in terms of two unproblematic notions: those of changes inside a system, and of discriminatory and other behavioural capacities modified by such changes. The stickleback model provided a crude illustration of the sorts of changes which might constitute the acquisition and processing of information. To end the chapter I want to emphasize two points.

First, unlike some varieties of functionalism, this approach does not insist that statements about conscious experience must be translatable into, or even logically equivalent to, statements about functions. Second, the view defended here does not absolutely require any particular functions to be actually performed in order for there to be raw feeling. Take the extreme case of the isolated vat-brain. Its isolation prevents our describing its internal processes as performing any functions except, perhaps, whatever functions can be characterized in terms of purely internal relationships among its components. All the same it is on my account the brain of a subject of raw feeling: there is something it is like to be it. That is because the occurrence of raw feeling—in sharp contrast to the occurrence of contentful thoughts—is entirely determined by what goes on inside the brain, and this brain is relevantly like that of an ordinary human being. What makes for raw feeling is not the fact that *functions* are performed, if they are. It is the fact that certain sorts of *processes* are going on. In normal cases those processes may well be identifiable on the basis of the functions they perform. More importantly, the fact that they are processes of raw feeling is intelligible to us on account of our understanding of the kinds of functions they perform, or are apt to perform. That is why the account offered in this chapter works (assuming it does work). But raw feeling does not require the actual performance of any functions. In particular it does not require the processing of information. Talking in terms of information has helped to make it intelligible how a purely physical system could be a subject of conscious perceptual experience, hence of raw feeling. But since even a brain in a vat can be that of a subject of raw feeling, there can be raw feeling without the processing of information.

6

The Character of Raw Feeling

My approach is broadly functionalist, but the inverted spectrum looks like a serious threat to it. The two different ways of seeing colours would seem to perform exactly the same functions. At any rate, like the positive and the negative of a film, they would perform exactly the same informational functions. So how could there really be two different ways of seeing colours? If I don't want to give up my whole approach, it may well look as if I must give up the claim that the inverted spectrum possibility is genuine. This apparent dilemma has forced some theorists into uncomfortable intellectual contortions. In fact, though, far from being a difficulty, the inverted spectrum idea, properly understood, flows naturally from it. It helps us towards a satisfyingly unified grasp of how raw feeling can have different characters—without involving an impenetrable privacy, or 'figment', or any kind of Cartesianism. So if there are independent reasons for accepting the inverted spectrum idea, or more strictly the Transformation thesis, they tend if anything to reinforce the validity of the approach.

After stating the problem I will examine what seems to be the most popular way of dealing with it among those who accept the inverted spectrum idea: the 'bald' psychophysical identity theory. I will also examine a version of this position which exploits a notion of 'inner sense'. In spite of its popularity, we shall find that this position is untenable. The rest of the chapter will be chiefly concerned to show how the approach outlined earlier provides for an unproblematic treatment of the Transformation thesis.

6.1 WHAT SEEMS TO BE THE TROUBLE

If you accept the notion of raw feeling, you will accept that there is a great difference between the total pattern of the raw feels you have when you see the full moon on a dark night, and the pattern you have when you see a dark disc silhouetted against the bright sky. And if the inverted spectrum idea is sound, it is at any rate logically possible that when both of us were looking at the moon together, your raw feels should have had the first pattern while mine had the second—and that this difference was just one instance of an overall 'positive–negative' difference in our visual raw feels whenever we were in the same perceptual situations. Yet because this difference had existed from birth it could not show up in our behaviour or behavioural capacities.[1]

There may seem no great problem about accepting the possibility of such a difference. Something analogous to 'crossed wires' might do the trick, as we noticed in Chapter 2. But now recall the Swiss Cheese principle. Relatively crossed wires would certainly constitute a physical difference between you and me. But the Swiss Cheese principle tells us that a physical difference *by itself* cannot make a difference in what it is like for subjects. And it is at any rate hard to see how crossed wires could amount to a difference that made a relevant difference. With or without crossed wires the processes inside the system would perform exactly the same informational functions—and, it seems, the same other functions too. So if we accept the Swiss Cheese principle, how can we insist on the inverted spectrum possibility?

6.2 WHY THE BALD IDENTITY THEORY WON'T HELP

A popular way of dealing with this problem today is to retain a functionalist approach to the mind in general but fall back on bald assertions of psychophysical identity for the case of raw feels. This hybrid doctrine is encapsulated in Putnam's words:

the most plausible move for a functionalist to make if such cases are really possible is to say, 'Yes, but the "qualitative character" is just the physical realization.' And to say that for this special kind of psychological property, for qualities, the older form of the identity theory was the right one.[2]

---

[1] Bear in mind that although the negative of a brightly lit scene is dark, it conveys all the contrasts which enable us to find our way about. Too much light (black negative) would leave us as helpless as too little (white negative).

[2] H. Putnam, *Reason, Truth and History*, 81. See also K. V. Wilkes, *Physicalism*, 101, 103; S. Shoemaker, 'The Inverted Spectrum'; P. M. and P. S. Churchland,

In spite of its plausibility and widespread popularity, we shall see that this hybrid doctrine is fundamentally mistaken.

Putnam invokes the 'older form of the identity theory'. But when you recall the history of the identity theory and the development of functionalism, his suggestion is odd. The chief motive for insisting on psychophysical identities was ontological: if sensations are brain processes we don't have to posit anything over and above the physical. But the mere assertion that such identities held was unsatisfactory. The identity statements might be true, but their truth was at any rate not obvious. Some explanation was still required of what it was about a particular physical state which made it an instance of a certain mental state. Hence the attractions of the view that what characterizes a mental state is its role in the causation of behaviour and other mental states.[3] Putnam took a rather different approach, impressed as he was by parallels between the mind–body distinction and the hardware–software distinction in computing. If any such functionalist conception is right, it makes the identity statements intelligible. But that is why the hybrid doctrine is so puzzling.[4] If having mental states is just a matter of having the right sort of functional organization, then the ontological purpose of asserting the identities is better served by the idea of physical realization. Functionalism removes the motivation for asserting psychophysical identities.[5]

But it is more than just odd to find functionalists adopting this hybrid theory and baldly asserting that raw feels are identical with certain brain processes. On one interpretation it is inconsistent. For functionalism entails the Swiss Cheese principle. (The converse is not true, if only because behaviourists can endorse the

---

'Functionalism, Qualia, and Intentionality'; P. M. Churchland, 'Reduction, Qualia, and the Direct Introspection of Brain States'; G. Graham and G. L. Stephen, 'Are Qualia a Pain in the Neck for Functionalists?'; J. C. Maloney, 'About Being a Bat'; E. Sober, 'Panglossian Functionalism and the Philosophy of Mind'; M. Tye, 'The Subjective Qualities of Experience'.

[3] For this view, see J. J. C. Smart, 'Sensations and Brain Processes'; D. M. Armstrong, *A Materialist Theory of the Mind*; and D. Lewis, 'Psychophysical and Theoretical Identifications'. For earlier versions, see R. Carnap, *The Unity of Science*, 76–92, and M. Schlick, 'Meaning and Verification'.

[4] It was Putnam who pointed out on another occasion that if the functionalist conception of mental states is correct, there is no point in bothering about psychophysical identities anyway: H. Putnam, 'Minds and Machines'. For a more systematic statement, see also his 'Philosophy and Our Mental Life'.

[5] See R. Kirk, 'Physicalism, Identity and Strict Implication'.

Swiss Cheese principle without endorsing functionalism.) And this principle entails that even if the raw feels involved in all actual pains are constituted by or realized in C-fibre firings (to use the traditional incorrect example), there are possible worlds where raw feels of the same kinds—ones with exactly the same character—are constituted by something different. So functionalism entails that having raw feels of that kind *cannot* be identical with C-fibre firings. At any rate it cannot be identical with them if Fs are type-identical with Gs only if every possible instance of an F is an instance of a G—in other words, if the identity thesis is supposed to give us a grasp of the nature of the things in question.

You might hold that it is sufficient for the identity of Fs and Gs that every *actual* instance of an F is an instance of a G, in which case the hybrid functionalist-cum-identity doctrine is not actually inconsistent. Unfortunately that interpretation lands the doctrine in the same trouble as the original identity theory. If you insist on using the word 'identity' to express the above point about pains, you cannot also hold that this claim gives their nature. You are still up against the intelligibility gap. So you cannot hold that your identity claim answers the sort of question that needs answering: the question of what it is about this C-fibre firing, for example, which makes it a case of pain. Merely asserting the alleged identities leaves all the main philosophical work still to be done.

Here it is instructive to notice a claim of Lycan's in his book *Consciousness*. He starts by insisting on a sharp distinction between a role and the occupant of that role. But he urges that it is a mistake to see this perfectly sound distinction as warranting the erroneous dogma of 'Two-Levelism': that Nature itself is divided into two levels, the physical and the functional. On the contrary, he maintains, there is in fact 'a multiple *hierarchy* of levels of nature, each level marked by nexus of nomic generalizations and supervenient on all those levels below it on the continuum'.[6] So the role/occupant distinction is relative. For example, at one level of nature we regard neurones as role-occupants: as what actually perform certain information-processing functions. But if we focus on a lower level, perhaps the molecular, then being a neurone is itself the performance of a role.[7]

---

[6] W. Lycan, *Consciousness*, 38.
[7] See ibid. 58 f. Compare Aristotle's relativization of the form–matter distinction.

These points are at least persuasive, and I won't challenge them. But Lycan goes further, concluding that the Identity Theory is 'just an empirically special case of Functionalism, one that (implausibly) locates all mental states at the same very low level of institutional abstraction—the neuroanatomical'. He claims that, contrary to what 'blind Two-Levelism' has suggested, 'there should be no purely conceptual or philosophical objections that apply to Functionalism that do not apply to the Identity Theory or vice versa, even if one is empirically less reasonable than the other'.[8] So he implies that there can only be empirical grounds, at most, for attacking the psychophysical identity theory while defending functionalism. But his assumptions are open to question. Functionalism surely isn't just the doctrine that mental states are identical with states performing certain roles. It is normally also taken to make claims about the level or type of description that applies to those roles. The idea may be summarized thus:

F. Mental states are states that perform roles describable at some relatively high level, and in certain fairly abstract, not narrowly physical terms (causal or information-processing terms, for example).

Which level and which terms are appropriate depends on the type of functionalism (see later). But it is of the essence that both level and terms are so chosen that they leave it open which physical descriptions apply. They even leave it open whether the system is physical or involves special spiritual ingredients. The psychophysical identity theory, on the other hand, is to the effect that:

I. Mental states are states specifiable in a recognizably physical vocabulary—perhaps that of neuroanatomy, perhaps even that of physics.

Thus the identity theory excludes even the possibility that mental states should have non-physical constituents.

There is no need to be drawn into a dispute over the boundaries of the philosophical or the conceptual. Suppose functionalism does have the implications roughly summarized in (F). Then Lycan has not shown that any conceptual or philosophical objections to the psychophysical identity theory (I) will automatically also apply

[8] Ibid. 59.

to functionalism. Given these elaborations of the two doctrines in question, his claim seems untenable.

And in fact the Swiss Cheese principle—my defence of which I take to be largely conceptual or philosophical—undermines (I) but not (F). As we have noticed, functionalism, hence (F), actually entails the Swiss Cheese principle. But evidently (I) is inconsistent with it. So the hybrid or half-hearted variety of functionalism advocated by Putnam and others is not a coherent response to the apparent challenge posed by the Transformation thesis.

6.3 FAILURE OF THE 'INNER SENSE' APPROACH

Some eliminativists concede that the ordinary concepts they reject still manage to pick out features of reality.[9] Since they find those concepts so confused it may seem a mistake to tax them with the intelligibility gap: to complain that they have not explained how whatever the concepts pick out can be intelligibly said to be identical with something physical. The complaint may sound especially inept when these eliminativists make a point of saying that folk-psychological concepts don't pick out natural kinds. Why shouldn't they confine themselves to the simple claim that in the special case of qualia, each individual instance is identical with some physical property?

But there is no way out here. As the quotation from Putnam illustrates, bald assertions of psychophysical identity are a response to the assumption that the inverted spectrum possibility is genuine. In order for that assumption to be intelligible, the ordinary concepts employed to describe that possibility in the first place must make some sense. So bald identity theorists can hardly claim exemption from the intelligibility gap objection. To illustrate these and related points I will examine the hybrid functionalism which was suggested by Paul and Patricia Churchland in their article 'Functionalism, Qualia, and Intentionality'.[10] Popular though their approach is, we shall see that it cannot work.

[9] See e.g. W. V. Quine, *Word and Object*, 264–6; P. M. and P. S. Churchland, 'Functionalism, Qualia, and Intentionality'.
[10] See also P. M. Churchland, 'Reduction, Qualia, and the Direct Introspection of Brain States'. Note that the Churchlands do not actually commit themselves to the view they defend in their article.

The Churchlands are among those who in effect dismiss the demand for statements of the alleged identities to be made intelligible. They propose to shift the responsibility on to the neurosciences. 'On the view argued here, the nature of specific qualia will be revealed by neurophysiology, neurochemistry, and neurophysics.'[11] However, a study of their suggestions reveals that this cannot be true—or at any rate not in the sense in which the inverted spectrum possibility has to do with qualia. (For the present let us ignore differences between what they mean by 'qualia' and what I mean by 'raw feels': see below.) Their conception of the nature of qualia in itself prevents bald identity statements of the kind they recommend from being true at all—regardless of whether the statements belong to psychology or to the neurosciences.

Their proposed solution has two main components. The first is that functionalists should build into the characterization of sensation states the condition that any such state involves an 'intrinsic property' whose presence is detectable by 'our mechanism of introspective discrimination'. Thus they suggest an 'inner sense' story—a relational story like Descartes's, but with purely physical items detected by a purely physical mechanism. The second component deals with the nature of such intrinsic properties and consists of the bald assertion of identities.[12] The intrinsic property alleged to be detectable by our introspective mechanism and said to be identical with some physical property must be supposed to be the sort of quale which is supposedly picked out in stories about transposed qualia. That is the whole point of this 'inner sense' approach.[13] The property is initially picked out by means of ordinary language or folk psychology; then it is said to be identical with something to be picked out by scientific means.

Unfortunately the inner sense story itself rules out anything like this sort of identity. It even rules out correlations between the folk-psychological qualities on the one hand, and the scientifically

[11] P. M. and P. S. Churchland, 'Functionalism, Qualia, and Intentionality', 130.
[12] For similar views, see Graham and Stephen, 'Are Qualia a Pain in the Neck for Functionalists?', and Maloney, 'About Being a Bat'. Graham and Stephen explicitly compare the relation between qualia and inner sense to the relation between trees and outer sense (74).
[13] That this is indeed the point emerges very clearly in P. M. Churchland's 'Reduction, Qualia, and the Direct Introspection of Brain States', where he suggests that we introspect our brain states directly.

characterized objects of our introspective mechanisms on the other. If you accept an inner sense story—any inner sense story, not just the Churchlands' version—you cannot consistently ident-ify raw feels with the physical objects of inner sensing. The inner sense story involves on the one hand a system in the brain capable of picking out physical properties from within some specifiable range, and on the other hand those scientifically identified prop-erties themselves. Let us concede for argument's sake that there are both kinds of things, and let us refer to the latter as 'C-qualia' (Churchland-qualia). Let R be the folk-quale I have now as I look at this red pencil, and let f be the C-quale supposedly identical with R. Exponents of the view under discussion maintain that functionalism is not affected by the inverted spectrum possibility: that a different folk-quale, say G, should have occupied exactly the same functional role as is currently occupied by R. We shall see that this story entails possibilities which undermine its own assertions of identity.

These possibilities arise from the assumed distinctness of C-qualia and the mechanisms which detect them. Given that the mechanisms and the C-qualia are distinct, there must be causal connections between them—otherwise there is no detecting the latter at all, hence no qualia. (No one would maintain that a C-quale unconnected to any introspective mechanism could be identical with a folk-quale.) Via these causal connections a given C-quale will normally combine with the workings of my intro-spective mechanism to produce a certain effect. However, any causal connection can be interfered with. By systematically mod-ifying the connections—transposing and reconnecting nerves, for example, or inserting 'inverters'—it must be possible to make that same C-quale produce a different effect on my introspective mechanism from the one it produces as things are. For example, it must be possible to make an instance of the C-quale f (supposedly identical with my red pencil quale) produce on my introspective mechanism exactly the same effect as would standardly be pro-duced on it by an instance of the C-quale g (standardly caused, *ceteris paribus*, by my seeing a green pencil). Suppose that f is a spiking frequency of 60Hz along a certain neural pathway, and g is a spiking frequency of 100Hz along the same pathway. Then the point is that by inserting a suitable transformer between that pathway and my introspective mechanism, an input of 60Hz could be made to produce the same effect as an input of 100Hz would produce as things are.

This difference in the effect produced on the introspective mechanism will alter the folk-quale. For on the inner sense view, the C-quale must be supposed to *work together* with the introspective mechanism to produce folk-qualia. Neither could do the job by itself. If a C-quale in isolation were sufficient for a folk-quale, the theory would have no role for the mechanism. But the theory still needs the C-quale: the mechanism by itself cannot be sufficient for folk-qualia. But now, the mechanism can only work on whatever inputs it receives. So if the connections are tampered with so that the inputs resulting from C-quale f are exactly as they would have been from g, the mechanism's contribution will be what it would have been if the C-quale actually were g. In that case the resulting folk-quale cannot still be F. To suppose it could be would be to imply, contrary to what we have seen the theory requires, that the mechanism's contribution makes no difference to the folk-quale. Given that there are causal connections, therefore, and given that they can be tampered with, it must be possible to tamper with them so as to alter the folk-quale.

It follows that on the assumptions we have conceded to exponents of the inner sense story, the same token C-quale (an instance of f) could have underlain my having either of two different raw feels or folk-qualia. Same C-quale, different folk-qualia. (Arguably it could have underlain my having G instead of R. But there is no need to insist on that. It's enough if the folk-qualia are different.) Hence, by Leibniz's law, on the inner sense account folk-qualia cannot be identical with C-qualia, or even necessarily correlated with C-qualia.[14]

Note that the argument is a reductio:

1. Let f (a C-quale of mine) be identical with R (a folk-quale of mine). [To be refuted.]
2. There must be connections between f and my 'introspective mechanism' [by the inner sense story].

[14] Note that the Churchlands themselves say there is 'no reason why the epistemological story for the faculty of inner sense should be significantly different from the story told for outer sense' (129). Since there's many a slip 'twixt the objects of outer sense and our perception of them, this remark seems to imply that the objects of inner sense might be perceived in more than one way. It is hard to see how this point could be reconciled with identifying C-qualia with folk-ditto.

3. A transformer can be inserted at any connection. [Empirical assumption.]

4. So by inserting a suitable transformer between *f* and my introspective mechanism, *f* could be made to produce the same effect on the latter as is actually produced by some completely different C-quale.

5. That difference would result in a difference in my folk-quale.

6. Therefore, on this inner sense account, R is not identical with *f*, contrary to (1).

7. Therefore this inner sense account cannot be true.

Note that the argument goes through even though we are talking about token identities. The point is that the same token of *f* could have been linked up with the same introspective mechanism in different ways, just as what is actually the hour hand of my watch—this same piece of metal—could have been linked up with the rest of the watch in the way the minute hand actually is. Clearly, if the aim is to say what it is for me to have an experience with this particular quale, and if I could have had exactly the same quale in the absence of this particular C-quale, the latter cannot be even token-identical with the former.

There may seem to be an easy way out. Why not define the C-quale as whatever physical property is actually put into the introspective mechanism? For example, if the effect of inserting a transformer is to produce an input with a spiking frequency of 100Hz rather than 60Hz, let the C-quale be the 100Hz input. Then, it may seem, the argument can't get started. But this suggestion is a dead end. The original idea was that a C-quale might be token-identical with a certain spiking frequency in a certain neural pathway; so the present suggestion is definitely a new one. Even so, it suffers from essentially the same fundamental defect as the original. If there is an introspective mechanism at all, folk-qualia could not be completely determined by things outside that mechanism. Suppose that impulses with a spiking frequency of 60Hz were made to occur in an isolated strand of neural tissue—unconnected to any brain or introspective mechanism. No one who had reflected on the point about cameras noted earlier would maintain that this would involve the occurrence of experiences. As we noticed, in order for there to be experiences there has to be an

organism or other system of the right sort. So it was never possible
to maintain that a folk-quale might be token-identical with some
physical property full-stop. At best the claim would have to be
that a folk-quale was identical with some physical property standing in suitable relations to a suitable system. And the futility of
such a claim should by now be evident. Perhaps, given the way my
own organism is set up, I have the red pencil folk-quale R when
and only when a certain particular type of physical process p
occurs. But that is a far cry from saying that R and p are identical.
Moreover, to say they were identical given the rest of the set-up
would still be mistaken. For the earlier argument showed that p
could perfectly well have occurred when I had some folk-quale
other than R. The bald identity 'inner sense' theory of qualia or
raw feels must be rejected.

For the same reason we must also reject the suggestion that the
nature of raw feels is not a task for psychology or philosophy but
for the neurosciences. The notion is inspired by folk psychology,
and there is no reason to expect that its boundaries will coincide
with those drawn by the neurosciences—any more than our
notions of colour coincide with boundaries drawn by physics.
The failure of raw feels to coincide with C-qualia in particular
makes this point especially vivid. If C-qualia exist, discovering
their nature is a task for the neurosciences; but we have seen that
raw feels are not C-qualia, and there is no reason to suppose that
the neurosciences need concern themselves with them. As to their
nature, the position defended here suggests it is a task partly for
philosophy, partly for psychology.

The above considerations show not only that raw feels could
not be identical with C-qualia. They also show that if there are C-
qualia, raw feels could not be identical with any physically specifiable items at all. For take any such item supposedly identical with
a given raw feel. Then by exploiting the gap between the relevant
C-quale and the introspective mechanism by the methods indicated, that item could have been physically modified so as to leave
the system with the same raw feel as it would have had if the item
had been left untouched. The occurrence of that particular raw
feel cannot therefore be identical with the presence of that item.

Even if there are no C-qualia, the considerations in the last
section provide strong reasons for supposing that raw feels could
not be identical with items specifiable in physical terms (rather

than in functional or similar terms). They suggest that in any system of the right kind—where inevitably there will be signals passing from component to component—physical modifications to outputs from one component could always in principle be compensated for by modifications to the component receiving the signals. So given any physical specification of an item supposedly identical with a system's having a given raw feel, it seems we could construct a different specification such that if it were realized the system would still have that same raw feel (other things being equal), contrary to the supposition.

The fundamental trouble with these hybrid approaches is that they fail to give due weight to the fact that in systems capable of raw feeling, physical differences in one area can be compensated for by differences elsewhere. Once that has been recognized, it becomes clear that, as with information processing in computers, the appropriate levels of description and explanation needed for explaining the nature of raw feeling must be above the physical.

6.4 THE INVERTER OPERATION

The problem raised by the inverted spectrum possibility might now look even more daunting. If we can't deal with it by the identity theory, what on earth are we to do? We seem to be deeper in the mud than ever. In fact the components of a solution are close at hand. We only need to develop the account given in the last chapter. A crucial feature was that perceptual processes caused by different external features have different characters for the system—different raw feels. Those processes in the stickleback which are caused by the silvery body of a mate have a different character for it from those which are caused by the red body of a rival. As we saw, it is only because they have different characters for the system that the system as a whole is in a position to assess its situation. By reflecting on this idea we shall eventually arrive at a coherent story about spectrum inversion and related ideas.

Although the various different characters for the system are in fact partly determined by the different features of the external world which impinge on its sense receptors, they are by no means wholly determined by them. To suppose they were would be to ignore the role of the structure of the perceiving system: of the sense receptors themselves, the processes of perceptual analysis which go to work on the outputs from the receptors, and the further processes inside the system. Thus character for the system—hence the nature of perceptual experience—is determined by external features working together with the structure of the total system. At the same time, if the rest of the system is held constant there will be a range of different kinds of process such that occurrences of any one of these kinds will constitute different occurrences of the same character. (That was the point of the stories about identical twins in Chapter 2.) For example, when the rest of my brain is held constant, perhaps a spiking frequency of around 60Hz in the activation of any subset of a certain (enormous) number of neurones in my visual cortex will realize the character my experience of the bright moon at night has for me, and a frequency of less than 3Hz in any subset of the same neurones will realize the character of my experience of total darkness.[15] This is the grain of truth in the bald identity idea—though for the reasons noted in the last section it falls well short of involving identities of the sort envisaged.

Given the way my brain is organized at present, we can suppose that a relatively high level of stimulation of my retinal cells is required in order to cause the corresponding cells in my visual cortex to fire at 60Hz. Similarly, it requires a very low level of stimulation for them to fire at less than 3Hz. However, since events at the retinas are distinct from events at the visual cortex, it must be possible to doctor the incoming signals so that characters for the system, or raw feels, are systematically switched round and we have an instance of something like the inverted spectrum. For this purpose we might use inverters.

An inverter is a device which performs the function of negation on a single binary input signal: if the device receives a 'o' it puts out a 'I' and vice versa. So let us suppose that overnight a tiny inverter were to be fitted to each nerve fibre leading from my own retinas. The result would be that the patterns of my raw feels

---

[15] Even with the *ceteris paribus* clause this is of course a simplification. For one thing, it seems that the visual system somehow integrates the total pattern of variations in illumination, so that the relative lightness a thing appears to have is not determined just by the absolute values of the amount of light it reflects. See e.g. Humphreys and Bruce, *Visual Cognition*, 32–6; C. L. Hardin, *Color for Philosophers*, 187–93.

would be like the negatives of the patterns I am actually having. The visual experience I had when I saw the full moon at night would be much like the one I should ordinarily have if I saw a football silhouetted against a uniformly bright sky. And so on. (Of course the inverters would require a source of energy on top of whatever might be got from the nerve fibres in which they were grafted. But that is an engineering problem.)

Now, if this operation had been performed on me at birth, my raw feels in any given situation would have been as they would be now if the operation had been performed on me overnight. (Recall the stories about the twins in Chapter 2.) The difference is that if the operation had been performed at birth instead of just recently, I should have been indistinguishable from a normal percipient by any possible behavioural test, since I should not have had any memories of things having looked different to me. That there would have been this systematic difference in my raw feels follows from two main considerations. First, as I suggested in Chapter 2 and have argued in the last chapter, raw feeling is wholly constituted by the processes inside the brain and does not depend on relations with the outside world. It follows that, second, the effect of the inverter operation would be that my raw feel processes would be similar to what they would have been if I had been living in a world in which the 'night' sky was bright, the 'moon' was a black object, 'coal' was white, and so on.[16]

Although I have not actually had the inverter operation, it happens that my identical twin sister, Emma, did: she had it at birth. It follows that she sees the relative luminances or lightnesses of things the other way round to me. This means that Emma and I illustrate the Transformation thesis.

This story at least seems to be sound. Nor does its soundness depend on its intuitive appeal. On our account of what it takes for something to be a subject of experience, input-driven perceptual processes interact with assessment processes, and their interaction constitutes there being characters for the system, or the having of

---

[16] If this suggestion involves too much strain, simply imagine that, as in the twins' stories in 2.7, I have lived all my life indoors, and that the alternative universe is coloured like the negative of my house. There are still difficulties— electric lamps are bound to be bright, shadows are dark, and so on—but my house has been specially vetted and provided with alternatives which don't noticeably impinge on my experience.

raw feels. The processes inside the head determine what those raw feels are. That point immediately provides scope for the Transformation thesis; and the inverter operation is just a way of illustrating it. It provides scope for inversions, transpositions, and other transformations simply because of the existence of an array of different types of external stimulation on the one hand, and different characters for the system on the other.

But now a cold and clammy thought comes to haunt us: the difficulty indicated at the beginning of this chapter. The stronger the appeal of the considerations just mentioned, the greater seems to be the pressure on the Swiss Cheese principle. For according to that principle, physical details in themselves cannot make a relevant difference. What matters is the patterns which the physical processes instantiate. And the difficulty is this: how is it possible that the patterns exemplified by Emma and me should be relevantly different? What could constitute such a difference? To deal with this and related questions it will be useful to consider a science-fictional example of Shoemaker's.

6.5 SHOEMAKER'S MARTIANS

The psychology of Shoemaker's imagined Martians is isomorphic to ours in all the ways covered by folk psychology. They also have raw feels: unlike Block's robot or the Machine Table robot they are not mere simulacra of sentient beings. But biochemically and neurophysiologically they are very different from us. In fact the physical realizations of their mental states are 'as different as they could possibly be from their realizations in us'.[17] And Shoemaker thinks that their raw feels would be radically unlike ours.[18]

The point is not that he thinks their raw feels would be inverted or transposed relative to ours. For in that case the *kinds* of raw feels they had would be exactly the same as ours, contrary to what he maintains. In that case, if a Martian and one of us were to be

---

[17] S. Shoemaker, 'The Inverted Spectrum'. Note that Shoemaker's conception of qualia is not dualistic.

[18] On p. 343 he says 'their experiences would not share any of the qualia our experiences have'. In a later article he maintains that sameness of the realizing *physical* states is necessary for sameness of qualia: 'Qualia and Consciousness', 513. But I think this claim is refutable by exploiting the arguments later in this chapter.

placed in the same perceptual situation, then although our corresponding raw feels would be systematically different, neither would have raw feels that the other could not have had in a suitably different situation. Shoemaker's contention contrasts strikingly with the Transformation thesis. He thinks that on account of the radical physical differences between them and us, the kinds of raw feels they had would be radically unlike any of ours.

There seem to be three mutually exclusive claims which might be maintained with respect to the raw feels of any given pair consisting of a human being and one of Shoemaker's Martians, both in the same perceptual situation: (I) The Martian's raw feels would necessarily be the same as the human's; (II) At least some of the Martian's would be radically unlike the human's; (III) The Martian's might be inverted or otherwise transposed relative to the human's, but could not be radically different. Which of these claims is correct? (I) is the position of someone—for example a behaviourist—who for some reason rejects the Transformation thesis. I will therefore ignore it. (II), as explained, is Shoemaker's view.[19] I think that if we reflect further on the general account of raw feeling defended here, it will become clear that the correct view is (III). However great the physical differences between the Martians and ourselves may be, given that they share all our discriminatory capacities their raw feels will not be radically different from ours.

6.6   A STRUCTURE OF CONTRASTS

The reason, in a phrase, is that differences between kinds of raw feel are determined by a structure of contrasts. Given a total set of discriminatory capacities there can be only one such structure, hence only one set of raw feels. There is scope for these raw feels to be associated with external features in more than one way, by inversion or transposition; but no scope for raw feels over and above those constituted by the structure of contrasts. Not that raw feeling is form without matter: in any particular instance it is constituted by a particular physical process. But what gives raw

[19] In fact (II) is weaker than Shoemaker's actual view: see n. 18 above. But since my argument will overturn the weaker claim, a fortiori it will overturn Shoemaker's stronger one.

feels their particular characters is the total structure of contrasts. I will explain and support these assertions.

We can start from the familiar point that (typically, at any rate) each sensory modality involves several dimensions. Colour vision involves dimensions of lightness, saturation, and hue; hearing has pitch, volume, and timbre. For each dimension in each sensory modality the range of different raw feels that a system could have in that dimension is determined by the range of discriminations it could make in respect of information in that dimension. We have seen that raw feeling is a matter of those processes which result from sensory stimulation acting directly on those which constitute assessment. So each kind of raw feel involves a process patterned in a way to which the assessment processes are sensitive. The process itself is no doubt physical, and has various physically definable properties. But the Swiss Cheese principle ensures that what matters is the pattern that the physical property instantiates, not its physical details, or indeed whether it is physical or not. And there can be no more to something's counting as a particular 'pattern' in this context than the fact that the assessment processes are sensitive to the contrasts between it and the other patterns involved in the kinds of raw feeling the system can have—contrasts not only within the dimension in question, but with the other dimensions in the same sensory modality and also with other modalities.

Here the example of the frog's eye and the frog's brain is relevant. The frog has perfectly good eyes but will starve surrounded by food in the shape of dead flies. Because the flies don't move, the frog can't identify them.[20] Quite generally, no matter how detailed the patterns of input from the eye may be, they will not affect perceptual consciousness unless the interpretation and assessment processes are correspondingly sensitive. If they are sensitive to a particular feature of the pattern, however, the system will be potentially capable of registering that sensitivity in some kind of behaviour. (I say 'potentially' to allow for shortcomings of memory and the like.) It is in that sense that the range of discriminations which the system could make determines the range of different raw feels it is capable of having. Without a corresponding sensitivity in the interpretation and assessment pro-

---

[20] J. Y. Lettvin *et al.*, 'What the Frog's Eye Tells the Frog's Brain'.

cesses, the presence or absence of a feature is irrelevant to what kind of raw feel is involved. Physiologists might detect many different patterns in the processes that occur; but unless the assessment processes are correspondingly sensitive the physiologically different patterns will not be the ones in question here. So the various sensitivities of the interpretation and assessment processes set up a structure of contrasts; and so long as that same structure is provided for, the raw feels involved—the *kinds* of raw feels, not necessarily their distribution—are bound to be the same.

These points need clarification: we shall do well to start from a simple example. Some creatures have only a very limited sensitivity to light. The tick is such a creature, of course, but (assuming it was a pure stimulus-response system) we saw that it lacked perceptual consciousness altogether. Suppose, however, that the creatures belonging to a certain zoological family qualify as subjects of perceptual consciousness, hence of raw feeling, but that the most they can do by way of perception is to distinguish between two types of external stimulation: light above some threshold intensity and light at or below that threshold. By my account of raw feeling, for each member of this family there are just two corresponding raw feels: one for the presence of light, the other for its absence. A vital point about the reasoning in the last paragraph is that it entitles us to reverse the quantifiers: there are two raw feels such that every member of this zoological family has one of them in the presence of light, the other in its absence. For there is just a single contrast involved here, just a binary sensitivity, and therefore no room for members of the family to differ from one another in respect of the raw feels they have in this sensory modality. This is emphatically not to deny that there is room for *physical* differences between the raw feel processes associated with light and darkness in the different species of the family. By the Swiss Cheese principle the physical processes might be very different indeed; but by themselves they count for nothing. All that matters is the contrasts to which these creatures' assessment processes are sensitive. Since there is just the one contrast, there are just two raw feels involved. And since the internal processes stand in that contrast independently of what their external causes may happen to be, there is scope for inversion. The contrast ensures that the processes have different characters, and their independence of their causes ensures that intersubjective inversion is possible.[21]

It doesn't matter what else is true about these creatures' sensitivity to light, so long as it is all-or-nothing. Obviously there is a whole range of possibilities. They might have no reaction at all to anything less than strong sunlight shining directly on to their surfaces. They might switch on only to illumination from within some very narrow band. They might react to differences of light intensity imperceptible to normal human beings, and that from very low to very high levels. But so long as the capacity in question is restricted to a simple on/off sensitivity, there is just the single contrast and consequently the single pair of raw feels.

The above reasoning applies not just to different species of the same zoological family. It applies to any creatures which share just this particular extremely limited pattern of sensitivity to light. So it applies to any Martian creatures there might be which have that limited sensitivity (not, of course, Shoemaker's Martians, who share our own rich sensitivity). Even though these Martian creatures might be physiologically very different from their psychologically equivalent terrestrial counterparts, the above reasoning shows that they would have exactly the same kinds of raw feels as the latter.

But that extremely simple on/off case was just an illustration. The argument applies quite generally, no matter how complicated the structure of contrasts may be. I conclude that Shoemaker's Martians themselves, since they share exactly our total pattern of sensitivities and hence our total structure of contrasts, must also share the same raw feels that we have. That is my argument for the position labelled (III) in the last section.

Many readers will have thought of an apparent objection. Contrasts alone cannot determine which items are contrasted. Why

---

[21] I once argued that spectrum inversion was impossible on the ground that it would entail that 'there are mental states which only *contingently* supply the information they do supply about the relative lightness and darkness of external things, when the only items of which that could possibly be true are items that could be perceived, not perceivings' ('Goodbye to Transposed Qualia', 42). What I failed to realize is that there could not be conscious perception unless there were internal states that contrasted *independently* of their external causes, hence independently of the information they conveyed. The above paragraph explains. In effect I was guilty of ultra-externalism.

shouldn't the same total structure of contrasts be realized by any number of different ranges of underlying raw feels, so that the Martians could have very different raw feels from ourselves? An example makes this objection vivid. Suppose we have a lot of monochrome pictures of the same scene, one in black and white and shades of grey, one in sepia, one in shades of red, and so on. In spite of their differences in hue they all convey the same information about the relative lightnesses of the scene they represent. In that particular dimension they share exactly the same structure of contrasts. So why shouldn't something analogous apply to the case of visual perception, and indeed to perception as a whole?

The objection is natural and the example intuitively appealing. All the same it is mistaken. Seeing why it is mistaken will further clarify and reinforce my account. Back again to the primitive creatures with on/off light sensitivity. Keep in mind that the only way they can have this sensitivity at all is by the occurrence of certain actual physical processes. Now, in the last chapter we saw that such processes—input-driven processes acting on those which constitute interpretation and assessment—alone are enough to constitute perceptual consciousness, hence raw feeling. (I will call them 'raw feel processes'.) Nothing further is required: Zombies are impossible. So in the case of our primitive creatures no further work has to be done to show that they have raw feels. What is needed is to show that the raw feels they have can be of only two kinds. I claim that my main argument, the 'structure of contrasts' argument, has already done that. But the present objection would require that kinds of raw feels should be determined by something over and above the structure of contrasts. It would allow two of our primitive creatures, *a* and *b*, to share the same structure of contrasts yet to have different raw feels. So it would require *a*'s raw feel processes to have some feature absent from *b*'s, the idea being that this dissimilarity determined that the two creatures had different raw feels. But there could be no such feature.

Suppose illumination above a certain threshold causes certain neurones in *a* to fire at a rate of 60Hz, and anything less leaves them not firing. And suppose that in *b*'s case illumination above that level causes certain neurones to fire at 100Hz, while anything less leaves them firing at around 20Hz. Each creature's assessment processes are differentially sensitive to whichever of these pairs of processes occurs. Their respective raw feel processes consist of those kinds of processes acting on their respective interpretation and assessment processes. Now, *a*'s raw feel processes certainly have some features lacking in *b*'s (and vice versa). For example, *a*'s input-driven processes involve less energy in a given perceptual situation than *b*'s do. But by definition neither creature's interpretation and assessment processes have any sensitivity to this particular difference. (Neither is in a position to contrast its own pair of on/off processes with the other's; nor could either of them contrast one member of its pair with another kind of process, since by definition these are the only raw feels they are capable of having.) Yet in order for *a*'s raw feels to be of different kinds from *b*'s, their characters for *a* would have to be different from their counterparts' characters for *b*. And characters for the system can only be determined by the sensitivities of the interpretation and assessment processes. Nothing else could do it—certainly not physical differences by themselves. So, since these additional sensitivities are absent, *a* and *b* cannot have different kinds of raw feels. The objection fails.

One reason why we suspect they could have had different kinds of raw feels may be that we tend to imagine other creatures' raw feels as being much like our own. Confronted with the story about the on/off creatures, we imagine ourselves experiencing limited visual experiences in response to light and its absence; and we seem capable of inserting many different kinds of experience into the two slots. There seems no limit to the number of different ways in which those slots might be filled. Perhaps we shut our eyes and notice that in daylight we are still aware of some light rather than total darkness; then we notice the slight redness of the light shining through our eyelids, and reflect that other colours would have served just as well. But these intuitive exercises are misleading. If a creature's only vision-like capacity is restricted to the extremely primitive one envisaged earlier, it lacks something that normally sighted people take for granted: the two-dimensionality of vision. So our two-dimensionally grounded intuitions can hardly fail to mislead us. Unlike such a creature, normally sighted people are capable of discriminating the different levels of illumination at different points in the two-dimensional array of light arriving at their retinas. So if we have normal vision, when we think about visual experience we tend to assume that any creature sensitive to light at all must enjoy something re-

sembling that kind of two-dimensional experience—even though
the creature might have less than our degree of visual acuity. But
clearly that is not so. There can be no reason why a creature's
light sensitivity should not stop at that mere sensitivity, and yield
no information at all about the spatial distribution of light of
different intensities. In that case the raw feels associated with
this simple capacity will be correspondingly limited. They will
certainly not be like the effects of light and dark on the eyelids of
normally sighted people, since those effects involve a sensation of
darkness or lightness over the whole two-dimensional visual field.
Normally sighted people would no doubt be at a loss if they had
to try to imagine what it would really be like to have raw feels
associated with that simple capacity. (I will discuss related points
in Chapter 7.)

It will probably have occurred to you that according to my
account there is no reason why the pure on/off raw feels should
not be associated with quite different sensitivities from the one I
have been discussing. It is not just that the raw feels themselves
could be transposed. If the argument is sound, exactly the same
pair of raw feels will be associable with on/off sensitivities of any
other kind: with such diverse sensory contrasts as the presence or
absence of sounds of certain kinds, bodily pressure, chemicals in
the atmosphere. And isn't that absurd?

On the contrary, it seems to be entirely correct, as well as being
consistent with my overall account of raw feeling. Consider: if
there is nothing but an on/off sensitivity, it imposes no constraints
whatever on the type of external feature that might cause it. The
character of raw feeling is in any case logically independent of
things outside the system. And in the on/off case the information
conveyed is absolutely minimal. So there is no reason why the
same pair of raw feels should not be associated with any pair of
external stimuli whatever. Two further considerations should help
to make this conclusion palatable.

The first is that the raw feels we ourselves actually have result
from an amazingly complex system of sensitivities. We can distinguish a virtual continuum of light intensities within a range
from total darkness to the brightest sunlight. We can register
different levels of illumination at each of a vast number of points
in the light mosaic which strikes our retinas. (It would take an
organized structure made up of millions of our primitive binary

perceivers to achieve anything comparable.) In addition we can discriminate things by colour—that is, we can discriminate them on the basis of their reflectances in respect of each of three main wavelengths. These two-dimensional sensitivities in turn enable us to register a lot of other kinds of information, including shapes, sizes, movement, relative position, distance, all of which affect our raw feels. Similarly with the other senses. Now, because the senses we actually enjoy involve such a range of complex capacities, it is extremely unlikely that there should be such a close isomorphism between the different sense modalities that it permitted the raw feels from one to convey *exactly* the same information as the raw feels from another. Our recognition of this fact no doubt helps to explain our intuitive reluctance to concede the possibility in question. The on/off cases are really so primitive that we can hardly grasp how radically they differ from our own.

The second relevant consideration which marks off our case from the primitive ones is related to the one just described. The original argument about 'structures of contrasts' applies not only to raw feels within one dimension of one modality, but to raw feels across modalities. Since raw feels from different sense modalities are in fact discriminable, that too depends on a structure of contrasts between modalities. The assessment processes evidently have to be differentially sensitive to inputs from the eyes and from the ears, for example, since these inputs equip us with capacities of different kinds. These different sensitivities constitute a structure of contrasts between those two modalities. When the other modalities are brought into the scheme the result is an extremely complex total structure. The complexity of this structure makes it hard for us to conceive of the simplicity envisaged in the on/off example. At the same time this complexity explains why in general we ought not to expect that the Transformation thesis could be exemplified across different sense modalities. (For an apparent exception, see the next section but one.)

It seems, then, that Shoemaker's Martians, so long as they share our discriminatory capacities, could not have raw feels of different kinds from our own. The reasons for this fit comfortably into the general account of raw feeling offered in the last chapter. The overall picture is coherent. However, there still appears to be a worrying loose end. If the Transformation thesis is true, different individuals may perceive things in different ways even if they share the same range of raw feels. So what determines that an individual perceives things in one particular way rather than in one of the alternative ways? We can put the question in terms of our primitive binary perceivers *a* and *b*, which share just two kinds of raw feels. What determines which way round they have those raw feels? What determines whether they both have the same raw feel in response to high illumination, and the other one in response to zero illumination, or whether their raw feels in the same situation are transposed relative to one another? As soon as these questions strike us we seem to be plunged into essentially the same difficulty as I raised at the beginning of the chapter. The Swiss Cheese principle rules out the suggestion that the explanation lies in merely physical differences. But if we appeal to the idea of a structure of contrasts, such a structure seems merely to determine which kinds of raw feels a system has, not which way round they are associated with external things. We have seen that the bald identity approach doesn't work. Yet now it looks as if a functionalist approach is thwarted too. Once again we find ourselves struggling in the mud.

I think the difficulty is only apparent—or rather there *is* a real difficulty, but it presents no threat to the Swiss Cheese principle or the argument of this section.

6.7 WHAT DETERMINES WHICH WAY ROUND?

The crucial consideration is that the question of which way round an individual's raw feels are associated with external features makes sense only in relation to some standard. For any given individual, it is an empirical question whether or not another's raw feels are associated with external things the same way or differently. It is also an empirical question once some standard has been fixed. No doubt this empirical question will generally be very hard to answer; but it raises no problems for our account.

Recall the case of my twin Emma and myself. Since she had the inverter operation at birth and I did not, we see relative lightnesses in opposite ways. By the argument of the last section there are only two 'ways round' available. Either the 'apparent lightness' feature of a person's raw feels is correlated with external lightnesses in the same way as mine is, or else it is correlated the other way round, like Emma's: inverted relative to mine. If for a moment we pretend there might exist actual cases of Transformation, then either the pattern of raw feels you have when you see the moon on a dark night is more or less like mine, or else it is like the pattern I have when I see a black disc silhouetted against a bright sky. Not that those of your raw feels which are associated with the extremes of lightness and darkness are bound to be either exactly the same as mine or else inverted relative to mine. Conceivably there is a continuum of intermediate values, in which case your continuum might be mapped to mine without the absolute values of your 'lightest' and 'darkest' coinciding with either of the absolute values of mine. Since such cases seem possible—for of course they would involve detectable differences in our respective discriminatory capacities—there are not just two raw feels capable of being associated with maximum light intensity or total darkness, but indefinitely many. But these possibilities are beside the point, which is that there are just two ways round for that variable property of a system's raw feel processes which is associated with relative lightnesses to be correlated with the intensity of illumination of the retina.

Given that there are just those two ways, we can call my way of seeing lightnesses K and Emma's L. So it seems to make sense to enquire of a particular individual whether they see relative lightnesses in way K or way L. It also seems to make sense to enquire what features of their organization, when compared with those of known instantiators of K or L, result in their also being instantiators of whichever of these two ways it may be. In contrast, there seems to be no sense in asking: 'What features of this individual's organization result in its perceiving things in the ways it does?'—absolutely, without any implied reference to a standard. Any subject of raw feels whatever perceives things as it does because it has the right kinds of capacities and internal processes; that goes without saying. But that question is pointless unless it presupposes some understanding of which ways of perceiving are in question. Unless we are going to be satisfied with a tautological answer such as 'It perceives things as it does', the necessary understanding depends on some agreed standard of comparison. Since the absolute question has no sensible answer, the worry raised earlier turns out to have been misconceived.

Even given agreement on a standard of comparison, though,

there will not be a general explanation of why two individuals share the same raw feels in the same situations, if they do, or of why they don't, if they don't. The position in general is very different from the special case of Emma and me. She and I started life with exactly similar brains, but the inverter operation ensured that her raw feels are as they would have been if she had been in an inverted world—or, for that matter, as mine would have been if I had been in an inverted world. Given our earlier arguments, the situation here is open to view. But it is obviously quite exceptional. Even in the case of our two binary perceivers *a* and *b*, who have just two kinds of raw feels at their disposal, there will generally be no straightforward procedure for discovering whether or not they share the same raw feels in the same situations. Of course there would be no problem if we knew they were exactly similar in all relevant physical respects, or that they differed only as Emma and I differ. But in general things won't be like that. If they belong to different species of their zoological family, they might have very significant physical differences. Nor could we use a simple rule like: 'If two individuals with the same discriminatory capacities both have inverters or both lack inverters, then they will both share the same raw feels in the same perceptual situations.' For there can be no guarantee that the presence or absence of inverters at one point is not compensated for by differences elsewhere in the total system. And there seems no limit to the number of possible physical realizations of such compensatory differences.

These considerations suggest that the *practical* difficulties in the way of discovering whether, for example, Shoemaker's Martians instantiate the Transformation thesis by comparison with us might be insuperable. But by now I think it is clear that there are no great *conceptual* difficulties in the way of such a project. The difficulties are real, but they don't seem to threaten the Swiss Cheese principle or the arguments of the last sections.

In Chapter 2 I pointed out that although the Transformation thesis is true, that is no reason to suppose that it is instantiated, especially among human beings. For as defended here it requires only a possibility, not actual cases. I also argued that, on the justified assumption that there are no actual cases, the Transformation thesis is consistent with acceptance of Wittgenstein's main private language argument. We noticed considerations which justify the claim that we can know and talk about one another's raw feels. Now, in the light of the account of raw feeling developed in this and the last two chapters it appears quite possible that scientific work should be capable of establishing that 'justified assumption' independently, and making certain that in human beings there are in fact no instances of the Transformation thesis. It might be difficult to trace the raw feel processes, ensure that there are no crossed wires, inverters, or whatever; but there seems no reason why it should be impossible. By the same token there seems no reason why actual instances should not be capable of being discovered if, contrary to all expectation, there were some.

I have been writing as if the positive–negative difference between Emma and me were an impeccable example of the Transformation thesis. But conceivably, even in this case, the structure of contrasts might lack the necessary symmetry. For example, while there seems to be a definite extreme of absolute darkness at one end of the scale, the notion of a corresponding absolute lightness is suspect. Let me therefore concede that examples of Transformation which involve absolutely no asymmetry in the structure of contrasts might not exist in any actual terrestrial perceivers. And so long as there is even a slight asymmetry in the structure, hence in the pattern of discriminatory capacities, instances would be in principle behaviourally discoverable—although it might take sophisticated testing equipment to sort them out. (Even the phenomenon of colourblindness was not scientifically recognized until the nineteenth century; and a positive–negative difference would be vastly less open to behavioural detection than much colourblindness.)

However, if there are in fact no perfect symmetries of appropriate kinds in terrestrial sense perception, there is no a priori reason why examples should not have existed, or even actually exist elsewhere in the universe. Indeed, there seems no reason why the Emma example should not have been modified so as to rule out the apparent asymmetry noted above: presumably we could arrange for a shut-off point at some high level of illumination, so that there was a definite limit at that end as well as at the other. For our purposes, the actual absence of instances of the Transformation thesis seems beside the point.[22]

---

[22] A point noted by S. Shoemaker, *Identity, Cause, and Mind*, 186 n. 7.

6.8   ALTERNATIVE VISION

There are devices by which blind people can learn to discriminate the relative lightnesses of things, hence further properties such as their shapes, by the mediation of other senses. One type, the 'tactile-vision substitution system'—a camera whose pixels are connected to a rectangular array of vibrating bristles fixed to the subject's back—represents light intensities by means of skin stimulations.[23] These devices may look like counter-examples to my claims about Shoemaker's Martians. They may appear to illustrate his own view that these Martians' raw feels might equip them with all the right discriminatory capacities, while being strikingly different from the kinds we ourselves have. In fact, far from undermining my position, these devices help to illustrate and reinforce it.

Consider someone for whom a tactile-vision substitution system is their only source of visual information—or at any rate of what would be visual information for a normally sighted person. You might think they don't really see at all, or at least don't have visual experiences, because these devices work through the sense of touch. What we get from touch is tactile experiences, not visual ones; therefore (it may seem) such devices could not produce visual raw feels. If that is right, these devices provide a way of detecting patterns of light intensity which is bound to be unlike that of normally sighted people. It cannot be the way I myself detect patterns of light intensity; but neither can it be merely the inverse of that way. It seems to be something completely different.

This objection ignores two crucial considerations. The first is the distinction between information that is genuinely for the system, and what would be information if only the system could deal with it appropriately. When patterns of light of various intensities fall on the tactile-vision device's camera, corresponding patterns of stimulation are produced on the subject's skin. So these patterns of stimulation are in principle capable of supplying the person with information about relative lightnesses. However, it is one thing for those patterns to be there; something else for the subject to be able to process them so as to acquire the sort of information

---

[23] See P. Bach-y-Rita, C. C. Collins, *et al.*, 'Vision Substitution by Tactile Image Projection', 963; G. Guarniero, 'Experience of Tactile Vision', 101–4.

that is in question. (Once again, recall the frog.) I am not committed to the implausible view that fitting a congenitally blind person with a prosthetic vision device would immediately enable them to process all the kinds of information required for visual experience. On the contrary, it is consistent with my position that they should take time to become capable of the right kinds of processing—for fresh neural pathways and new types of interpretation and assessment processes to come into operation. The situation after the subject has had some experience of the new device can be expected to be both physiologically and psychologically different from what it was at the start. Indeed that is what the empirical evidence suggests. Subjects report that in time they acquire new sensations;[24] and that is entirely in line with the view that those whose raw feel processes endow them with the right capacities do actually have visual raw feels.

The second crucial point comes in two instalments. First, as we have seen, what matters when the character of an individual's raw feeling is in question is not the distal causes of the signals whose processing constitutes the raw feeling, but the nature of the signals and the processing themselves. Second, we know that what matters about the nature of the signals and the processing is not their physical character *per se*, but their patterns and relationships. Of course, within a given actual system it matters a great deal which pattern is instantiated. The key has to fit *this* lock. But the point is that there could perfectly well be a differently constructed system where a different pattern played exactly the same role as the first pattern in the first system. There is no magic in the specific ways in which the signals in a system are patterned.

We can now see why the present objection fails. The objection would work only if using a tactile-vision substitution system could never yield anything but tactile sensations, tactile raw feels—never visual ones. But we have seen that this assumption goes against not only the theoretical considerations, but the empirical evidence. The theoretical considerations suggest that the mere fact that in normal circumstances stimulation of the skin produces tactile sensations does not entail that in all possible circumstances in which the skin is stimulated (and the person is not anaesthetized) the upshot will be tactile sensations. Whether or not the subject

[24] See Guarniero, 'Experience of Tactile Vision'.

has tactile sensations will depend not only on the distal stimulation, but also on the internal processing of the signals resulting from that stimulation. Moreover, the fact that the subject starts off by experiencing the stimulation as tactile does not entail that it must necessarily remain so, since new neural pathways may be formed together with new ways of processing the incoming signals, with the result that the subject has types of raw feeling that are also— for the subject—new. The empirical evidence also suggests that such subjects do in fact acquire 'two-dimensional' visual sensations. So this example is no counter-example to my claim that the kinds of raw feels a system can have are determined by the structure of contrasts determined by the pattern of its sensitivities and discriminatory capacities. On the contrary, it is a virtue of the account defended here that it accommodates such examples in a way that does full justice to the empirical evidence.

There may still be lingering doubts. What about the thoughts suggested by monochrome pictures, briefly discussed two sections back? We noticed that different monochrome pictures may be in different colours yet still convey the same information about relative lightnesses. If we recall Anna's original condition of monochromatic vision, it seems conceivable that she should have seen things *either* in shades of grey *or* in shades of sepia *or* in shades of blue *or* . . .[25] If that is a genuine possibility it appears to be a counter-example to my position on kinds of raw feels. For I maintain that what determines the kinds of raw feels that an individual is capable of having is a structure of contrasts correlated with a structure of discriminatory capacities. Since it looks as if Anna would have had exactly the same discriminatory capacities regardless of which single hue might have provided the basis for her monochromatic vision, hasn't something gone wrong?

This case does require me to spell out a feature of my position more clearly; but it is far from being a counter-example. The right approach will emerge if we start by considering a famous imaginary example of Frank Jackson's. Mary, though normally sighted, has been brought up in surroundings purged of all colours but shades of grey. She learns about colour vision from books and

---

[25] In case this suggestion strikes you as just a philosophical fancy, the following occurs in a psychology textbook: '. . . the rod-monochromat sees all wavelengths as gray, whereas the cone-monochromat sees them presumably as one hue' (Y. Hsia and C. H. Graham, 'Colour Blindness', 405).

from black-and-white television, but she has no experience of the actual colours of grass, the sky, ripe tomatoes, and so on until she is eventually released from her grey prison. At present I am not concerned with Jackson's argument, which will be discussed in the next chapter.[26] The point now is that there is nothing wrong with Mary's colour vision. She has all the necessary capacities: all that is lacking is actual encounters with coloured objects.

Now it is conceivable, though no doubt improbable from a physiological point of view, that a defect at the 'front end' of someone's visual system should have the same effects on their experience as Mary's incarceration in the grey prison had on her. Suppose Fritz suffers from such a defect. The rest of his visual processing system is normally equipped to receive full colour information; but its defective front end deprives him of inputs carrying the appropriate information. So Fritz's raw feels are like Mary's. Now, we can imagine that somewhat different defects in Fritz's input processing might have had correspondingly different consequences. That particular one leaves him with raw feels like Mary's. But another might have left him with the kinds of raw feels that would have been produced if he had been normally sighted and living in a world of shades of sepia—or of blue, or of . . . The idea of this modified Fritz will at first annoy verificationists. But they need not worry: my account entails that such differences are in principle empirically detectable. (In any case, those who deny the possibility would not have raised the present objection.)

Notice that Fritz, with or without the modification, has capacities that ordinarily colourblind people no doubt lack. If they do lack those capacities, we should not expect that their raw feels would resemble the ones we have when we see representations of the world in some one colour. There is a moral here for the Martian story. I have been assuming that Shoemaker's Martians share exactly our powers of perceptual discrimination. In particular I have been assuming that their assessment processes match ours exactly. However, we are now in a position to see how they could have shared our behavioural capacities while their internal perceptual sensitivities went beyond ours. Conceivably their input processing might have been selectively deficient, analogously to

---

[26] See F. Jackson, 'Epiphenomenal Qualia', to be discussed in 7.6 below.

that of the modified Fritz. The result would be that their raw feels would belong to a different range from ours, just as Shoemaker claimed. But it is crucially important that any such differences would depend on differences in their internal sensitivities, which, although they would not actually show up in behavioural differences, would be potentially capable of showing up in that way. They would actually show up if the deficiencies in their input processing were to be corrected.

We have examined some unusual kinds of vision. At first sight they may have appeared to threaten my account of perceptual consciousness. On closer consideration, however, they have enabled us to see the power of that account.

6.9 WHERE DOES THIS LEAVE FUNCTIONALISM?

It should now be clear that the difficulty raised at the beginning of the chapter was only apparent. The Transformation thesis does not after all conflict with the Swiss Cheese principle. Yet the Transformation thesis does conflict with some varieties of functionalism. To define my position more clearly I will spell out the nature of that conflict, and why I am still happy to describe my position as broadly functionalist. We noticed in the last chapter that there are several ways of distinguishing varieties of functionalism. For my purposes I need just two dichotomies: between 'surface' varieties of functionalism and others; between 'definitional' varieties and others.

Surface functionalism regards the character of the internal processing as irrelevant provided there is the right relation between sensory inputs, behavioural outputs, and other states. All kinds of functionalism—indeed all sane theories of the mind whatever—are agreed that if something has mental states at all, its behaviour and dispositions must at any rate have their origin within it.[27] However, with that necessary condition taken for granted, surface functionalism imposes no further conditions on the nature of the

[27] Another Aristotelian echo: see e.g. *Ethics*, 1111ᵃ23. I don't mean to rule out the possibility of individuals whose bodily components are spatially scattered, as imagined by P. F. Strawson (*Individuals*, ch. 3) and D. C. Dennett ('Where Am I?'). These possibilities are of spatially dispersed *persons*: the causes of their behaviour still lie within their scattered selves.

internal processing. Surface functionalism is obviously close to behaviourism; but from a theoretical point of view it is sharply marked off from it. For even surface functionalism insists that many if not all mental states are internal states, not just a matter of dispositions. The pure behaviourist maintains that suddenly remembering you have forgotten to turn off the cooker, for example, is nothing over and above the fact that you suddenly acquire a disposition to go to the cooker and turn it off, or something of the sort. But all functionalists will insist that your suddenly having that thought necessarily involves some sort of internal occurrence—though it may be expected to cause you to acquire certain dispositions.[28]

Surface functionalism is plainly incompatible with the Transformation thesis. Ignoring the nature of the internal processing as it does, it cannot provide for purely internal differences such as those between the ways in which Emma and I see the relative lightnesses of things. In any case surface functionalism must be rejected because the Block machine and the Machine Table robot are counter-examples. Any adequate functionalism must be deep.

The other dichotomy is between *definitional* functionalism and other varieties. Definitional functionalism maintains that particular mental states can be actually defined in functional terms, that is: logically necessary and sufficient conditions for their occurrence can be given in those terms.[29] In view of the last paragraph the definitions will have to be in 'deep' terms. Non-definitional varieties of functionalism, on the other hand, confine themselves to using functional notions in order to make clear the general nature of mental states. The approach I am taking is non-

[28] It is not always clear which are surface varieties of functionalism and which are deep. Putnam's machine functionalism is certainly a surface variety. On the other hand the causal functionalisms of Armstrong and Lewis appear to be varieties of deep functionalism because they appear to impose conditions on the nature of the internal causation of behaviour. Dennett seems to commit himself to surface functionalism when he suggests that 'every mental phenomenon is intentional-system-characterizable': *Brainstorms*, p. xvii; *The Intentional Stance*, 68. For his behaviouristic tendency, see too *Consciousness Explained*, 311, 389, 398, and the discussion at 5.6 above.

[29] Nomologically necessary and sufficient conditions would not be good enough, if only because they would not rule out the Zombie possibility. See 3.1, 3.2, 3.4. Shoemaker has asserted that functionalism, 'as a general theory of mind', should be definitional ('Absent Qualia are Impossible', 311). If so, my position is not functionalist—but so what?

definitional. I am using broadly functionalist ideas with a view to overcoming the philosophical perplexities which surround the questions of the existence and nature of raw feeling. Certainly I have offered a statement of necessary and sufficient conditions for something to be a subject of raw feeling. But that doesn't mean that particular raw feels are definable in functional terms.

If the definitions did not have to be correlated with the definiendum by logical necessity there would be no difficulty. In that case we might define certain raw feels as 'the kind of raw feels RK has when he sees a ripe tomato in ordinary daylight'. But such definitions are hardly illuminating. Of course they might be informative. If you already know which raw feels are referred to, learning that some other individual has them would be a definite addition to your knowledge. But such definitions throw no light on the nature of the raw feels in question.

Unfortunately I don't think we could do much better. Characterizations like the one just mentioned are steeped in folk psychology. The notion of raw feeling itself depends on folk-psychological notions for its explanation, and the same seems to be the case for 'see'. Our usual ways of classifying raw feels are according to their typical causes and effects, given in traditional or folk terms (for example 'pink elephants', 'a scratching sound'). It is true that, as our scientific understanding of our environment and our internal workings improves, we become able also to use scientific concepts in these descriptions ('the taste of copper sulphate', 'a sound with a frequency of 440Hz').[30] But the raw feels, regardless of whether they are characterized in folk or austerely scientific terms, are far from being wholly determined by their external causes. They also depend very largely on the peculiar human perceptual apparatus. From this it follows that the only way to arrive at a truly scientific characterization of types of raw feel—if that were possible—would be via some reference to that apparatus. Suppose we had a scientific characterization, H, of the human perceptual apparatus. Then we could at any rate pick out one kind of raw feel by defining it as 'the one typically caused, in a system conforming to H, by exposure to predominantly green

[30] Following the lead of Feyerabend and Rorty, Paul Churchland has presented the prospects for much more radical developments in this direction in the most imaginative and dramatic ways. See his *Scientific Realism and the Plasticity of Mind*.

light'. ('Typically' here stands for something like 'when the system is functioning properly and circumstances are normal'.) This definition would apply not only to that type of raw feel as it occurred in human subjects, but also to the same type if it existed in Martians or robots. ('The kind of magazine typically found in dentists' waiting-rooms' applies to magazines also found elsewhere.) But that too would not be very illuminating. We have noted the futility of attempting illuminating definitions of words such as 'hill' or 'gnarled' independently of the traditional or folk schemes for describing physical objects and countrysides. I suspect it is similarly futile to look for illuminating definitions of individual raw feels.

There are other objections to the project of finding functional definitions of individual mental states, but I will not pursue them here.[31] For the reasons I have given, the attempt seems pointless, and it is not part of my project. What matters is to understand how there can be such states, and in particular how there could be states of raw feeling. That, I maintain, has been explained in this and the last two chapters.

With that account of raw feeling, I think the intelligibility gap has been bridged. But for some readers this assertion may come as a surprise. How can I claim to have bridged the intelligibility gap, they will demand, when I have not explained the necessity of the link between a particular physical and functional set-up—the set-up instantiated by me, for example—and its being like THIS for me to see things as I do? But I believe I have already explained that necessity too. Perhaps the gap has not yet been seen to have been bridged.

[31] See e.g. J. Hornsby, 'Physicalist Thinking and Conceptions of Behaviour'.

7

The Gap has been Bridged

The intelligibility gap is not all-or-nothing: there are stepping-stones. To begin this final chapter I will recall the main ones, and make as vivid as I can the questions that may still seem perplexing. The objection mentioned at the end of the last chapter is one of several. But I will not repeat or do much to elaborate my earlier arguments: I will mainly be considering further points. A central task will be to examine the difficulties raised by Nagel in his famous article 'What Is It Like to Be a Bat?'. He proposed that 'an organism has conscious mental states if and only if there is something it is like to *be* that organism—something it is like *for* the organism'.[1]

7.1 IS THERE STILL A MYSTERY?

If we acknowledge that a physical theory of mind must account for the subjective character of experience, we must admit that no presently available conception gives us a clue how this could be done. The problem is unique. If mental processes are indeed physical processes, then there is something it is like, intrinsically, to undergo certain physical processes. What it is for such a thing to be the case remains a mystery.[2]

Here Nagel despairs of being able to bridge the intelligibility gap—which I claim has now been done. Five questions will help us distinguish the main components of the gap. The first is this:

1. How could the essence of consciousness, raw feeling, be constituted by something purely physical?

---

[1] T. Nagel, 'What Is It Like to Be a Bat?', 392 f.

[2] Ibid. 399 f. Fodor is even more pessimistic: 'Nobody has the slightest idea how anything material could be conscious. Nobody even knows what it would be like to have the slightest idea about how anything material could be conscious. So much for the philosophy of consciousness.' (J. A. Fodor, 'The Big Idea: Can there be a Science of Mind?', *The Times Literary Supplement*, 3 July 1992, 5).

This question is directed at physicalists of all persuasions. Most philosophers and psychologists are likely to be at least minimal physicalists, so answering it has been one of my main objectives. The first step was to make clear that even minimal physicalism commits you to the Strict Implication thesis. You must accept that all interesting truths about raw feeling are strictly implied by the totality of truths statable in purely physical terms. But that is not an answer to the question. It is just a way of bringing out what has to be done. Any satisfactory answer must include an answer to the question how the truths about raw feeling *could* be strictly implied by the totality of physical truths. At first that may seem to make minimal physicalism harder to sustain, not easier. How could we possibly explain a necessary connection from the physical to the mental, especially when that necessary connection has to embrace kinds of raw feeling? Still, recognizing the problem is an essential step towards solving it.

The second step was to notice that what at first appeared to be a problem only for physicalists was in fact a problem for everyone, including dualists. Being forced to acknowledge the Swiss Cheese principle, we were forced to accept that no advantage could be gained by resisting minimal physicalism. Even if the actual world turned out to include non-physical items as essential components of mental states, their existence would not make the task of understanding the nature of raw feeling any easier. In this debate, the issue of dualism versus physicalism is a red herring. As we have seen, there can be no a priori reasons why what might conceivably be done by non-physical means should not have been done by purely physical means. Dualists or physicalists, then, we're all in it together. True, dualists don't have to answer question (1) as it stands. But they do have to answer a modified version:

1a. How could the essence of consciousness, raw feeling, *have been* something purely physical?

(1) carries the implication that raw feeling is in fact constituted by something purely physical while (1a) implies that it isn't. But both require an answer to the second of my five main questions:

2. How could the Strict Implication thesis hold?

A closely related question is: How is it that anything is a subject of raw feeling—something it is like something to be—*at all*? Yet another is: How can the logical possibility of Zombies be ruled out? The first and principal part of my answer to question (2) was set out in Chapters 4 and 5. It consists of an account of what it takes for something to be a subject of raw feeling—assuming that the something is purely physical. The key component is an account of what it takes for something to be a subject of conscious perceptual experience. It requires the system to have the Basic Package: the capacities to acquire information about the environment, to store that and other information, and to initiate and control behaviour on the basis of incoming and stored information, when all this information is *for* the system in the realistic sense explained. And it requires some incoming perceptual information to act directly on the system's main assessment and decision-making processes. A crucial feature of this story is that when incoming perceptual information is directly active in that way, there will be internal processes with certain characters for the system. These processes constitute the system's having raw feels, hence constitute there being something it is like to be it. Subjects of raw feeling in general are defined on the basis of that account of subjects of conscious perceptual experience.

If that account is sound the main burden of question (2) has been removed. For, as a brief consideration of some of the central ideas of connectionist models of cognitive processing has suggested, no philosophical perplexities appear to be raised by the question of how a purely physical system could meet the conditions specified. As we noted just now, to support that account of raw feeling involved refuting the possibility of Zombies—contrary to a powerful intuition.

Some of the apparent force of question (2) derived from another intuition, that of the inverted spectrum. To deal with that aspect of the question I showed in the last chapter how, properly understood, the Transformation thesis was quite compatible with the general account of raw feeling given in Chapters 4 and 5. The full answer to question (2) includes that discussion in Chapter 6, which of course provides my answer to a distinct question:

3. How could the Transformation thesis hold?

So questions (1), (2), and (3) have been dealt with explicitly in previous chapters. The two remaining questions have been dealt with only implicitly. The first uses the Transformation thesis as a springboard.

7.2 THE INVERTED SPECTRUM STRIKES AGAIN—OR DOES IT?

Some readers may suspect that I have failed to take the measure of the inverted spectrum objection to functionalism. Properly understood, they may think, that objection would demolish my account of raw feeling and leave the intelligibility gap as wide as ever. I think this idea is mistaken and arises from confusion; but it goes deep and needs to be taken seriously. I will deal with it piecemeal in this and the following sections.

We saw earlier that there are just two 'ways round' in which it is possible to see relative lightnesses. There is K, which is the way I see them, and there is L, which is the way my twin Emma sees them after the inverter operation. The worry now may perhaps be expressed like this. Nothing I have said gives us a grasp of why a given way of seeing relative lightnesses, for example K, should be constituted by one particular type of functional and internal organization rather than by a different type which, on my account, would constitute seeing relative lightnesses in the other possible way, L. Suppose the relevant functional and internal set-up in my case is F. Then the worry is that no explanation has been given of why F should constitute seeing relative lightnesses in way K rather than way L. This thought is expressed by the question:

4. Why should one functional and internal set-up go with one way of perceiving things rather than with any other which the system's structure of contrasts would allow?

As it stands, this question is rather obviously misconceived. If a set-up of type F really does *constitute* my seeing relative lightnesses in way K, there is no possibility that it should have been accompanied by a different way of seeing lightnesses. The claim that F constitutes my seeing in way K logically implies that I could not have seen in way L so long as F continued to be the relevant set-up. According to the account in Chapters 4, 5, and 6, having raw feels, and hence, in particular, seeing lightnesses in one way rather than another, is nothing but the occurrence of processes satisfying the relevant conditions and constituting a certain structure of contrasts. We saw that these conditions provide for just two ways of seeing relative lightnesses; and we saw how such differences could exist—in spite of the fact that there seems no prospect of actually defining the kinds of set-up in question. So, given a particular type of functional and internal organization, the associated way of seeing relative lightnesses is thereby determined. It is strictly implied by a description of that organization. (Remember that K is defined by reference to *my* way of seeing: we are talking about comparisons with a standard.) So after all my account provides all the explanation that could consistently be required of why a given functional and internal set-up is associated with a particular way of seeing relative lightnesses. The apparent objection has evaporated.

7.3 THE QUESTION OF NECESSARY CONNECTION

You may still not be satisfied. In an attempt to bring your worry into sharper focus you may be inclined to press something like the following question:

5. How *could* there be a necessary connection from the functional and internal set-up that I instantiate to its being like THIS for me to see red things as I do?

The question is still not clear. But behind it we can discern two key assumptions. One is that the character of each individual's particular way of perceiving things is revealed to that individual. The other is that this character, as so revealed to the individual, is logically and conceptually remote from any details of functional and internal organization, so that even if the ways we perceive things are constituted by our respective functional and internal organizations, there is bound to remain an unbridgeable gulf between such organizations and our raw feels.[3] How could I connect my way of seeing red things with whatever relevant functional and internal set-up I happen to instantiate? What conceptual glue could possibly do the job?

---

[3] Compare the 'property objection' to the old identity thesis. It was to the effect that phenomenal properties are irreducible, hence cannot be identical with physical properties. See J. J. C. Smart, 'Sensations and Brain Processes', objection 3 and reply, and p. 332 of the useful Bibliography in J. Cornman, *Materialism and Sensations*.

The first assumption may look like a suitable case for Wittgensteinian treatment, since it could be construed as presupposing
just the kind of privacy that Wittgenstein showed to be impossible.
But many people are inclined to think his arguments fail to
do justice to the thoughts about raw feeling that I have been
developing, so perhaps some version of the assumption is de-
fensible. Apart from that consideration, it is plausible to suggest
that the ways in which we know how we perceive things are
different from the ways in which we might come to know which
functional and internal organizations we instantiate. If, as I have
argued, I see relative lightnesses in one of just two logically possible 'ways round', then it seems I have access to THIS way round in
a peculiarly straightforward manner. After all, there is general
agreement that I could detect a sudden switch in the way I see
lightnesses; so it is natural to conclude that I know how I actually
do see lightnesses. Anyway, I will let the first assumption pass.

The second assumption—that the character of our ways of
perceiving is logically and conceptually remote from any details of
functional and internal organization—is a different sort of animal
altogether. It is probably the biggest single obstacle to acceptance of my type of account of raw feeling. Here the intelligibility
gap seems to be at its most impassable. Yet the objection is
bogus.

It may be taken in either of two senses. In the first it can quickly
be seen to be mistaken; in the other it is superficially more interesting. Suppose 'THIS' were to be taken to mean *whatever may
actually be* the way I see red things. In that sense anyone could
understand what I was referring to by 'THIS'. There is no particular
problem about it. More to the point, in that sense I have already
explained how there is a necessary connection from my functional
and internal set-up to its being like THIS for me to see red things as
I do. The former actually constitutes the latter, as we saw when
discussing the last question (4). In fact, if 'THIS' is taken in that
way, question (5) is essentially the same as question (4), and has
already been answered.

So we must suppose that 'THIS' is to be taken in such a way
that the question can be properly understood only by those
who understand the demonstrative in the special way the speaker
understands it. We might say they will be able to project themselves imaginatively into the speaker's point of view, and somehow

or other grasp what it is like for the speaker to see red things.[4] In
that case, though, there is no reason why the apparent logical or
conceptual gap in question should be an objection to my account
of raw feeling. For the concepts in terms of which we can explain
what it takes for something to be a subject of conscious experience
are bound to be quite different from the ones in terms of which
subjects themselves think of or characterize their experience. The
first set of concepts won't necessarily enable you to arrive at the
second. Yet that doesn't prevent truths stated in terms of the first
from strictly implying truths stated in terms of the second. I will
elaborate these points.

7.4   AN IMPOSSIBLE REQUIREMENT

The driving thought behind question (5) is that if 'THIS' is construed in the second way—so that it is properly understood only
by those who know what it is like for the speaker to see red
things—the necessity of the corresponding connection has not
been explained. But consider what form an explanation could
possibly take. The unstated assumption seems to be this: in order
to show that there is a *necessary* connection, there would have to
be a chain of a priori reasoning whose main premiss was the
proposition that I instantiate such-and-such a functional and
internal set-up, and whose conclusion was the proposition that I
see red things like THIS. Without some such assumption it is hard
to understand how the complaint could be made explicit at all.
However, once it has been made explicit we can see what is wrong
with it. No such chain of a priori reasoning could possibly be
supplied.
   Given any system with the right functional and internal organization, which of course includes the Basic Package and directly
active incoming perceptual information of the right sorts, there
will be something it is like for that system to see colours. That
claim lies at the heart of my position, and I have been defending it
in the last three chapters. In fact I have supplied a chain of a priori
reasoning explaining the necessity of the connection from the right

---

[4] Compare Quine's well-known remark about indirect quotation: '. . . we project ourselves into what, from his remarks and other indications, we imagine the
speaker's state of mind to have been' (*Word and Object*, 219).

kind of organization to its being like THIS for me to see colours—
when 'THIS' is construed in the first way. In other words I have
explained how truths stated in physical and broadly functional
terms can strictly imply truths such as those about how I see
colours. That takes us as far as my answer to question (4). But the
situation is radically different when 'THIS' is construed in the
second way. In that case the conclusion of the chain of reasoning
would have to be on the lines of 'So THIS is what it's like for this
system to see red things!'. And the trouble is that in order to be
able to understand that conclusion we must be able to connect
'THIS' with the right sort of experience, the right sort of raw feel.
We must know what it is like to have that sort of raw feel. To
know such a thing, in the sense the present objection requires,
involves being able to project ourselves imaginatively into the
system's own point of view. This might be possible if either we
ourselves have had that sort of experience, knowing it to be of the
kind referred to; or at any rate we have some well-grounded
imaginative conception of that sort of experience. (More on this
later.) But such knowledge cannot be actually *acquired* from any
chain of a priori reasoning. Therefore no sound chain of a priori
reasoning could have as its conclusion a statement of the kind in
question. It follows that the unstated assumption referred to in the
last paragraph imposes an impossible requirement on explanations
of raw feeling.

You might follow every detail of the functional and internal
story yet still fail to know, in the sense just indicated, what it
was like to have the experience. For example, you might have
been blind from birth, and unable to conjure up an adequate
imaginative conception of the experience of seeing a red tomato.
Quite generally, there is an inevitable gap between knowledge of a
system's functional and internal set-up, and knowledge (in that
sense) of what it is like for that system to see red things. The first
kind of knowledge, by itself, is not capable of supplying the
second. Not only does this gap exist: its existence is necessitated
by the nature of raw feeling, so there is no hope of bridging it. It is
simply the difference between knowing what it *is* for something to
be a subject of raw feeling, and knowing what it is *like* to be such
a subject. Clearly, then, it cannot be an objection to my account of
raw feeling. If a thing can't be done at all, the fact that my
account hasn't done it is no objection. For equally clearly, the

existence of that gap is entirely consistent with the truths about consciousness being strictly implied by purely physical truths.

7.5 NAGEL'S CHALLENGE

My position can be further reinforced by looking at it from the point of view of Nagel's challenging attack on physicalism and functionalism. He maintains that what he calls 'the subjective character of experience' 'is not analysable in terms of any explanatory system of functional states, or intentional states', nor 'in terms of the causal role of experiences in relation to typical human behaviour'. His central, most distinctive reason for this claim is encapsulated in these words:

(N) If physicalism is to be defended, the phenomenological features must themselves be given a physical account. But when we examine their subjective character it seems that such a result is impossible. The reason is that every subjective phenomenon is essentially connected with a single point of view, and it seems inevitable that an objective, physical theory will abandon that point of view.[5]

Let us examine this line of thought. The example of bats is intended to illustrate it. Especially but not only on account of their system of echolocation, they are radically alien to us. Nagel thinks it is pretty obvious that we cannot hope to tell what it is like to be such a creature. No doubt we could understand all the details of bat physiology.[6] But understanding such objective physical facts gives us no way into an understanding of bat phenomenology: it leaves us ignorant of what it is like to be a bat. To acquire this special type of knowledge we should need to acquire, or at least to be able to approach, the bat's own peculiar point of view.

What is to be counted as a creature's 'point of view' in this context? Two main construals seem possible. One would have it that individuals share the same point of view only if they share the same kind of total system of cognition and perception. Presumably each species of sentient animal has its own point of view of that

[5] Nagel, 'What Is It Like to Be a Bat?', 392 f.
[6] For some fascinating relevant details, see N. Suga, 'Biosonar and Neural Computation in Bats'.

kind. Human beings have one point of view; bats another. On the other construal, point of view would be relativized to some component of the total system, and might be common to quite different species. They would share the same point of view if they enjoyed a particular type of sense-perception, including of course its associated kinds of raw feels. So if a subspecies of human beings were to acquire a bat-type echolocatory system of perception, which brought with it characteristically microchiropteric (or batty) raw feels, they would share the same point of view with bats in that respect. Alternatively any of us might share that point of view with bats if a special prosthetic echolocatory system could be built—a kind of 'Virtual Reality' helmet which, after an initial period of training, gave you bat-type echolocatory perception. Our examination of prosthetic vision suggested that there are no a priori reasons against that possibility. So far as I can see, the purposes of Nagel's main argument would be adequately served by this second construal, although he himself usually seems to be assuming the first.

But now, what exactly is he attacking under the name 'physicalism'? Minimal physicalism is committed to the Strict Implication thesis: the totality of truths statable in the austere physical vocabulary strictly implies (but is not strictly implied by) all truths ascribing mental states, including states of raw feeling (see 3.3). Has he any quarrel with that? At any rate he seems to agree that physicalism commits you to the Strict Implication thesis. The relation between physical processes and mental processes 'would not be a contingent one'.[7] But does he also assume that the Strict Implication thesis is sufficient for the kind of physicalism he is attacking? Consider the first sentence of (N): 'If physicalism is to be defended, the phenomenological features must themselves be given a physical account'. Clearly we need to know what would constitute an 'account'. We already know that Nagel would not be satisfied with a merely physical or neurophysiological description of the bat's echolocation system. That is just the sort of objective knowledge that he sets in contrast to knowledge of what it is like (for the bat) to be a bat. The required sort of 'account' must constitute *some* kind of account of what it is like for the bat. And

---

[7] Nagel, 'What Is It Like to Be a Bat?', 399 n. Notice, by the way, that in that article Nagel assumes without argument that the Zombie possibility is genuine (392).

the critical question is this. Must the account actually *convey* a knowledge or understanding of what it is like for the bat? We have seen that such an account would be impossible. No physical, functional, or neutral account of what is involved in a system's perceiving things in a certain way will by itself convey a knowledge or understanding of what it is like to perceive things in that way. So any variety of physicalism which entails that such an account is possible must be mistaken.

And some varieties do appear to carry that implication. In his classic article 'Sensations and Brain Processes', for example, Smart says:

When a person says, 'I see a yellowish-orange after-image', he is saying something like this: 'There is something going on which is like what is going on when I have my eyes open, am awake, and there is an orange illuminated in good light in front of me...'[8]

He insists that the psychophysical identity theory doesn't commit you to the untenable view that the meaning of a sensation report is given by a statement in terms of brain processes.[9] However, he does maintain that something like the meaning of a sensation report can be given in the 'topic-neutral' terms suggested. The trouble is that while 'I see a yellowish-orange after-image' conveys what it is like for the speaker, Smart's topic-neutral statement doesn't. It fails to convey what it is like—except to those who already know what it is like to see an orange. Now it is reasonable to assume that a person blind from birth does not necessarily know what it is like to see an orange. So the topic-neutral statement would not convey that information to such a person. It therefore does not do what Smart seems to require it to do. By our earlier argument, the same goes for any attempt to provide neutral equivalents to reports of experience.

Although Smart's suggestion appears to commit him to the claim that there can be topic-neutral *translations* of sensation reports—equivalents which are actually synonymous—he later repudiated this suggestion. Instead the neutral expression is 'meant to give in an informal way what a sensation report purports to be about'.[10] We saw earlier that Armstrong similarly rejects the

---

[8] Smart, 'Sensations and Brain Processes', 167.
[9] Ibid., reply to Objection 2.
[10] Smart, *Philosophy and Scientific Realism*, 96.

project of providing translations, and aims only to 'do full justice' to the nature of mental states by means of purely physical or neutral concepts. Of course both these declarations are fuzzy. What does a sensation report 'purport to be about' if not the character of the sensation? Can 'full justice' be done without conveying that character? But this is not a historical work, and we need not pursue the question of how to interpret Smart. My own approach avoids any suggestion that the actual character of experience could be conveyed in purely physical or neutral terms. And for the reasons given above I endorse Nagel's point that if any physicalistic doctrine entails that it could be conveyed in those terms, that doctrine must be mistaken. (I need not defend this point further. If it turns out to be mistaken, that is a further reason why Nagel's arguments are no threat.)

It is worth emphasizing the remarkable point whose identification we owe to Nagel. If I am right, it is possible to provide, in sufficiently neutral terms, logically necessary and sufficient conditions for there to be a subject of conscious experience—for there to be something it is like something to be. But if Nagel is right, it is not possible to provide *translations* in those terms of any statement ascribing either consciousness in general, or some particular state of consciousness. Consider the paedagogically useful though implausible suggestion that 'x is in pain' *means* something like 'x is in a state which is typically caused by damage to x's body, and which typically causes x to wince, groan, or scream, depending on the degree of damage'. The remarkable point I think Nagel is right to insist on is that retaining the word 'means' in that position ensures not only that this particular statement as a whole is false, but that any comparable statement would be false—any such statement whose right-hand side was formulated exclusively in physical, behavioural, or broadly functional terms. However, his point applies only to the project of finding topic-neutral translations or synonyms for mental statements. It has no force against the project of finding topic-neutral statements which are logically necessary and sufficient for the truth of mental statements. It has even less force against the more general project of 'doing justice' to the phenomena in topic-neutral terms.

Minimal physicalism is clearly immune to the particular objection we have been considering. Minimal physicalism is still physicalism, in that it supports the ontological claim that there is nothing in the world over and above what is covered, in their way, by descriptions in purely physical terms. No one whose physicalism is of this strictly ontological variety need be worried by the fact that it is impossible to give a physical or neutral characterization of what it is like for the bat which has the effect of transforming someone who does not already know what it is like into someone who does.

However, Nagel seems to think he has a much more general objection to physicalism. If he has, we must still try to decide how to take his word 'account'. We have ruled out (a) a description of the organism's workings in physical or physiological terms. We have also ruled out (b), an account conveying an actual knowledge of what it is like for the organism. And with this latter we link the idea of an account which gives the *meaning* of descriptions of the organism's experience. There are, though, two further possi-bilities: (c) an account giving logically necessary and sufficient conditions, in sufficiently neutral terms and in an explanatorily useful way, of the fact that the organism's experience has a sub-jective character; (d) an account that does justice to the phenomena of the subjective character of experience in the sense explained in Chapter 3. (Presumably (c) entails (d), but not conversely.)

Several remarks suggest that Nagel would accept both (c) and (d) as ways of providing an account of 'the phenomenological features'—which he thinks physicalism cannot provide. For example, he says that 'a physical theory of mind must *account for* the subjective character of experience' and that 'physicalism is a position we cannot understand because we do not at present have any conception of how it might be true'.[11] Either type (c) or type (d) would 'account for' the subjective character of experience on any ordinary understanding of the phrase, and either would give us a conception of how physicalism might be true.

Surely physicalism must provide something on the lines of (c) or (d). But I think I have done just that in the last three chapters. I claim to have given logically necessary and sufficient conditions for raw feeling in an explanatorily useful way. Even if you think the conditions I have given are actually not logically necessary and sufficient, I still maintain that what I have said would qualify

---

[11] Nagel, 'What Is It Like to Be a Bat?', 399, 401.

as an account of type (*d*): I claim to have done justice to the subjective character of experience. If that is correct, Nagel's (N) is not cogent. We can endorse his claim that 'every subjective phenomenon is essentially connected with a single point of view', and also that 'an objective physical theory will abandon' that single point of view, without conceding that a physical (or at any rate physicalistically acceptable) account of phenomenological features is 'impossible'. Indeed, with our present understanding of the sort of account that is required, (N) no longer even looks like an argument.

Nagel's objection to physicalism may perhaps be stated in terms of two classes of concepts. One consists of the concepts of physics and functionalism, together with any further concepts agreed to be 'neutral'. These concepts are supposed to be capable of being grasped by sentient beings of any kind, regardless of their point of view, that is, regardless of the particular character of their perceptual equipment. If there were bats with enough intelligence, they could grasp the concepts of astronomy or quantum electro-dynamics as well as human beings: their blindness would be no obstacle. Such universally accessible concepts may be termed 'viewpoint-neutral'. The other main class of concepts is 'viewpoint-relative'. They are the concepts in terms of which we can charac-terize our experience: they convey what it is like to have the experiences we have. They include, among others, the concepts of the so-called secondary qualities. No doubt intelligent bats would have their own concepts for characterizing the experiences associated with echolocation; intelligent fish would be able to characterize experiences associated with their 'lateral lines'; and so on. But—so the argument goes—you cannot in general grasp the viewpoint-relative concepts needed to characterize a certain kind of experience unless you either share the relevant point of view, or can at least imaginatively project yourself into it. You must have experiences of the kind in question, or be able to imagine what they are like.[12]

---

[12] The 'viewpoint-neutral'/'viewpoint-relative' distinction seems to coincide with one of the distinctions McDowell labels as 'objective/subjective'. See his 'Functionalism and Anomalous Monism', especially 395 f. It seems to me that he could consistently accept the Strict Implication thesis, which connects the subjec-tive to the objective without implying that subjective concepts are objective in his sense.

In these terms the core of Nagel's argument seems to be: since physicalism is restricted to viewpoint-neutral concepts, it cannot give an account of viewpoint-relative concepts. And my reply is this. First, I concede that translations or synonyms for statements using viewpoint-relative concepts cannot be constructed in purely physical or neutral terms. Purely physical or neutral statements can never actually *convey* a grasp of the character of experiences. But second, that is only an objection to some excessively optimistic varieties of physicalism. It is not an objection to minimal physicalism, which confines itself to maintaining the Strict Implication thesis. And it is clearly not an objection to the present work, which aims to explain what it takes for there to be subjects of experience in general, hence how it is that there are organisms with an 'inner' life, which there is something it is like to be.

It is tempting to think that Nagel may have been led astray by the potential ambiguity of 'account'. In any case he faces a dilemma. Either he requires physicalism to give an account of phenomenological features that has the remarkable property of transforming someone who doesn't already know what it is like to have such experiences into someone who does, or he does not. If he does require it to give an account of that sort, we must concede that it cannot do so; but we can insist that there is no need for physicalists to provide such an account.[13] If he does not impose this requirement, then the fact that an objective physical theory doesn't take a single point of view will not prevent physicalism from giving a satisfactory account of phenomenological features.

Towards the end of 'What Is It Like to Be a Bat?' Nagel offers some suggestions about what he calls 'objective phenomenology'. The aim of this project would be to develop frameworks of viewpoint-neutral concepts that would make it possible, for example, 'to explain to a person blind from birth what it was like to see'.[14] It would be inappropriate to offer any extensive criticisms of his remarks under this heading, since he puts them forward only tentatively. But three comments will help to clarify my own position.

---

[13] McGinn has used an assumption like Nagel's as the basis for arguing that although a solution to the mind–body problem exists, it is inaccessible to us: beyond our cognitive powers: C. McGinn, 'Can We Solve the Mind–Body Problem?'. See also his book, *The Problem of Consciousness*. For criticism, see R. Kirk, 'Why Shouldn't We Be Able to Solve the Mind–Body Problem?'.

[14] Nagel, 'What Is It Like to Be a Bat?', 402.

The first is that ordinary talk between sighted people and people blind from birth actually does enable the latter to grasp at least the general structure of visual experience. They can come to know such things as the following. Normally sighted people are able to see objects by means of light reflected or emitted from them. When our eyes are open and it is light, they are continuously receiving a two-dimensional pattern of stimulation. Thanks to accurate focusing, differences in the intensity of light coming from different objects and different parts of the same objects are registered on the retinas. At any instant we are constantly receiving masses of detailed information about the shapes, sizes, and relative positions of the objects at which our eyes are directed. Light comes in different wavelengths; and surfaces with different fine structures tend to reflect characteristically different mixes of wavelengths. People with normal colour vision are sensitive to such differences, so that they can discriminate surfaces on the basis of such differences—colour differences—alone. And so on. Now, a description of the colours of the sunset doesn't enable the person blind from birth to know what the experience is like in the full sense relevant to the earlier discussion. But, given the sort of background information just indicated, it does enable them to fix the experience in a conceptual structure which makes sense of it. So it enables them to acquire some *degree* of understanding of what the experience in question is like. Indeed, I suspect it would facilitate their recognizing various kinds of visual experiences if they were suddenly to gain their sight.[15] To that extent the aim of 'objective phenomenology' might be secured by means of ordinary language.

Now, we must assume that objective phenomenology is for the benefit of other sentient creatures, not for insentient systems such as the Machine Table robot. So my second comment is that there is no point in trying to construct an objective phenomenology so thoroughly viewpoint-neutral that it excludes even such general concepts as *experience* or *sensation*. Whatever their particular modes of perception might be, the potential beneficiaries of the project will have or be able to acquire such concepts. The terms of objective phenomenology might as well, therefore, be those of

---

[15] These remarks are consistent with the line suggested by G. Evans in 'Molyneux's Question'.

ordinary language. And although colour concepts, for example, might have only limited use when conversing with people blind from birth, there seems no reason to abstain from using them altogether in such talk. It helps to improve blind people's grasp of the way those concepts work.

My third and last comment on the project of objective phenomenology is that, if it is combined with considerations of the kinds offered in the last three chapters, it should enable people who lack a certain sensory modality to establish, in favourable circumstances, the truth values of statements describing individuals' experiences in that modality. To see how this might be so we can turn to the so-called 'argument from knowledge'.

7.6   THE ARGUMENT FROM KNOWLEDGE

There is a strand of argument in Nagel's paper which has a different emphasis from the one I have taken to be central. I have concentrated on points relating to the contrast between two classes of concepts: the viewpoint-relative ones which cannot be grasped except by those with the right point of view, and the rest, the viewpoint-neutral concepts. The present line of argument emphasizes a different point, which has to do with knowledge. Its best presentation is due to Frank Jackson.[16] Though much criticized, it is attractive; and the fact that its critics are not in agreement suggests it still has something to tell us. It purports to show that there is a kind of knowledge which physicalism cannot account for. Our earlier conclusions will enable us to see what is right, as well as what is wrong, with the reasoning.

We have already met Jackson's Mary, who has normal vision but has been kept from birth in a colourless environment. She is a superb scientist. From books and black-and-white television she has acquired a complete knowledge of the physical and physiological facts about colour vision, together with a complete knowledge of the relevant (neutrally characterized) causal and functional facts, and a grasp of all those implications of this knowledge that bear on the nature of colour vision. Evidently she has all the background that 'objective phenomenology' could impart. How-

---

[16] F. Jackson, 'Epiphenomenal Qualia'. An earlier version of the argument is given by L. Nemirow in his review of Nagel's *Mortal Questions*.

ever, when she eventually emerges from her grey world and sees the sky, ripe tomatoes, grass, and so on for the first time she immediately acquires new information—or so it seems. For she learns what it is like to see the blue sky, red tomatoes, green grass. (Not that exposure to blue light is sufficient for knowing what it is like to see blue things, since that requires what we may call conceptual knowledge as well. Babies see the blue sky, but that doesn't automatically supply them with that sort of knowledge.) It follows, according to the argument from knowledge, that there is a kind of information which goes beyond what can be supplied by information about the physical and neutral or functional facts, together with their entailments. Physicalism, however, appears to imply that information about the world, in particular about colour vision, is exhausted by these latter kinds of information. So physicalism is false. (The reasoning we explored earlier may be seen as paralleling this argument from knowledge, with 'facts' substituted for 'information'. I will make connections in the course of the discussion.) Let me start the examination of the argument by summarizing what I take it to be:

1. If physicalism is true all information is derivable from physical and neutral information.   [*Assumption*]

2. Before she is released Mary already has all the information relating to colour vision that is derivable from physical and neutral information.   [*Assumption*]

3. Yet it is only when she is released that Mary comes to know what it is like to see the blue sky.   [*Assumption*]

4. So before she is released there is a piece of information—namely, information about what it is like to see the blue sky—which Mary lacks, and which she acquires when she is released.   [*From 3*]

5. Therefore there is a piece of information which is not derivable from physical and neutral information.
     [*From 2, 4*]

6. Therefore physicalism is false.   [*From 1, 5*]

This argument appears valid and its premises are plausible. However, each premise has been disputed, and a fallacy of equivocation has been discerned in the use of 'information' ('knowledge' in some versions).

Premiss (1) is plausible because if there are pieces of information over and above those derivable from physical or neutral information, it looks as if a purely physical account of reality would leave something out. However, it has been objected that knowing what it is like to see blue things, for example, is not a matter of just grasping facts, but involves the acquisition of certain sorts of abilities.[17] Another suggestion, at odds with the first, is that when Mary sees the blue sky for the first time she acquires a 'new perspective'—a 'first-person perspective'—on the information she already has.[18] Since no reason has been given why physicalists should concede that knowing the physical and neutral truths should necessarily endow the knower with the relevant special sort of ability, or the special first-person perspective, it is concluded that physicalists need not concede (1). (This parallels the point made three sections back.)

An alternative suggestion is that physicalists can concede (1) on condition that 'information' is taken in a restricted sense. The sense would have to be one which requires all genuine information to be expressible in viewpoint-neutral terms and therefore does not involve any special abilities or perspectives. They can insist that in this sense (1) is consistent with the assumption that Mary acquires 'new information' when she is released. For this assumption can be taken to introduce a different, wider sense of 'information', one which does involve special abilities or perspectives. (This is why the argument may be said to depend on a fallacy of equivocation.)

Premiss (2) has been disputed on the ground that there is a special class of 'physical facts' which Mary could not be guaranteed capable of acquiring in a grey world.[19] I do not quite follow the suggestion, but in any case it is beside the point if we understand the phrase 'physical facts' in the way both physicalism and the knowledge argument require. For it will serve all the purposes of both physicalism and the knowledge argument if we take the physical facts, hence physical information, to be those expressible

[17] See L. Nemirow, review of Nagel's *Mortal Questions*, 475. For a version of this objection see D. Lewis, 'Postscript to "Mad Pain and Martian Pain"', 131 f.

[18] See T. Horgan, 'Jackson on Physical Information and Qualia', 151. See also M. Tye, 'The Subjective Qualities of Experience', who writes of 'new epistemic access', and P. M. Churchland, 'Reduction, Qualia, and the Direct Introspection of Brain States'.

[19] See Earl Conee, 'Physicalism and Phenomenal Qualities', 301.

by means of what I am calling physical statements. I know of no reason why someone living in a grey world shouldn't be able to acquire all the relevant physical and neutral information. So I shall take it that (2) is true.

Finally, the thought expressed in premiss (3) has been challenged in two ways. One challenge is implied by the last two paragraphs: the sense of 'information' (or 'knowledge') in which Mary acquires new information or knowledge when she sees the blue sky for the first time is different from that in which she knows all the relevant physical and neutral truths. If this is correct, then even though physicalists can still accept (3) as true, it is irrelevant. The other challenge is to insist that (3) is actually false because (1) is true. If physicalism is true, then all the relevant truths are supervenient upon or, as I prefer to put it, strictly implied by the physical and neutral truths. (1) is true, and so physicalists must bite the bullet and maintain that if (2) is true, (3) is false. If Mary really knows all the relevant physical and neutral truths about colour vision, *eo ipso* there is no class of relevant truths about colour vision that she does not know.

One of these objections to the argument from knowledge requires premiss (2) to be false, the rest assume it can be true. Some imply that premiss (1) is false, one implies it is true. Some concede that premiss (3) is true, one requires it to be false. So even if the argument is misconceived it has smoked out some striking differences among proponents of physicalism. Now, my own physicalism is minimal. It consists in acceptance of the Strict Implication thesis together with the statement that there is nothing in the world whose existence is not guaranteed by the totality of austerely statable physical truths. And I have already committed myself to agreement with Nagel's point about viewpoint-relative concepts. Many concepts, including especially those in terms of which we characterize experiences, cannot be fully grasped except by those who can adopt the point of view of those who have them. They must have actually had experiences of the kinds in question, or be otherwise capable of imaginatively constructing them. Since Mary's extensive theoretical knowledge cannot supply her with either the experience of seeing the blue sky or the capacity to construct that experience, she will not be able to derive a knowledge of what it is like to see the blue sky from that knowledge. She can find out as much as objective phenomenology can impart; but she cannot cross the unbridgeable gap discussed earlier in this chapter.[20] So according to my account premisses (2) and (3) are perfectly acceptable, as are steps (4) and (5). On the other hand there is no reason why minimal physicalism should concede premiss (1) in the sense required for the argument to go through—the sense in which knowledge of what it is like to see the blue sky is included with the information to be derived. So it follows from my earlier conclusions that the argument leaves minimal physicalism unscathed.

However, it also follows that the argument seriously threatens any variety of physicalism which commits itself to premiss (1) in the required sense. There seem to be just two ways in which such a physicalism could escape being demolished by the argument. One is to take up eliminativism. I have already explained why I reject that option. The other way, noticed a little way back, would be to compensate by defining 'information' in a specially narrow sense. The trouble with this way out is that it in effect concedes Nagel's point about viewpoint-relative concepts. It does nothing to show that he is wrong in maintaining that there are many concepts, hence many truths, which cannot be grasped except by those who share the same point of view. So in the end that special reconstrual of the word 'information'—or for that matter of 'knowledge'—seems pointless. If you altogether reject concepts which cannot be grasped except by those who share a certain point of view, then you are not going to be bothered by the argument from knowledge. You have a problem in explaining why so many wrong concepts—including, for example, all those such as 'blue', 'sweet'—appear to be capable of expressing truths and are so useful, reliable, and practically indispensable; but eliminativists have never let that sort of consideration bother them. But if you accept that there are indeed perfectly acceptable truths expressible in terms of those concepts, you gain nothing by refusing to describe the acquisition of one of those truths as the acquisition of information. So it is hard to know what motive there could be for such a refusal.

Part of the motivation may have been a misconception about

[20] See 7.4. In *Consciousness Explained*, 441–7, Dennett says much that is consistent with the line taken here. However, I think he blurs the distinction between what objective phenomenology could impart, and that inside knowledge of what it is like which the argument from knowledge attempts to exploit.

what minimal physicalism commits you to. It does commit you to the view that all the interesting truths about raw feeling are strictly implied by the totality of purely physical truths. It does not commit you to the view that an understanding of the purely physical truths, and of how it can be that they strictly imply the other truths, confers upon you a full *understanding* of all those other truths. Mary, in her grey world, knows not only that English speakers use colour words such as 'blue'. She also knows in what circumstances they use them—indeed in what circumstances *she* would use them—except for not actually having experienced colours. So if Mary is given details of the surface of some object, for example a piece of blue cloth, she is capable of working out that a normal English speaker would describe it as blue. So she is capable of working out that the statement 'This piece of cloth is blue' is strictly implied by the totality of purely physical truths. Given further information about a normally sighted person gazing at the same piece of cloth, she is also capable of working out that the statement 'This person is having the experience of seeing something blue' is true. She knows, then, *that* these statements express truths. But there is a sense in which she doesn't know just *which* truths they express. Certainly she knows a lot about the use of the statements; but she lacks the kind of understanding of them that normally sighted English speakers have. Yet what else she needs in order to acquire that kind of understanding is very little. All she needs is the actual experience of, for example, the clear blue sky. (She already knows that clear skies are blue.)

My suspicion, then, is that if those who propose to avoid the argument from knowledge by restricting the use of 'information' or 'knowledge' had been fully aware of the points just noted, they would have lost interest in making the restriction. They would have realized that there is no reason why non-eliminative minimal physicalism should insist on premiss (1). The argument from knowledge is no threat to it, or indeed to the position set out in the last three chapters.

7.7 'FACTS BEYOND THE REACH OF HUMAN CONCEPTS'

Let me now say something explicitly about Nagel's famous claim that there are 'facts beyond the reach of human concepts'. He supplies a clear enough paraphrase of this claim. It is to the effect that 'there are facts which do not consist in the truth of propositions expressible in a human language'.[21] Understood that way, the claim is entirely compatible with the minimal physicalism I have been defending. It is no part of minimal physicalism that all truths be expressible in some particular language, whether that be the austere language of physics, or ordinary English, or Chinese, or any human language. It requires only that all truths about mental states be strictly implied by the totality of narrowly physical truths. Since Nagel's claim depends on the points about viewpoint-relative concepts that we have been discussing, and since I have argued that these points are consistent with minimal physicalism, that claim does not imply that the truths in question are not strictly implied by the physical truths.

If some intelligent bats used a language, there is no reason why we shouldn't be able to learn enough of it to discuss such things as astronomy and physics with them. But we should not be able to acquire their kind of grasp of the terms in which they described the experiences they had by means of their sense of echolocation. That kind of grasp would require us to know what their echolocatory experiences were like from their point of view; and this we cannot know because we lack the necessary equipment to have such experiences—though, as we noticed, we might acquire suitable prosthetic equipment. But there is nothing mysterious about this state of affairs. Those propositions about bat experience whose truths are not expressible in a human language don't imply the existence of things beyond our reach, or aspects of reality that we cannot have any inkling of. The *only* thing they imply is the unproblematic fact that there are kinds of experience we ourselves are not able to have.

The lack of mystery is further emphasized by a point similar to one made earlier about Mary. In spite of her ignorance of what it is like to see colours, she was able to discover the truth values of statements about colour experience. Similarly, in spite of our ignorance of what it is like to be a bat, we could in principle discover the truth values (in the language of intelligent bats) of statements about the experiences of bats. Of course we should need to acquire a lot of physical, functional, and other objective-

---

[21] Nagel, 'What Is It Like to Be a Bat?', 396.

phenomenological background knowledge about the bats and their language. But there are no a priori reasons why we should not be able to do so. Then, having learnt their language as far as possible, we should be in a similar position with respect to them as Mary was with respect to people who had had normal experiences of colour. We should be able to discover the truth values of statements about bat experience even though we lacked the kind of understanding of them that only actual bat-like experiences could provide.[22]

I accept, then, that there is one sense in which the facts about bat experience are 'beyond the reach of human concepts'. But I reject the suggestion that there is anything mysterious about this, or problematic for minimal physicalism. For, as just noted, there seem to be no a priori reasons why we should not be able to obtain as detailed a knowledge as we desired of those aspects of reality in virtue of which the propositions in question were true. Moreover, in order to acquire the concepts necessary for characterizing the experience of any given kind of creature, it would only be necessary to acquire perceptual equipment of the sort such creatures enjoyed. (Of course the practical difficulties may be insuperable.)

I have adopted Nagel's own assumption that facts are true propositions. On that assumption I have argued that minimal physicalism leaves no facts out of account—even though there are plenty of facts not 'expressible in a human language'. Assuming minimal physicalism, such facts—such truths—are still *strictly implied* by the physically statable truths, and could in favourable circumstances be seen to be so. Nagel is therefore in no position to reproach minimal physicalism with failing to account for some facts: it accounts for all the facts that are accountable at all.[23]

Although Nagel's position about the facts of perceptual experience in 'What Is It Like to Be a Bat?' did not logically commit him

---

[22] The last paragraph brings out an interesting point about the claim of Nagel's that I have used as the heading for this section. His *paraphrase* of that claim was that 'there are facts which do not consist in the truth of propositions expressible in a human language'. We have just seen that such truths are potentially within our reach, at least in the sense that we can discover such truths. So strictly speaking they are not after all, in his sense, 'facts beyond the reach of human concepts'.

[23] You may prefer not to take facts to consist in the truth of propositions. But no matter how you construed them, I would argue that the above reasoning can be reconstrued correspondingly.

to a non-physicalist metaphysics, in *The View from Nowhere* he seems strongly inclined in that direction. He remarks:

The strange truth seems to be that certain complex, biologically generated physical systems, of which each of us is an example, have rich non-physical properties. An integrated theory of reality must account for this, and I believe that if and when it arrives, probably not for centuries, it will alter our conception of the universe as radically as anything has to date.[24]

If the account advocated here is anything like correct, however, these remarks are excessively pessimistic. We don't need a whole new science. The Strict Implication thesis seems to be true; and I have tried to explain how it can be true. If my account is even roughly correct, minimal physicalism is not threatened by the facts of consciousness.

7.8 'THE REAL NATURE OF HUMAN EXPERIENCE'

A thought pervading Nagel's article is that we are unlikely to 'get closer to the real nature of human experience by leaving behind the particularity of our human point of view and striving for a description in terms accessible to beings that could not imagine what it was like to be us'.[25] Here and elsewhere—for example when he says on the same page, 'it is a mystery how the true character of experiences could be revealed in the physical operation of [an] organism'—he seems to be attacking not minimal physicalism but the view that we could obtain a better knowledge of what it is *like* for us to have the experiences we do by learning more about the physical facts involved. I agree that we couldn't get better knowledge of that kind in that way. To get more of that kind of knowledge would presumably require exercises in imagination, more experience, more reading of novels and poetry, more viewing of plays and films—or possibly objective phenomenology. So I support his attack on those who think we could. However, when physicalists have used phrases such as 'the real

---

[24] T. Nagel, *The View from Nowhere*, 51.
[25] Nagel, 'What Is It Like to Be a Bat?', 399. Cf. 402.

nature of human experience' or 'the true character of experiences', they may have meant them in the sense of 'the underlying or constitutive nature of experiences'. In this sense the quest would not be for a better knowledge of what it is like to be the subject of experiences. It would be for a better knowledge of what it is for something to have experiences—just what I have been trying to provide.

Admittedly, if my position is correct, the underlying or constitutive nature of experiences is not physical, but broadly functional. That is, what makes it the case that experiences are going on is not the fact that what is going on is physical (assuming it is), or that it falls under such-and-such physical descriptions. It is the fact that it satisfies certain conditions which may be described as broadly functional. So I think Nagel is right to attack those varieties of physicalism, such as the old psychophysical identity thesis, which have supposed the underlying nature of experience to be physical, and have suggested that the nature of experiences could be, in his words, 'captured in a physical description'.[26]

An associated question for Nagel is 'whether any sense can be made of experiences' having an objective character at all. Does it make sense, in other words, to ask what my experiences are *really* like, as opposed to how they appear to me?'[27] The way he puts this question suggests that he has not clearly separated out the two issues we have just distinguished. On one side there is the question of improving our grasp of *what it is like* for this or that individual or kind of individual to have experiences. No amount of improvement in physical or functional knowledge can improve that kind of knowledge. This is the valid point to do with bats. However, there is another question: what is the nature of experiences— what is it for something to have experiences? This is a perfectly valid question. Indeed, after a certain amount of discussion it can be made reasonably clear—and answered.

---

[26] Paul M. Churchland thinks that by discovering more about the physical processes involved in perception on the one hand, and about the external physical world that impinges on us to trigger those processes, we can enrich the character of our experience enormously: see e.g. *Scientific Realism and the Plasticity of Mind*, esp. 25–36. I entirely agree with this important point. But it is not the same as the claim that such investigations would help us towards a better grasp of what it is now like to have the experiences we actually do have.

[27] Nagel, 'What Is It Like to Be a Bat?', 402.

7.9   A LAST LOOK AT THE INTELLIGIBILITY GAP

At first it seemed possible to present the intelligibility gap in a single question. How could the firings of neurones, however complex, amount to THIS? Put like that, the question was elusive. But we have teased out a number of more manageable components. A necessary preliminary was to dispose of Wittgensteinian and eliminativist worries. With them out of the way, the Strict Implication thesis proved a valuable instrument for clarifying the issues. And the Swiss Cheese principle enabled the issue of dualism versus physicalism to be left on one side, where it belongs. It was then possible to focus on what has turned out to be the central question: how could the Strict Implication thesis hold? How could the facts expressible in a narrowly physical vocabulary absolutely fix the facts of consciousness? My answer was reached by developing the line of thought powerfully advocated by Armstrong—that perception is a matter of the acquisition of information. In the course of that development the relevant notion of information was itself explained in unproblematic terms. A system is a subject of conscious perceptual experience if, and only if, it has the Basic Package of capacities, all concerned with information that is *for* the system, realistically construed, with some perceptual information acting directly on its main assessment processes. If this is correct, we have an answer to the question of what it is for a system to have a point of view and an 'inner' life. So far as the essence of consciousness, raw feeling, is concerned, we noticed that it will be present wherever the right kinds of processes are present, even if those processes are cut off from whatever might be necessary for the system to interact with its environment. With these conclusions the main work of bridging the intelligibility gap was completed.

This explanation of how the Strict Implication thesis could be true shows immediately that the Zombie idea, however intuitively appealing, does not represent a genuine logical possibility. On the other hand, science-fictional examples like the GIANT and the Machine Table robot illustrate the genuineness of a different possibility. There could be insentient systems whose behavioural capacities matched our own. Their internal processing would be of the wrong kind to make them subjects of conscious experience.

The Transformation thesis—my cleaned-up version of the inverted spectrum idea—seemed at first to be at odds with my main position because the Swiss Cheese principle seemed to rule out the possibility of differences of the sorts envisaged. However, further development of that position showed how the Transformation thesis is in fact entirely consistent with both it and the Swiss Cheese principle.

In this final chapter I have been trying to remove any remaining obstacles to acceptance of the claim that the intelligibility gap has finally been bridged. Of course some readers will remain unconvinced. No doubt the position set out in Chapters 4, 5, and 6 is defective in various ways. But the real question is whether it is altogether misconceived. To show that it is, it won't be enough to rely on intuitions—for example the one I myself once found compelling, the idea that Zombies are a genuine logical possibility. Argument is required.

In conclusion, let me emphasize that bridging the intelligibility gap does nothing to diminish a real gap we have already considered: the one between two positions that we, as conscious subjects, occupy. One is our position as agents and thinkers in the world, centres of consciousness with our own needs, interests, and ways of conceptualizing reality. The other is our position as objects of attention from others. Others need not share our interests, ways of perceiving, or conceptual schemes. We may be wholly alien to them—they might even be intelligent bats. Clearly there is no necessity by which the concepts in terms of which they describe us and attempt to explain our behaviour should mesh in smoothly with those in terms of which we ourselves think. A particular instance of this real gap lies at the heart of our problem. For good reasons we are impressed by the power of the scheme of description and explanation offered by physics. This scheme applies to each of us, in its way, whether we are human beings, robots, sticklebacks, or bats. But its application to us completely ignores our own ways of thinking. Indeed it ignores the fact that we think at all. Sufficiently alien and biased investigators could conceivably arrive at full physical descriptions of our workings without even coming to realize we were conscious subjects. There is some symmetry here, since people have normally not given much thought to the physical descriptions which might be true of themselves, even if they have belonged to that tiny minority with some knowledge of physics. So there is a real gulf between the two kinds of conceptual scheme. Evidently it reinforces the feeling that what is described in the viewpoint-neutral terms of physics could not possibly fix the phenomena of experience that we describe as subjects. Showing that in fact there is no logical gap—that the physical truths strictly imply the truths about raw feeling— evidently leaves this real gap unaffected. And the real gap continues to make it easy for us to think we can detect a logical one.[28]

[28] This is the reply to Nagel's remark that 'a theory that explained how the mind–brain relation was necessary would still leave us with Kripke's problem of explaining why it nevertheless appears contingent' ('What Is It Like to Be a Bat?', 400 n.).

BIBLIOGRAPHY

Armstrong, David M. (1968). *A Materialist Theory of the Mind* (London: Routledge & Kegan Paul).
—— and N. Malcolm (1984). *Consciousness and Causality* (Oxford: Oxford University Press).
Bach-y-Rita, P., C. C. Collins, *et al.* (1969). 'Vision Substitution by Tactile Image Projection', *Nature*, 221: 963–4.
Bacon, John (1986). 'Supervenience, Necessary Coextension, and Reducibility', *Philosophical Studies*, 49: 163–76.
Bennett, Jonathan (1965). 'Substance, Reality and Primary Qualities', *American Philosophical Quarterly*, 2: 1–17.
Bisiach, E. (1988). 'The (Haunted) Brain and Consciousness', in *Consciousness in Contemporary Science*, ed. A. J. Marcel and E. Bisiach (Oxford: Clarendon Press).
Block, Ned (1981). 'Psychologism and Behaviourism', *Philosophical Review*, 90: 5–43.
Carnap, Rudolf (1932/3). 'Psychology in Physical Language', *Erkenntnis*, 2; reprinted in *Logical Positivism*, ed. Alfred J. Ayer (Glencoe, Ill.: The Free Press), 1953.
—— (1934). *The Unity of Science* (London: Kegan Paul).
Carruthers, Peter (1989). 'Brute Experience', *Journal of Philosophy*, 86: 258–69.
—— (1992). 'Consciousness and Concepts' II, *Proceedings of the Aristotelian Society*, supp. vol. 66: 41–59.
Churchland, Paul M. (1979). *Scientific Realism and the Plasticity of Mind* (Cambridge: Cambridge University Press).
—— (1981). 'Eliminative Materialism and the Propositional Attitudes', *Journal of Philosophy*, 78: 67–90.
—— (1985). 'Reduction, Qualia, and the Direct Introspection of Brain States', *Journal of Philosophy*, 82: 8–28.
—— and Patricia Smith Churchland (1981). 'Functionalism, Qualia, and Intentionality', *Philosophical Topics*, 12: 121–45.
Conee, Earl (1985). 'Physicalism and Phenomenal Qualities', *Philosophical Quarterly*, 35: 296–302.
Cornman, James (1971). *Materialism and Sensations* (New Haven, Conn.: Yale University Press).
Crane, Tim (1991). 'All God Has to Do', *Analysis*, 51: 235–44.
Dennett, Daniel C. (1969). *Content and Consciousness* (London: Routledge & Kegan Paul).

Dennett, Daniel C. (1978). *Brainstorms* (Hassocks, Sussex: Harvester).
—— (1978). 'Where Am I?', in his *Brainstorms*, 310–23.
—— (1987). *The Intentional Stance* (Cambridge, Mass.: MIT).
—— (1988). 'Quining Qualia', in *Consciousness in Contemporary Science*, ed. A. J. Marcel and E. Bisiach (Oxford: Clarendon Press), 42–77.
—— (1991). *Consciousness Explained* (Boston: Little, Brown).
Dretske, Fred I. (1981). *Knowledge and the Flow of Information* (Oxford: Blackwell).
Dummett, Michael (1978). *Truth and Other Enigmas* (London: Duckworth).
Evans, Gareth (1985). 'Molyneux's Question', in his *Collected Papers* (Oxford: Clarendon Press), 364–99.
Farrell, B. A. (1950). 'Experience', *Mind*, 59: 170–98.
Fodor, Jerry A. (1975). *The Language of Thought* (New York: Thomas J. Crowell).
Graham, George, and G. Lynn Stephen (1985). 'Are Qualia a Pain in the Neck for Functionalists?', *American Philosophical Quarterly*, 22: 73–80.
Gregory, Richard L. (ed.) (1987). *The Oxford Companion to the Mind* (Oxford: Oxford University Press).
Guarniero, G. (1974). 'Experience of Tactile Vision', *Perception*, 3: 101–4.
Hacker, P. M. S. (1990). *Wittgenstein: Meaning and Mind* (Oxford: Blackwell).
Hardin, C. L. (1988). *Color for Philosophers* (Indianapolis: Hackett).
Harrison, Bernard (1973). *Form and Content* (Oxford: Blackwell).
Horgan, Terence (1984). 'Jackson on Physical Information and Qualia', *Philosophical Quarterly*, 34: 147–53.
Hornsby, Jennifer (1986). 'Physicalist Thinking and Conceptions of Behaviour', in *Subject, Thought, and Context*, ed. Philip Pettit and J. McDowell (Oxford: Clarendon Press).
Hsia, Y., and C. H. Graham (1965). 'Colour Blindness', in *Vision and Visual Perception*, ed. C. H. Graham (New York: Wiley).
Hubel, D. H., and T. N. Wiesel (1959). 'Receptive Fields of Single Neurons in the Cat's Striate Cortex', *Journal of Physiology*, 148: 574–91.
Hume, David (1740/1978). *A Treatise of Human Nature*, ed. L. A. Selby-Bigge, second edition revised by P. H. Nidditch (Oxford University Press).
Humphrey, Nicholas (1984). *Consciousness Regained* (Oxford: Oxford University Press).
—— (1992). *A History of the Mind* (London: Chatto & Windus).
Humphreys, Glyn W., and Vicki Bruce (1989). *Visual Cognition* (Hove and London: Lawrence Erlbaum Associates).

Jackson, Frank (1977). *Perception* (Cambridge: Cambridge University Press).

—— (1982). 'Epiphenomenal Qualia', *Philosophical Quarterly*, 32: 127–36.

Jaynes, Julian (1976). *The Origin of Consciousness in the Breakdown of the Bicameral Mind* (Boston: Houghton Mifflin).

Kim, Jaegwon (1978). 'Supervenience and Nomological Incommensurables', *American Philosophical Quarterly*, 15: 149–56.

—— (1984). 'Concepts of Supervenience', *Philosophy and Phenomenological Research*, 45: 153–76.

—— (1987). '"Strong" and "Global" Supervenience Revisited', *Philosophy and Phenomenological Research*, 48: 315–26.

Kirk, Robert (1974). 'Zombies v. Materialists', *Proceedings of the Aristotelian Society*, supp. vol. 48: 135–52.

—— (1981). 'Goodbye to Transposed Qualia', *Proceedings of the Aristotelian Society*, 82: 33–44.

—— (1982). 'Physicalism, Identity and Strict Implication', *Ratio*, 24: 131–41.

—— (1986). 'Sentience, Causation, and Some Robots', *Australasian Journal of Philosophy*, 64: 306–19.

—— (1986). *Translation Determined* (Oxford: Clarendon Press).

—— (1991). 'Why Shouldn't we be Able to Solve the Mind–Body Problem?', *Analysis*, 51: 17–23.

—— (1992). 'Consciousness and Concepts', i, *Proceedings of the Aristotelian Society*, supp. vol. 66: 23–40.

—— (forthcoming). 'Conscious Experience and the Concept of Experience'.

Kripke, Saul (1972). *Naming and Necessity* (Oxford: Blackwell).

Lettvin, J. Y., *et al.* (1959). 'What the Frog's Eye Tells the Frog's Brain', *Proceedings of the Institute of Radio Engineers*, 47: 1940–51.

Lewis, David (1972). 'Psychophysical and Theoretical Identifications', *Australasian Journal of Philosophy*, 50: 249–58.

—— (1983). 'Mad Pain and Martian Pain', *Readings in the Philosophy of Psychology*, i, ed. Ned Block (Harvard University Press, 1980), 216–22; reprinted with a Postscript in David Lewis, *Philosophical Papers*, i (New York: Oxford University Press), 122–32.

Locke, John (1975). *An Essay Concerning Human Understanding*, ed. P. H. Nidditch (Oxford: Clarendon Press).

Lockwood, Michael (1989). *Mind, Brain and the Quantum* (Oxford: Blackwell).

Lycan, William G. (1981). 'Form, Function, and Feel', *Journal of Philosophy*, 78: 24–50.

—— (1987). *Consciousness* (Cambridge, Mass.: MIT).

McCulloch, Gregory (1992). 'The Very Idea of the Phenomenological',

Proceedings of the Aristotelian Society, 93: 39–57.

Macdonald, Cynthia (1989). *Mind–Body Identity Theories* (London: Routledge).

McDowell, John (1985). 'Functionalism and Anomalous Monism', in *Actions and Events*, ed. Ernest LePore and Brian P. McLaughlin (Oxford: Blackwell), 387–98.

—— (1985). 'Values and Secondary Qualities', in *Morality and Objectivity: a tribute to J. L. Mackie*, ed. Ted Honderich (Oxford: Blackwell), 110–29.

—— (1986). 'Singular Thought and the Extent of Inner Space', in *Subject, Thought, and Context*, ed. Philip Pettit and J. McDowell (Oxford: Clarendon Press), 137–68.

McFarland, David (ed.) (1987). *The Oxford Companion to Animal Behaviour* (Oxford: Oxford University Press).

McFetridge, I. G. (1985). 'Supervenience, Realism, Necessity', *Philosophical Quarterly*, 35: 245–58.

McGinn, Colin (1989). 'Can We Solve the Mind–Body Problem?', *Mind*, 98: 349–66.

—— (1991). *The Problem of Consciousness* (Oxford: Blackwell).

Maloney, J. C. (1985). 'About Being a Bat', *Australasian Journal of Philosophy*, 63: 26–49.

Marr, David (1982). *Vision* (New York: Freeman).

Melzack, Ronald (1992). 'Phantom Limbs', *Scientific American*, 266: 90–6.

Murdoch, Iris (1970). *The Sovereignty of Good* (London: Routledge & Kegan Paul).

Nagel, Thomas (1974). 'What Is It Like to Be a Bat?', *Philosophical Review*, 83: 435–50; reprinted in *The Mind's I*, ed. D. Hofstadter and D. Dennett (Hassocks, Sussex: Harvester, 1981), to which references apply.

—— (1986). *The View from Nowhere* (New York: Oxford University Press).

Nemirow, L. (1980). Review of T. Nagel's *Mortal Questions, Philosophical Review*, 89: 473–7.

Parfit, Derek (1984). *Reasons and Persons* (Oxford: Clarendon Press).

Pears, David (1988). *The False Prison: A Study of the Development of Wittgenstein's Philosophy*, ii (Oxford: Clarendon Press).

Penrose, Roger (1989). *The Emperor's New Mind* (Oxford: Oxford University Press).

Putnam, Hilary (1975). *Mind, Language and Reality: Philosophical Papers*, ii (Cambridge: Cambridge University Press).

—— (1975). 'Minds and Machines', in his *Mind, Language and Reality*, 362–85.

—— (1975). 'Philosophy and Our Mental Life', in his *Mind, Language and Reality*, 291–303.

—— (1975). 'The Meaning of "Meaning"', in his *Mind, Language and Reality*, 215–71.

—— (1975). 'The Nature of Mental States', in his *Mind, Language and Reality*, 429–40.

—— (1981). *Reason, Truth and History* (Cambridge: Cambridge University Press).

Quine, W. V. (1960). *Word and Object* (Cambridge, Mass., New York, and London: MIT and Wiley).

Robinson, Howard M. (1982). *Matter and Sense* (Cambridge: Cambridge University Press).

Rumelhart, David E., J. L. McClelland, and the PDP Research Group (1986). *Parallel Distributed Processing*, i and ii (Cambridge, Mass.: MIT Press).

Ryle, Gilbert (1949). *The Concept of Mind* (London: Hutchinson).

Schlick, M. (1949). 'Meaning and Verification', in *Readings in Philosophical Analysis*, ed. H. Feigl and W. Sellars (New York: Appleton-Century-Crofts), 161–70.

Searle, John (1980). 'Minds, Brains and Programs', *Behavioural and Brain Sciences*, 3: 417–57; reprinted in *The Mind's I*, ed. D. Hofstadter and D. Dennett (Hassocks, Sussex: Harvester), 1981.

Shoemaker, Sidney (1981). 'Absent Qualia are Impossible', *Philosophical Review*, 90: 581–99; reprinted in his *Identity, Cause, and Mind*, 309–26.

—— (1981). 'The Inverted Spectrum', *Journal of Philosophy*, 74: 357–81; reprinted in his *Identity, Cause, and Mind*, 327–57, to which page references apply.

—— (1984). *Identity, Cause, and Mind* (Cambridge: Cambridge University Press).

—— (1991). 'Qualia and Consciousness', *Mind*, 100: 507–24.

Smart, J. J. C. (1959). 'Sensations and Brain Processes', *Philosophical Review*, 68: 141–56; reprinted, slightly revised, in *The Philosophy of Mind*, ed. V. C. Chappell, to which page references apply.

—— (1963). 'Materialism', *Journal of Philosophy*, 60: 651–62.

—— (1963). *Philosophy and Scientific Realism* (London: Routledge & Kegan Paul).

Sober, E. (1985). 'Panglossian Functionalism and the Philosophy of Mind', *Synthese*, 64: 165–93.

Stout, G. F. (1931). *Mind and Matter* (Cambridge: Cambridge University Press).

Strawson, P. F. (1959). *Individuals* (London: Methuen).

Suga, N. (1990). 'Biosonar and Neural Computation in Bats', *Scientific*

American, 262: 34–41.

Tolman, E. C. (1932). *Purposive Behaviour in Animals and Men* (New York: Appleton-Century-Crofts).

Tye, Michael (1986). 'The Subjective Qualities of Experience', *Mind*, 85: 1–17.

Weiskrantz, L. (1986). *Blindsight: A Case Study and Implications* (Oxford: Clarendon Press).

Wiggins, David (1980). *Sameness and Substance* (Oxford: Blackwell).

Wilkes, Kathleen V. (1978). *Physicalism* (London: Routledge & Kegan Paul).

—— (1984). 'Is Consciousness Important?', *British Journal for the Philosophy of Science*, 35: 223–43.

Williams, Bernard (1978). *Descartes: the Project of Pure Enquiry* (Harmondsworth: Penguin).

Wittgenstein, Ludwig (1953). *Philosophical Investigations*, trans. G. E. M. Anscombe (Oxford: Blackwell).

—— (1968). 'Notes for Lectures on "Private Experience" and "Sense Data"', ed. Rush Rhees, *Philosophical Review*, 77: 275–320.

—— (1969). *On Certainty*, ed. G. E. M. Anscombe and G. H. von Wright (Oxford: Blackwell).

Wootton, R. J. (1976). *The Biology of the Sticklebacks* (London: Academic Press).

INDEX

absent-minded driver 155–7
'absent qualia', *see* Zombies
analogy, argument from 43
anti-realism about sensation language
    38–40, 44–5, 54
    see also Dummett; Wittgenstein
argument from knowledge 226–31
Aristotle 51, 110 n., 171, 178 n.
Armstrong, D. M. 13, 23 n., 50 n.,
    86 n., 108 n., 177 n., 207 n., 220,
    236
    on 'inner sense' 125–7, 153
    on perception 152–4, 155
Artificial Intelligence 130–1
    see also connectionism
assessment and interpretation 129–30,
    171, 172, 191
    determine characters for the system
        146–7, 195
    illustrated by stickleback 140–2,
        146–7
    needed for the Basic Package
        109–11
    'main' processes distinguished
        145–6
    not present in Block's robot 22–3
    and decision making 150
    realistic view of 116–17, 119–23
    and richness of perceptual
        information 145
    see also Basic Package; information
        for the system

Bacon, J. 81, 82
Basic Package 109–11, 129–30, 137,
    140, 157, 162, 165, 167, 169
    see also assessment and
        interpretation; GIANT;
        information for the system
bats 218, 219, 223, 232–3
    see also Nagel
behaviourism 21–4, 39, 40, 60, 161
    see also Block's robot; Machine
        Table robot
blindsight 162–4, 168–9
Block, N. 21, 23 n., 115 n.

Block's robot 21–3, 39, 42, 207
bundle theory 15–17
brain in a vat 50–5

Carnap, R. 13, 177 n.
Carruthers, P. 146 n., 152, 155–7,
    158 n.
'Cartesian materialism', *see* Dennett
characterization of experience 28, 39,
    48, 45–6, 47–9, 53–4, 70, 124,
    208, 216, 220–2, 223, 229, 233
characters for the system 147–50,
    164, 186, 195, 212
    identified with raw feeling 152
    see also assessment and
        interpretation; raw feeling
Churchland, P. M. 66, 67, 208, 235
Churchland, P. M. and P. S. 180–6
colour-blindness 1, 201
concepts 125, 127–9, 135, 145, 151,
    157, 216
Conee, E. 228
connectionism 130–5
consciousness:
    does not require language 152,
        158–62, 169
    and Leibnizian 'mill' 100
    not all-or-nothing 160, 167–9
    and physical processes 3–4, 37, 42,
        44, 86, 94
    problems of 2–5
    raw feeling as the essence of 24,
        210–11, 236
    see also behaviourism; bundle
        theory; conscious subjects;
        Dennett; dualism; eliminativism;
        epiphenomenalism; experience;
        'inner sense'; perception; raw
        feeling; relational ('act-object')
        accounts of perception
conscious subjects 3, 50, 51–2, 88,
    100, 136–74
    and the Basic Package 109–11
    contrasted with pure stimulus-
        response systems 106–9, 111
    and directly active perceptual